Building an Import/ Export Business
Fourth Edition

Building an Import/ Export Business

Fourth Edition

Kenneth D. Weiss

John Wiley & Sons, Inc.

Published by John Wiley & Sons, Inc., Hoboken, New Jersey
Published simultaneously in Canada

Wiley Bicentennial Logo: Richard J. Pacifico

For general information about our other products and services, please contact our Customer Care Department within the United States at (800) 762-2974, outside the United States at (317) 572-3993 or fax (317) 572-4002.

Wiley also publishes its books in a variety of electronic formats. Some content that appears in print may not be available in electronic books. For more information about Wiley products, visit our web site at www.wiley.com.

Library of Congress Cataloging-in-Publication Data:

Weiss, Kenneth D. (Kenneth Duane), date.
   Building an import/export business / Kenneth D. Weiss.—4th ed.
      p. cm.
   Includes bibliographical references and index.
   ISBN 978-0-470-12047-7 (pbk.)
   1. Trading companies.   2. Export marketing.   3. International trade.
I. Title.
   HF1416.W43 2007
   658.8—dc22   2007012090

10 9 8 7 6 5

The fourth edition of *Building an Import/Export Business* is dedicated to the managers and staff of the United States Department of Homeland Security. They have the very difficult task of allowing legitimate trade to flow while blocking imports and exports that might bring harm to the United States.

This huge and relatively new government agency includes the Transportation Security Administration (TSA), which protects the nation's transportation systems to ensure freedom of movement for people and commerce. It also includes United States Customs and Border Protection (CBP), which is responsible for protecting the nation's borders against terrorists and terrorism while facilitating the flow of legitimate trade and travel. In addition, it includes the United States Immigration and Customs Enforcement (ICE), which is charged with finding and eliminating vulnerabilities in the nation's border, economic, transportation and infrastructure security.

Imagine 30,000 sealed shipping containers entering the United States every day through ports on all borders, and the enormous task of deciding which ones to detain and inspect. It boggles the mind, yet it is being done to the best of the DHS's ability, guided by ever-changing legislation and its interpretation. I congratulate everyone who is involved in this difficult but vital endeavor.

Contents

Acknowledgments

It might seem strange to acknowledge the Internet, but that is exactly what I am doing. Unlike the first edition of this book, for which none of the information came from the Internet, this fourth edition draws heavily on electronic information. The new world of high technology helps authors as much as it does international traders.

For example, the Web site of the U.S. Food and Drug Administration, at www.fda.gov, has become user-friendly and extensive. Detailed information, which used to be nearly impossible to obtain, is now freely available. Access is limited to people with computers, high-speed connections, and knowledge of how to search, but that now includes most of us.

I also owe debts of gratitude to friends and acquaintances who have told me of their recent adventures in international trade. Some of these are included in the text. They give life to concepts that might otherwise be difficult to grasp.

Introduction

"The Mighty Micro-Multinational," an article in the July 2006 issue of *Business 2.0* magazine, told of a small company based in San Francisco. Its chief technical officer lived in the Dominican Republic and worked mainly on the beach. From there he chatted by instant messenger and e-mail with associates in Serbia and Ireland and sometimes made international calls through the Internet. The company's business was shipping fruit from Mexico and California to Washington State, concentrating it and shipping the concentrate to California, then producing juice and sending it to warehouses in California and Wisconsin. Its customer service center was in the Philippines and the accounting department in India. This is the kind of world you can step into when you embark on an import/export business.

Millions of people in the United States and abroad dream of owning their own business. Of the thousands of us who try, many fail, many succeed to some degree, and a few become highly successful. Reading this book will increase your chances of landing in the third category.

I have never seen success and failure statistics just for people who start import and/or export businesses, but they are probably similar to the statistics for businesses in general. I will say in this book that importing is easier than exporting, but there is money to be made either way. For example, I know a fellow Rotarian who raises and sells farm animals. He unintentionally met an importer from Ecuador, whose first order led to a significant business exporting live pigs to South American countries.

This is an enormous business. In 2005, two-way trade between the United States and Canada came to $472 billion dollars. It was $281 billion with China, $271 billion with Mexico, and $225 billion with Japan (data taken from http://dataweb.usitc.gov/scripts/cy_m3_run.asp).

Thousands of companies of all sizes combine to produce these startling figures. Also, nations are trading more and more as interest in foreign goods increases, transportation costs and customs duties decrease, and procedures such as international payment are simplified.

Two journals of commerce publications, the *Directory of United States Importers* and the *Directory of United States Exporters*, together list more than 60,000 companies. The listings give indications of company size, and many if not most of the firms have just a few employees and small volumes of shipments.

People who want to start businesses often ask me which products they should deal in to make big money fast. In responding, I usually try to lower their expectations and then tell them that what really matters is the customer. If they can find a person who is willing and able to buy something from them, all the other details can usually be worked out. I will talk about this in more detail later in this book.

I hope that each of my readers will end up in that select group of highly successful international businesspeople. Reading this book will not guarantee it but will definitely help.

There are several books, articles, and Web sites that can introduce you to importing and exporting. Beware, though, of any that promise to set you up in business quickly and easily for a few hundred dollars. There are some that will take your money and not provide much more than product ideas and names of suppliers.

The following information sources are mentioned in this introduction. Some other good ones are the publication *Importing into the United States*, which is described in a later chapter, and *Export Basics*, on the Web site www.export.gov/exportbasics/index.asp.

- *Business 2.0* magazine's article, "The Mighty Micro-Multinational," in the July 2006 issue, http://money.cnn.com/magazines/business2/business2_archive2006/07/01/8380230index.htm.

- The *Directory of United States Importers* and the *Directory of United States Exporters*, available from Commonwealth Business Media. Address: 400 Windsor Corporate Park, 50 Millstone Road, Suite 200, East Windsor, NJ 08520-1415; Phone: (877) 203-5277; Web site: www.piers.com/impexporder.

I

Your Big Idea:
Is It Any Good?

A lot of mediocre ideas have been turned into successful businesses, and many great ideas have fallen by the wayside. Still, you will have a better chance of succeeding if you start with a good idea rather than with a bad one. Let's look at a couple of import/export business ideas and how you might analyze them: handicrafts from Ecuador and home safes to Mexico or Central America.

IMPORTING HANDICRAFTS FROM ECUADOR

Ecuador, especially the town of Otavalo, is one of the world's greatest areas for buying handicrafts. The local people are famous for their colorful textile items, jewelry, paintings, and so on. Suppose you visit Otavalo and decide to build a business importing crafts to the United States. First, you might search on the Internet to see whether anyone else is doing this. Otavalo has been there for a long time, and it is not likely that you are the first person to be attracted by its products.

A quick search on the Internet suggests that you may not have many competitors. How can this be explained? People usually buy handicrafts when they visit a country, and aren't very interested in them if they don't. Also, crafts sell better in our materialistic society if they are utilitarian. They must be useful in some way. Of course, there is another possible explanation—that some of your competitors do not have Web sites.

If you decide that some of the Ecuadorian crafts are attractive and useful, and can probably be sold in the United States, you will want to look into the matter of finding an honest, reliable supplier. Suppose that you search on the Internet and find an Ecuadorian export promotion organization known as CORPEI, which promises (by e-mail) that you will have no trouble finding excellent suppliers.

When you look at the market, however, you find that most of the sales of similar products are made at ethnic fairs and festivals and that these markets are pretty well supplied. This worries you a little. You don't want to work on weekends.

Moving on to other details, you find that transportation of the products will be relatively easy and that import regulations on the items from Otavalo will not be especially burdensome. Still, you come back to the vital questions of how and to whom you will be able to sell the various items. If you cannot find good answers to these questions, you should probably look for another business idea.

EXPORTING HARDWARE

Now, suppose you are looking on the Internet one day and you come upon the Web site www.madeinusa.org. From the 30 categories of merchandise you select hardware because you worked for a long time at Home Depot or Lowe's and know the products well. You want a fairly high-ticket item and one that cannot be produced easily in all countries. Safes for homes and offices catch your eye. Since several companies make safes, you expect to be able to line up a supplier. You can either buy from the supplier and resell or set up a transaction between the supplier and a foreign buyer and receive a commission.

Since these products are too heavy to ship by air, you will have to find markets in countries that you can ship to by land or by sea. Also, since you cannot make money exporting just one safe at a time, you will have to find someone in each country to import a quantity of the safes and sell them to his or her customers.

You know from reading newspapers that crime has been increasing in Mexico and some Central American countries, so many people there should want to own safes. These countries can be reached by land or by sea. Maybe you even know someone in Mexico City or San Salvador who can help you find a qualified importer/distributor. If you do not know such a person, your state or federal department of commerce will help you.

You look into U.S. export controls and Mexican and Salvadoran import controls on safes and conclude that none of them will pose a significant obstacle. Then you move on to the problem of money, because you will probably have to stock the distributor's warehouse at your expense, perhaps with payment guaranteed by an instrument called a *letter of credit* (to be explained later).

If you can get over the financial hurdle, you might be able to set up a profitable business venture.

Let's look at two more examples, in a little more detail.

IMPORTING "WORLD CLOCKS"

Suppose you are looking through an export promotion catalog from Taiwan and see a small clock that tells the time in major world cities. This item seems to be functional as well as decorative, and you decide to look into it, even though you know that world times are available on the Internet. You ask for a catalog and price list and receive them immediately by e-mail. Then you show the appropriate catalog page to several friends, taking care to not reveal the supplier's name and address.

Since most of your friends seem to like the product, you decide to take the next step. Your order a half dozen items as samples. After some discussion with the supplier, you agree to pay for the clocks through PayPal, and the company in Taiwan agrees to pay to send them by airmail. You might have been able to get one sample free, but free samples have become less common and you wanted more than one.

While you wait for the samples, you go to www.usitc.gov to

consult the United States tariff schedule. You become quite confused but finally determine that there is a small duty on clocks, another on clock cases, and a slightly larger duty on the batteries. You determine that each of these three pieces must be marked in a conspicuous place with the country of origin. In addition, the clock movement must be marked with the name of the manufacturer and the number of jewels, including substitutes for jewels. The tariff schedule will be explained later in this book.

While waiting, you think hard about who might want to buy world time clocks. You decide that they will sell best as gifts for people who travel internationally. Also, you decide that gift-givers will be likely to buy such items from hard-copy and online catalog merchants, so these will become the end point of your distribution channel.

Soon the samples arrive. They are marked SAMPLES, NO COMMERCIAL VALUE, and no duty is charged. They look good but not great, and the packaging isn't as strong or as attractive as you think it should be. The instructions seem clear but have a few mistakes in English. You decide, based on prices you have seen in the market, to set the suggested retail price at $19.95.

From the Internet and a book in your local business library, you identify companies whose product lines include gifts for travelers. You send them a description of your product and ask if they would consider selling it. Since only one responds, you phone them all and find three buyers who are interested. You send each of them a sample, your suggested retail price, and your price to them of $10 including shipping. Your calculations show that you can make an acceptable profit if you sell to the buyers for $10.

Then you call the buyers again and find one who likes the product and wants to talk with you. Fortunately, she isn't far away, so you make an appointment to see her. You try to anticipate all her questions and develop a "sell sheet" that will answer them. A sell sheet contains the information that you will provide in a sales presentation. Then, you can leave it with your customer.

When you are face-to-face with the buyer, she agrees to put the item in her catalog but will purchase only a small quantity at a time. She wants you to have a larger quantity, in stock in the United States, so she can get them from you when she needs them.

She wants just two cartons of 60 clocks each but wants you to have at least five cartons in stock. You quickly figure your cost for the five cartons and decide to accept her order. She offers to send it to you in writing within a week.

So, you are in business. You ask the supplier for a firm quotation on seven cases of 60 clocks, sent to you by airfreight. It arrives by e-mail: $270 per case plus $450 for shipping for a total of $2,340. You agree to pay via a sight draft, with documents provided against payment, and send your order. International payment methods and commercial documents such as orders are described later on. You ask the supplier to correct the instructions, use stronger, more attractive packaging, and ship in multiwall cardboard cartons. He agrees.

Just 10 days later you receive a call from Jumping Air Freight. Your goods are in! Unfortunately, since the value is more than $2,000, you will need to file a *formal* customs entry, and that is somewhat complicated. The airfreight company puts you in touch with a *customs broker* who can handle this, for a fee of course. You tell the broker to go ahead and to call you when the shipment is ready to pick up. Luckily, you have a vehicle large enough to hold the seven cartons.

You go to your bank and find that it has received a small package of documents from the exporter. The bank presents you with a *draft* for the cost of the clocks and the airfreight, which you agree to pay. Then you receive the documents and take them to the customs broker. The next day, the broker calls you, and the merchandise is yours for the taking. Later you will be billed for the customs duty and the broker's fee.

The clocks look good, but the instructions and the packaging have not been improved. You understand that this could not be done so quickly. The exterior packing is pretty strong, and there doesn't seem to be any damage to the merchandise.

Your cost turns out to be $1,890 for the clocks, $450 for shipping, $75 for customs duty, and $190 for the services of the customs broker—a total of $2,605. This comes to $6.20 per clock, assuming none is damaged or defective. Since you expect to get about $9.70 per clock, after paying for shipping, your *gross margin* will be $3.50, or 36 percent of your selling price. That sounds pretty good.

You realize that whether you can make money with the clocks depends on your ability to sell them through catalog dealers or other outlets. You do a quick calculation of your office, telephone, and other fixed costs and see that they will come to about $2,000 per month. That means you will have to sell 571 clocks per month to break even (2,000/3.5), which does not include any compensation for your time. If you want to make just $1,000 per month from the business, you will have to sell 857 clocks every 30 days.

Well, it's a start. If you can add other items to build a product line and market them well, you will have a going concern.

EXPORTING PRINTER PAPER

Now that you have started importing, you decide to try to export. You go to a Web site, www.export.gov, to search for trade leads and to find a company in Cameroon that wants to import several kinds of paper products. The most important of these is printer paper, about which you have some knowledge.

By corresponding with the importer, you are able to get specifications as to the types and quantities of paper she wants. You ask about shipping and payment and are told that the goods should be sent by sea to the port of Douala with shipping and insurance prepaid. The importer is willing to pay through a letter of credit issued by the Commercial Bank of Cameroon.

You start your search for suppliers with the *Thomas Register of American Manufacturers*, which you buy on a CD-ROM for about $10. There you find several companies. You call some and find, to your delight, that most of them are not represented in Cameroon and are willing to ship to that country, provided they have payment in advance or firm guarantees of payment.

A friend tells you that because of its nature, printer paper is not subject to any special U.S. export restrictions. We will cover this subject later in the book. To find out about import restrictions, you check with the desk officer who handles Cameroon at the U.S. Department of Commerce. Also, you contact the National Technical Information Service in Washington, D.C., and order a Commercial Guide to the country. You consider contacting a commercial attaché from Cameroon but do not find one in the United States. On the Internet you find one in Ethiopia, but that's far from Cameroon and there is no fax number or e-mail address.

Since many paper manufacturers have similar products, you select one to deal with because you know of the company and have established, by phone, a good working relationship with a person in the export sales department. You get a price of $25 per case of 10 reams of 20 pound, 96 US/108 Euro Bright paper, delivered to a U.S. port. The supplier says that each box weighs 50 pounds, and that he can load 1,150 boxes in a 20-foot container.

Then you contact a freight forwarder to help you develop a price quotation. The numbers are as follows.

Cost Item	Amount
1,150 boxes of paper delivered to Port Newark	$28,750
Freight forwarding and related charges	300
Ocean freight from Newark to Douala with surcharges and insurance	3,660
Banking and miscellaneous charges	300
TOTAL COST	**$33,010**

There are a couple of other important details, one of which is profit. You have to earn enough to justify the time and the risk, but you cannot quote more than other companies unless you can offer something of value besides the paper. You decide to add 10 percent to the merchandise cost, or $2,875. That makes your quotation, delivered to Douala, $35,885 (33,010 + 2,875).

The other important detail is how to arrange the payment, and this presents a problem. You could scrape up the $33,000 but are not sure you want to take the risk. The supplier, based on your very limited track record, isn't willing to give you enough credit. What to do?

Finally, the supplier suggests that you get the order written to his company. He offers to pay you a 5 percent commission, which means you will make just half as much as you counted on, but he offers to pay the 5 percent commission on any future orders you get from the same customer. Finally, he says that he wants the letter of credit guaranteed by Citibank in New York. You decide to agree to these conditions.

When you recalculate your price to the importer, it goes down, because you are changing from a 10 percent markup to a 5 percent commission. Then it goes back up a little because of the cost of confirming the letter of credit.

After more contact by phone and e-mail, your customer agrees to buy and sends her purchase order, which you forward to the supplier. The customer's bank opens a letter of credit to the supplier, who succeeds in getting it confirmed by Citibank. The supplier ships, gets paid, and sends your commission.

It all worked out pretty well. Maybe there is some future in this business of arranging export transactions—for a commission.

BROKERING COMPUTER EQUIPMENT

I have an acquaintance who advertises himself as an "international products search broker and manufacturer's representative." His idea is to help people find the best source for products they want to buy, arrange a deal, and earn a commission. He will deal with any product but specializes in laptop computers and related equipment. Will this idea work for him? Would it work for you? Read on. In a few chapters you should be able to form an opinion.

SOURCES OF INFORMATION AND HELP

This chapter is about analyzing product ideas, or product/market combinations, to determine whether the one you have in mind seems viable. This is a vital part of your preparation to do business. There are various Web sites that will help you with this process. One is NetMBA at www.netmba.com/marketing/market/analysis, and a more sophisticated one is KnowThis.com at www.knowthis.com/tutorials/marketing/marketingplan1/3.htm.

The following sources of information are given in chapter 1.

- PayPal, an online payment solutions company. Address: 2211 North First Street, San Jose, CA 95131; Phone: (402) 935-2050; Web site: www.paypal.com.

- WWW.USITC.GOV, the United States International Trade Commission, an independent federal agency. Address: 500 E Street, SW, Washington, DC 20436; Phone: (202) 205-2000; Fax: (202) 205-2340.

- WWW.EXPORT.GOV, the U.S. government's export portal, which is sponsored by several federal agencies specializing in exporting. Phone: (800) USA-TRAD(E).

- *Thomas Register of American Manufacturers*, a publication of Thomas Publishing. Address: Five Penn Plaza, New York, NY 10001; Phone: (212) 695-0500; Fax: (212) 290-7362; Web site: www.thomaspublishing.com.

- National Technical Information Service's (NTIS) publication, *Commercial Guide*. NTIS is part of the U.S. Department of Commerce. Address: 5285 Port Royal Road, Springfield, VA 22161; Phone: (703) 605-6000 or (800) 553-NTIS; Fax: (703) 487-4146; Web site: www.ntis.gov.

2

Is This Business for You?

This chapter is really about you. I am assuming that you are interested in starting your own business and are thinking that it could be an import and/or export business. The discussion that follows covers some personal characteristics that will affect your ability to be successful. Then you will see 20 important questions, the answers to which can be the beginning of your business plan. We will conclude with two brief financial examples, which can help you decide whether your business is likely to pay off economically.

HAVE YOU FAILED YET?

Yes, the question sounds strange, but it is one that many bank loan officers ask. The idea is that many entrepreneurs fail the first time, but they learn from their failures, and the kinds of personalities that led them to try once will make them try again and again until they ultimately succeed.

Another way of looking at this is to ask yourself what experience you have had in business. Importing and exporting are definitely businesses that require knowledge of purchasing, marketing/ selling, finance, and other functions that go along with being your own boss.

If you are weak in this area, I suggest taking a course for entre-preneurs or at least reading some of the many good books on how to start and manage a small business.

HOW IS YOUR FINANCIAL SITUATION?

I often meet people who want to start businesses but have little or no capital and not much borrowing capacity. One group that stands out in my mind is a trio of men who came to meet me but were all low on funds and had all been through bankruptcy within the past two years. I paid the lunch bill and wished them well.

You normally need some money to register your business and for basic office equipment, communications, and so forth. Then, if you plan to buy merchandise for import or export, you will probably have to pay for it before you can sell it and collect from your buyer. In addition, you may have to lay out cash for trans-portation, storage, and other services.

As we saw in chapter 1, many people make a living acting as agents or brokers and do not take title to or possession of mer-chandise. Doing business this way limits their need for capital, but even so, they usually set up small offices and have communication and other expenses. Also, if you plan to quit your job to start this business, you will need money to live on, probably for several months.

This means that you should have several thousand dollars in the bank before you start. You may be able to borrow part of the money but only if you have business experience, cash, and collat-eral. We will talk more about financing in the next chapter.

INTEREST IN AND KNOWLEDGE OF THE WORLD

Did you hate geography in school? If you did, it may come back to haunt you. Long after the United States began fighting in Afghanistan and Iraq, I read in the September 26, 2006, edition of the *Washington Post* that 88 percent of Americans could not locate

Afghanistan on a blank map; 75 percent could not locate Iran or Israel; and 63 percent could not locate Iraq. It really helps to know where countries are located, which ones are friendly with the United States, which have strong currencies, and so forth.

This may be a foolish example, but suppose you are selling to someone in El Salvador and the buyer suggests paying you in colones. It would be useful for you to know that colones have no value because El Salvador adopted the U.S. dollar in 2001.

Suppose you are buying from a company in Thailand and there is a military coup, which did occur in September 2006. Would you worry about receiving your shipment? You probably would not worry if you knew that Thailand often had nondemocratic changes of government and there was usually not much economic disruption. This was especially true in 2006, partly because the king favored the military action of overthrowing the elected prime minister.

If your knowledge of the world is weak, you would do well to subscribe to the *New York Times*, read *U.S. News and World Report*, and listen to the news on *BBC World* regularly on the radio or watch it on TV. Whatever you do in life, the knowledge gained will not hurt you.

FAMILIARITY WITH FOREIGN CULTURES AND LANGUAGES

There are many stories, some true and some probably made up, about mistakes related to culture that have caused embarrassment or worse. Type "cultural blunders" in a search engine and you will find several. I was recently on the receiving end of one when a young lady from Latin America called me to ask some questions about importing. She had heard that Americans were direct and straightforward, but she overdid it. She was *so* direct and straightforward that I quickly lost interest in doing business with her.

When you meet people and receive their business cards, what do you do? If you are meeting someone from Asia, especially, and don't spend a couple of seconds reading the information on the card, you will have committed a blunder.

Those of us who are frequently in contact with people of other cultures gradually learn about them and develop a sort of sixth sense that tells us when we are beginning to say or do something that might be offensive. Until you develop this sixth sense, tread carefully and ask questions. For example, if you are traveling overseas and are invited to dinner, don't automatically take the kind of present you would take in the United States. Ask a local friend what to take and what, if anything, to refrain from taking.

Language is an important part of culture and a reflection of it. Alaskans have names for several kinds of snow, and desert dwellers for several conditions of sand. A common expression in Spanish, *se cayó*, literally means "it fell," which a Latino will usually say instead of "I dropped it." Ask for a "boot" in England and you will be shown the trunk of a car instead of an item of footwear.

I suggest trying to learn a little of the language of the country or countries you expect to do business with. Besides books and tapes, an excellent source is Transparent.com, which will send you one word a day of your favorite language and will let you hear it used in a sentence. Please don't tell on me, but I use three e-mail addresses and get a word a day in each of three languages.

When you need to use a translator (for written work) or an interpreter (for oral conversations), be sure you have someone who is competent. Overseas, U.S. commercial offices can usually help you find good people. Above all, *never* use a computer or Web-based translation without having it checked by a human who is fluent in both of the languages involved. An electronic translation can be helpful as a starting point but cannot capture the many nuances of a language.

PERSISTENCE, PATIENCE, AND JUDGMENT

Persistence, to a point, is usually a virtue in business. You are not likely to be very successful in the first few months, so be prepared to give your business some time to develop. On the other hand, if you are losing money or barely breaking even, you may judge that the time has come to change your business model or to close for a while. In the printer paper example in chapter 1, we talked about changing from a buy-sell to a commission agent model.

With individual customers, too, you should be persistent to a point. If you are importing ground coffee from Colombia and think it would be an excellent product to sell to a major store chain, you will certainly not make a sale immediately. It will take several contacts with both local and regional buyers. An acquaintance of mine was in exactly that position. Not long after he stopped trying, the store chain started selling a similar product from a different vendor.

A word of advice here is to take stock at least every month of customers you are working on and the status of each and decide whether, and if so how, to continue your pursuit of them. Every year take stock of your business as a whole and prepare a pro forma (projected) income and expense statement for the year to come. If you can't project a profit that will justify continuing in the business, you might have to change course or take a job for a while.

ATTENTION TO DETAIL

In international trade, as with any business, you have to give the buyer exactly what he or she asks for. Before the days of computers, I received an export order for rolls of paper for calculators and adding machines. I found a supplier, made the necessary arrangements, and shipped the product. All would have been fine except that someone, we'll never know for certain who, had typed "3/8 inch" instead of "5/8 inch" for the diameter of the cores. The rolls got to the buyer in perfect condition, but he couldn't use them.

Details can be especially critical when they relate to payment. Suppose you are exporting electric motors and getting paid with a letter of credit that specifies 100 boxes each containing 10 motors. If for some reason you ship 10 boxes each containing 100 motors, you will technically be in violation of the terms of the credit, and your payment may be delayed.

So, if you are a broad thinker who doesn't like to be bothered with details, you might want to find a different kind of business.

CONTACTS WITH BUYERS OR THE ABILITY TO MAKE THEM

It is certainly possible to start an import or export business by finding an attractive product and then looking for buyers, and this is the way it is usually done. Selling, however, is usually much harder than buying. If you have or can find someone who wants to buy a product from you, and will give you the specifications, you can probably find and supply the item. If your friend will tell you how much he or she is willing to pay, so much the better.

For example, there is a substantial Bolivian community in an area of northern Virginia that, a few years ago, was hungry for Bolivian products. The first people who started importing to the United States, from companies such as Dillman in Cochabamba, had no trouble selling, because the buyers, owners of Latino stores, needed these products on their shelves.

On the export side, in 1992 the U.S. Congress enacted legislation that permitted exports of agricultural goods and medicines to Cuba for humanitarian reasons. A Virginia firm, Virginia Apple Trading Company (VATC), realized that apples were in demand in Cuba. Perhaps the common belief that "an apple a day keeps the doctor away" makes this delicious fruit "humanitarian." In any case, VATC could legally sell and had no trouble finding buyers who wanted this product.

TWENTY IMPORTANT QUESTIONS

Now, let's look at the 20 questions. Your answers to these can be the beginning of your import/export business plan.

1. **Why are you thinking of starting a business? What are your objectives?**

   If your answer is "to make money," you should probably spend extra time on good planning with realistic financial projections.

If you basically want to experiment with international trade and perhaps deduct some travel expenses from your income for tax purposes, you are at a lower level of commitment and can start your business in a less formal way. If you are unemployed and want to start a business because you don't feel like looking for a job, please think again. Some people who are in this position succeed, but many would be better off getting more work experience, even at low salaries.

2. What do you have going for you?

Once in a while I read of someone who, for example, bakes cookies for a church supper and 10,000 people ask where to buy them. For most of us, however, starting a business is a lot harder, and every asset you have may be called into play. If you have business training and experience, capital, product knowledge, contacts with buyers, travel experience, or foreign languages, you'll be in a much stronger position than if you lack these things.

3. Do you plan to import, export, or both?

Small-scale importers outnumber exporters by a wide margin. I think this is because selling is usually the harder part of the business, and if you import, you will be selling in your own environment (the United States). If you export, however, you can get free help from federal, state, and often local government organizations. I do suggest picking one or the other, at least at first. It's hard enough to start one business; you don't want to be starting two at the same time.

4. Do you plan to work as a merchant, an agent, a broker, or some combination of these?

The easiest way to go into this business is usually by buying and reselling, which makes you a merchant. Unfortunately, this model usually requires quite a bit of money and involves risk. You might, for example, buy and sell some goods and not be able to collect from your customer.

Some people begin as commission agents, and you can be a

selling or a buying agent for a U.S. or a foreign company. There is usually a formal written agreement by which the *principal* designates a firm or individual to act his agent in return for a commission on completed transactions.

The third alternative is for you to just try to broker, or arrange, deals between unrelated parties. You can try to collect a commission from either party to the transaction, or from both. This model does not always require written contracts. Brokers usually do not take title to or possession of products, but there are some who do. Produce brokers, for example, work very differently from real estate brokers.

5. **When you start, will you be working full-time or part-time?**

Many people try to start businesses on a part-time basis, and sometimes they do well. Often, however, they find themselves under a lot of pressure and have to surreptitiously make phone calls or do other work on their small ventures while they are being paid to do something else.

Another option is for one person to work on a new business while a partner keeps pulling in a salary. This can work well if the one salary covers the couple's expenses.

A final option is simply to quit work and try to build up the new business. This maximizes the chance of being successful but it entails a risk that you will use up all of your savings and have to go back to work. This recently happened to a person I know. He and his partner are still working at their business in the evenings and on weekends.

6. **Who, if anyone, can help you with the work in the beginning?**

Even a very small business involves buying, selling, accounting, and a variety of other tasks, and most people aren't good at all of them. It is very helpful to have a partner or an employee and/or to subcontract some functions such as preparing tax returns.

One importer I know, from Bolivia, is working full-time on his new business while his wife continues at her regular job but also has specified responsibilities in the new firm. So far, the arrangement is working very well.

7. What is your target market?

This is among the most important questions. If you "shotgun" your products at millions of people, you may not hit any of them. Use a rifle at first. Instead of offering hand-tooled leather to anyone in the United States, try hand-tooled leather menu covers to Peruvian restaurants. That is a market you can identify and contact. Instead of trying to export fire extinguishers to anyone in the world, try selling them to hardware stores that sell to middle-income consumers in selected countries in which most household stoves use gas.

8. How do you plan to sell to customers in the target market?

If you can find a product that will bring customers running to you, you'll be among the fortunate few. Most people have to attract customers by promotion and then sell to them. You will probably need a plan for promoting sales and a "sell sheet" to use in meetings with potential buyers.

For example, suppose you want to import from Russia a system to detect computer network invasions and attacks. If you pick banks as a target market, you might advertise in *The Banker* magazine and develop a sales presentation for bankers. If you want to sell that Russian product in Colombia, you might look for a local agent and use a sales presentation that shows that person how much money he or she can make by selling the new system.

9. Which type(s) of product(s) do you plan to deal in?

The best answer to this question is that you will deal in a product for which you already have a customer. If you cannot do that, try looking for a product that you like and know a lot about, that is available in sufficient quantity, and that can be transported to and entered (through customs) into your market country. Whichever product you choose, you will probably find that companies in the United States import it, export it, or both. Nearly every product is traded internationally, and you may find a way to get a piece of the action.

10. **What will be your sources of supply—companies and countries?**

Both importers and exporters usually try to deal with companies that produce merchandise, rather than buying from intermediaries. Middlemen have a role to play, but each one has a profit and costs that increase the price to the consumer. There is information later in the book about how to find manufacturers in the United States and abroad.

If you import, you will probably find potential suppliers in several countries. Some factors to consider in selecting a country from which to buy are its reputation for quality, its cost structure, transportation to the United States, and customs duties.

11. **How will you ship your merchandise?**

There are several different methods of shipping. Small items can be handled by couriers. You might use airfreight for larger shipments and sea or land for still larger ones, but the decision also varies with such factors as the value and fragility of the cargo. *Intermodal* shipments are very common; your organic apple juice from New York State to India might be moved to its destination by truck, ship, train, and possibly oxcart to some small stores.

In international shipping there are a number of standardized terms such as FOB and CIF. It is important that you understand these; the main ones are explained later in this book.

12. **Which method of international payment do you plan to use?**

Inexpensive, secure payment is vital to any business. In international transactions there is an extra element because money must cross international boundaries. This has been made easier by new methods of payment but, in some cases, is complicated by counterterrorism measures.

Unfortunately, in most or all countries there are unscrupulous people who try to order merchandise from overseas and not pay for it. I once heard of a small businessman in Taiwan who received an order for live birds from a buyer in the United States. He invested all his capital in purchasing and shipping the birds, did not get paid, and was out of business almost before he started. There are steps you can take to prevent this from happening to you.

13. **Which U.S. and foreign government regulations will concern you?**

International traders are subject to the laws of multiple juris-dictions—federal, state, and local—in both the exporting and the importing countries. There are also bilateral and multilateral agreements that come into play with regard to many transactions. This book explains some of the regulations and gives you information about how to find out about many of the others.

14. **What will be your company's name and form of organization?**

Should your business bear your name or a trade name that you create and register? Should you incorporate, and if so, which kind of corporation should you select? Your answers to these questions have important implications for liability and taxation. This book will give you ideas about how to make these decisions, but it is suggested that you consult a lawyer and/or an accountant. They can give expert guidance that will probably pay off in the long run.

15. **What will you do for an office and office equipment?**

Many people start businesses in their homes, and that has become easier and more acceptable than it used to be. You will save a lot of money, but of course there are disadvantages. You will have to find another place for business meetings, and you may suffer from being too close to your spouse and kids, the refrigerator, and the garden tools.

Equipping a home office is not difficult, but, of course, there are costs involved. This book will give you some guidance as to the things you should have and those you can do without. You should avoid spending money for that big office and 100-gigabyte computer until there is cash coming in.

16. **How will you communicate with your suppliers and customers?**

There is an art to knowing when to use phone, fax, and e-mail, and a science to picking the most cost-effective services. For example, many small traders now use the Internet as a telephone with services such as Skype. This book will help you explore some of the options.

On the subject of communications, you can now start to practice speaking and writing in clear, simple English with no colloquial expressions. If you tell your foreign supplier that he is "pulling your leg" or that your best customer just "kicked the bucket," confusion will reign.

17. **Which service companies will you need, and how will you select them?**

You may want to use the services of an accountant and/or an attorney to help set up your business. Then you will need a bank, an Internet provider, a telephone company, and perhaps an insurance broker. When you start doing business, you will need a freight forwarder and perhaps a customs broker, a courier service, and others. This book will give you more information about these kinds of companies and how to select them.

18. **Where will you get information and help as your business develops?**

You will often need clear, accurate, up-to-date information about such things as trade regulations and transportation costs, and you would like to be able to get information quickly and at a reasonable cost. This book will give you ideas about how to do it. There is a lot of free help available, but much more for exporters than for importers.

You might also want to look for help with general aspects of organizing and operating your business. It is available in some areas from business mentors, the International Executive Service Corps, the Alternative Board (for a price), and other organizations.

19. **How much will you invest, and where will the money come from?**

No matter how you start the business, you will have to make some investment. It is wise in the beginning to determine your start-up costs, including equipment, the cost of your time, and "working capital" to see you through until you start to make a profit.

Once you have a bottom-line number, you will know whether you have enough money. If you don't have enough, you will know how much more you need and can look at possible sources. You can consider various kinds of loans as well as capital investment by friends and relatives. A later chapter will look at these options.

20. What is your income and profit potential?

After you figure out the start-up costs, you should project sales and then project your income and your expenses. The difference between income and expenses is what you will have left to put back into your business and for personal use. Let's look at two brief examples that will help you understand the financial side of small import and export businesses.

IMPORT MERCHANT EXAMPLE

Suppose you decide to import a product or products, take title to and possession of them, stock small amounts in your basement or garage, sell them, and ship them to your customers. Perhaps you plan to sell by means of a manufacturer's representative, who will receive a 15 percent commission. You work from home to keep costs to a minimum. Summarized operating results, after a few months in businesses, are as follows.

Item	Dollars	Percent
Sales for the month	20,000	100
Less cost of merchandise	−12,000	60
	=8,000	40
Less commission on sales	−3,000	15
	=5,000	25
Less operating expenses	−2,000	10
Profit before owner's salary and income tax	=3,000	15

Note that all figures are given as a percentage of sales. Note also that monthly sales of $20,000 have produced a nice part-time income but not a full-time income. If you want to, you can work with these numbers to see how the bottom line will change if you increase or decrease sales, pay more or less than 60 percent for your merchandise, pay a higher or lower rate of commission, or change your level of operating expenses. For example, you will see that if the $2,000 is a fixed cost (not changing with the level of sales), a 10 percent increase in sales will result in more than a 10 percent increase in your gross profit.

EXPORT AGENT EXAMPLE

Now, suppose you are working as an export agent. Your business model is to book orders from foreign buyers for products of U.S. manufacturing firms. You might have five or six principals who produce related goods so you can offer a full line of, for example, industrial lighting fixtures. You receive commissions from your principals that average 14 percent of sales, and you pay 6 percent to your own agents in foreign markets. You might be able to do without these agents but would have higher travel and communication (phone and fax) expenses. You work from a small rented office and try to keep expenses to a minimum. Your operating results might be summarized as follows.

Item	Dollars	Percent
Sales for the month	200,000	100
Commissions earned	28,000	14
Less foreign agents' commissions	−12,000	6
Net sales	=16,000	8
Less operating expenses	−6,000	3
Profit before owner's salary and income tax	=10,000	5

Note that I have the agent selling 10 times what the merchant was selling and making just over three times as much profit. This is because the agent is performing fewer functions and taking very little risk. As an agent your main investment is your time, and theoretically that is worth whatever you would earn if you were to use it some other way.

SOURCES OF INFORMATION AND HELP

You might want to buy a book in which there is some kind of self-assessment for potential entrepreneurs. Of course, you can find self-assessment tools on the Web also. One is the entrepreneurial self assessment, from a Canadian organization. The Web address is very long, however: www.bdc.ca/en/business_tools/ entrepreneurial_self-Assessment/Entrepreneurial_self_assessment .htm. You might also try one from the Chamber of Commerce of West Alabama, on the Web at www.youronestopcenter.com/ entrepreneur-test.php.

The following are the sources of information mentioned in this chapter.

- *New York Times*, a great daily newspaper. Web site: www .nytimes.com.

- *U.S. News and World Report*, a weekly magazine. Web site: www.usnews.com.

- *BBC World* a source of news distributed via a nightly news program broadcast on most Public Broadcasting Service television stations, public radio stations, and their Web site, www.bbcworld.com.

- Transparent.com is the Web site for Transparent Language, which provides language-learning solutions in over 100 languages. Address: 12 Murphy Drive, Nashua, NH 03062; Phone: (603) 262-6300; Fax: (603) 262-6476.

- *The Banker* magazine is published monthly by Financial Times. Web site: www.thebanker.com.

- International Executive Service Corps is a private, not-for-profit organization that recruits and assigns U.S. volunteer experts to assist businesses in developing and emerging-market countries worldwide. Address: 901 15th Street, NW, Suite 1010, Washington, DC 20005; Phone: (202) 589-2600; Fax: (202) 326-0289; Web site: www.iesc.org.

- The Alternative Board brings together owners of privately held businesses to solve challenges and seize new opportunities. Board members meet monthly to learn from one another's successes and mistakes and grow their businesses to the next level. Address: 1640 Grant Street, Suite 200, Denver, CO 80203; Phone: (800) 727-0126; Fax: (303) 839-0012; Web site: www.tabboards.com.

3

Setting Up Your Business

Technically, it is possible to import or export without setting up a business. There are, however, several reasons for formalizing your venture. With a registered business you can give it a name other than your own, which normally sounds better. Also, you might be able to sell shares of stock to raise money. You may want the protection against judgments resulting from lawsuits that an incorporated business provides. Finally, you might want to sell to individuals in the United States. To do this legally, you will need a sales tax number, and to get that, you will need an employer identification number. This all says to me: Register your business.

FORMS OF ORGANIZATION

The four types of business organization in the United States are as follows:

1. Sole proprietorship
2. Partnership
3. Corporation
4. Limited liability company

There is a lot of information on the Internet about forms of business organization. State laws vary, but the information that follows is applicable in most jurisdictions of the United States.

Sole Proprietorship

A sole proprietorship is your business, all yours. In general you can use this legal form if there will be no co-owners, your income and expenses will be small, and you will deal only with products that are not likely to cause any sort of illness, injury, or damage. This is because, as a sole proprietor, your personal assets will be at risk if anyone should sue your business.

Technically, if you start doing business under your name, you will automatically be the owner of a sole-proprietorship business. In your state there might be a form to fill out and send with a small amount of money, but this is no longer common. If you use a name other than your own, you will have to register that you are doing business as (DBA) a name that is not your own. There is a section later in this chapter on registering your business name.

As a sole proprietor you will make all business decisions and take all the glory or bear all the blame for the results of these decisions. There are real risks. For example, if you import and distribute dried fruit and someone becomes ill, or claims to have become ill, after eating it, that person can sue you and may be awarded most of your personal assets.

As a sole proprietor the gain or loss from your business will pass to your personal income tax return. You may, however, need to file certain kinds of business tax returns. Some of these are discussed in a later section.

Partnership

A partnership is as easy to form as a sole proprietorship except that there is usually a formal *partnership agreement*. There are sample agreements available on the Internet and in books of legal forms. Such an agreement normally states what each partner will contribute to the business (cash, time, etc.), what each will receive in salary or other benefits, who will be responsible for paying taxes on profits (usually the same for all partners), how the partnership would be terminated, and how disputes will be resolved.

There can be any number of partners, and there can be both "general" and "limited" partners. The word *limited* refers mainly to decision-making and to liability. It is for someone who wants to invest money and perhaps contribute in other ways but does not want to make important decisions or be held liable if there are judgments against the business.

Most business advisors do not recommend partnerships. They can be worse than rocky marriages. The kind of person who wants to own a business usually does not want to share decision-making with anyone else. Also, partnerships are often dissolved when one of the partners leaves the business, unless the departing partner can sell his share with the agreement of the remaining partners.

In this form of business, each partner's share of profit or loss is transferred to his or her personal income tax return. Of course, profits are taxed and losses can be deducted. As with a sole proprietorship, there are other tax reports that may have to be completed.

Corporation

A corporation is a more formal kind of business organization. It makes your business a separate legal entity, or corpus, which can raise capital by selling shares of stock and can theoretically continue with new owners when the original owners are gone.

Moreover, a corporate form of ownership helps protect your personal assets from legal judgments. This can, for example, keep you from having to sell your house to pay the medical bills of the young man who falls when a wheel breaks on a roller blade that you imported, even if he was skating 90 miles per hour on gravel. Incorporation will not *always* protect your personal assets, however. If a jury decides that you knowingly handled a dangerous product and incorporated specifically to avoid liability, you may have to pay a judgment.

A corporation must be registered with your state government. The fee is usually a few hundred dollars (e.g., $120 in Maryland), and nowadays most states have the required forms on the Internet. The forms are simple; however, there are several variations, such as "stock," "nonstock," and "close" corporations. I recommend consulting a lawyer or an accountant to be sure you are making the right choice. Many companies advertise on the Internet offering to help you incorporate your business, but for this function it's probably better to speak with someone you know and trust.

Some people might suggest incorporating in states such as Delaware that have relatively favorable tax laws. I have found, however, that this is not worthwhile for most small businesses. The saving is very small, and you will be required to register in your own state as a "foreign corporation." This will increase your record-keeping and reporting burden. Also, if you dissolve the corporation, you will have to remove it formally from both states and pay for the privilege of doing so.

The corporation will have to pay taxes on its net profit. Then it can retain some profit to use for expansion and distribute the remainder to shareholders, who will pay a dividend tax on the money they receive. Losses cannot be deducted from the owners' income for tax purposes but can be carried forward and deducted from profits in the future. On the other hand, a corporation can save you money because some kinds of taxes, insurance, and other expenses are deductible.

Import/export businesses should be incorporated from the start if they deal with products that can be dangerous in any way, and that includes nearly all products. Babies can choke on anything. This warning applies more to importers than to exporters, because they are closer to the customers. An aggrieved customer will sue whoever in the distribution channel is handiest, and whoever has the deepest pockets. In mid-1977, many companies that were importing from China learned this the hard way.

A variation that you might want to look into is the "subchapter S" corporation, or "S corp." The S stands for "small," and the procedure is to incorporate and then elect the S option. This legal form involves restrictions on the number of owners, public stock offerings, and other aspects of the business, but it gives you protection against liability and still lets you pay taxes as an individual.

Limited Liability Company

The form of organization known as a limited liability company (LLC) is relatively new in the United States. It exists in every state but is not the same in every state. It usually lets you pay taxes as an individual and gives you some protection from liability. In most states there must be at least two owners, and there can be shares of stock, but stock *certificates* do not have to be issued. An LLC can have foreign shareholders, which a subchapter S corporation cannot have.

Because of differences in liability, you are supposed to tell the people with whom you deal what kind of business organization you have. Thus, if it is a limited liability company, the name should include the initials "LLC." If it is a corporation, the name should include "Inc."

YOUR TRADE NAME AND LOGO

Assuming you want to do business in a name other than your own, you will have to select a name, make sure it has not been taken by someone else, and register it.

People tend to deal with companies the names of which they know and have favorable opinions. Whole Foods is a great name. It is easy to remember and describes the company's products in just two words.

In Laredo, Texas, I once saw a store that was named Shirt on You. I would never go there; I hated the name. On the other hand, there is, or was, a store in Guatemala named Q Kiss. I thought that was a fabulous name. To see why, pronounce it the way you would in Spanish (COO-kice).

If you can't think of a name you really like, think of three words and put their first letters together, like IBM. A three-letter name stands out in people's minds, and most consumers don't know or care that the company referred to used to be called International Business Machines.

The general rule is that you can't use a name that is so like or similar to another name that it might cause confusion. The geographic reach of this restriction depends on various factors. You would not be able to use the name IBM anywhere for a business that imports or exports computers, because the name is owned by a company that sells worldwide. You might be able to use it for a local company in a different line of business (maybe Instant Beverage Merchants).

To see if the name you have in mind is already taken, first do a search on the Internet. You can go on the Web to www.Network Solutions.com to see if anyone has registered a Web site using your name. A final step is to search the files of the U.S. Patent and Trademark Office at www.uspto.gov. That will show you if your chosen name is registered with the United States government and, if so, by whom and whether the registration is "alive" or "dead" (no longer in use).

Be careful to verify that the name you select does not have an insulting or vulgar connotation in the language of any of the countries you plan to deal with. To do this, it's best to check with an acquaintance who knows those languages well. Here is a simple example, in this case of a product name, from the Web site www.bytelevel.com:

> In August 2002, the British sportswear manufacturer Umbro was denounced as "appallingly insensitive" for naming a running shoe the Zyklon. That's the same name as the lethal gas used in extermination camps during the Second World War.

The final step is to register your company name, which you will do in your state when you register your business. In Maryland, where I am located, the cost is just $25 for a sole proprietorship. If you want to protect the name nationwide, go back to the Patent and Trademark Office's Web site and complete the proper trademark registration form. The cost in 2006 was $225 or $275 depending on the type of registration. Be sure to use block letters. If you use a stylized font, other people might be able to use the name with other styles. You can also register your trade name in other countries, but this is complicated and expensive, and enforcement of your rights may be impossible.

If you want a visual symbol that will identify your company in people's minds, perhaps you can find a stock design or a logo on the Web site of a company that supplies business cards and letterhead stationary. You could have a custom logo designed but will probably have to pay the designer, and then printing cards and other items might be more expensive. Your logo is a form of trademark; you can register it, and you should not use one that already belongs to a company with which consumers might confuse your firm.

OPENING A BANK ACCOUNT

Even with a sole proprietorship I suggest opening a special bank account for your business. There will be some costs involved but probably not more than $10 a month.

You may be tempted to go with your friendly neighborhood bank, but its personnel will probably not be able to give you advice on international payments. It's better to try to get in with a bank that has a letter of credit department somewhere in the United States. This effectively limits you to a large banking firm that operates internationally, such as Bank of America, Citibank, or JP Morgan Chase, although there are smaller banks, such as Bremer in Minnesota, which can meet all your needs.

You may have trouble opening an account at a major bank if you are new in business and offer an initial deposit of $1.99. Competition among banks has increased, however, and this is not as severe a problem as it used to be.

I suggest trying to open a checking account and a revolving line of credit at the same time. This will make you more important to the bank, and you may need the credit line when you start paying for merchandise and other expenses.

If you are forming a sole proprietorship or a partnership, just go to the bank with identification and a copy of whichever document you have to show that you registered your business or trade name. If you have a corporation, take your employer identification number and a corporate resolution that says you are entitled to open an account for the firm. In some states you may have to take your articles of incorporation and/or a corporate seal.

Once your account is open, try to build a good banking relationship by occasionally speaking with an officer and by never writing a check for which you don't have sufficient funds. If you make a mistake in this regard, you will have to pay a fee to the bank. Also, the payee might ask you to pay the fee charged by his bank and write a letter of explanation, and your reputation will be harmed.

SETTING UP YOUR OFFICE

Importing and exporting is a business that requires at least some office space and equipment. Many people start at home to save money, but this has disadvantages.

First, local zoning laws may restrict the number of employees and business visitors. Second, you may not have much space to store merchandise. You can solve this problem by renting a storage room, but that will add to your costs. Third, you will have to find some other place to meet business visitors. For some visitors, coffee shops and restaurants will do, but for others you might need to rent space by the hour from an executive suites company, your chamber of commerce, or a friend who has an office with an extra room. Once in a while you might have a visitor, especially a customer from overseas, who will want to meet in your office and will be concerned if you don't have one.

Your basic equipment might be as follows:

- Desk and chair with good lumbar support.
- IBM-compatible computer, and perhaps a laptop for traveling.
- A multifunction machine (printer, copier, fax, and scanner).
- Telephone with answering machine and perhaps a cellular phone to which calls can be forwarded when you go out (for your three-hour lunches, of course).
- Filing cabinet and miscellaneous office furniture (computer table, lamp, etc.).

This equipment might cost you between $4,000 and $8,000, depending on its quality and whether you buy it new or used. If you buy a used computer, make sure it has sufficient capacity to run the newer software and store your valuable files. Also use some kind of backup system regularly, take care to keep your antivirus program up-to-date, and use a good firewall.

It's usually not a good idea to use your personal phone line for business, especially if you have a spouse and/or teenagers in the house. A second line will give you a business listing in a telephone directory, and your monthly charges will be deductible. You will probably want a cellular phone, too, and many cellular phone services now work internationally. When I land in San Salvador and turn on my phone, it connects to a local provider and resets itself to the correct time. Then I can call home on that long ride from the airport to say I have arrived safely.

You will be making some international calls, and service providers have plans that will reduce the cost of direct dialing. Calling will be even cheaper if you use calling cards, but not those from the major companies like AT&T. If you call a lot to any region of the world, go to a deli or beer/wine store that caters to people from that region and ask which cards work the best and are the least expensive.

Another option is to use Internet telephony. These services are rapidly being improved. Some of my calls are made through the company Skype, on the Web at www.skype.com. I can "skype" my associate in Peru and talk as long as I want to and not spend a penny.

STATIONERY AND PRINTING NEEDS

With a computer, ordinary software, and special paper, you can create your own business cards, stationary and envelopes, invoices, and other business forms. You don't have to spend money for printing, although it can pay off if you plan to use a large quantity of any item. For example, you might want to send a mass mailing to potential customers or exhibit at a trade show and give cards to everyone who visits your booth.

One of several Internet sites you can look at is www.vistaprint .com. They offer free business cards if you don't mind using a standard design and having their small advertisement printed on the back. They also have reasonable prices for stationary, brochures, and other items.

If you plan to do much international mailing, you might order lightweight stationary; however, most of your foreign correspondence will probably be by e-mail. Your cable or DSL modem will replace a pile of paper.

If you work from home and don't want your home address to appear on your business documents, you can rent a post office box or use a local mail box service. You can make your post office box your first stop when you drive anywhere on business, and mileage will be deductible from that point to your last (business) stop. Of course, there will be a cost involved, and every dollar counts to a start-up. Also, using a post office box may lead some correspondents to think that you are trying to hide your physical address and may not be reputable. Your image is very important in the import/export business.

ACCOUNTING AND TAXATION

Do you like accounting? Does anyone like accounting? Most people don't, but it is a vital business function. You need financial records in order to

- Know where you income is coming from;
- Know what you are spending money on;
- Know how much you are earning or losing;
- Know whether your operating results and financial status are getting better or worse;
- Fill out your income tax statements; and
- Apply for a loan or a line of credit, etc.

In the beginning you can create your own simple accounting system, but I suggest buying a ready-made one such as the Dome Monthly Record. With this system you can do your accounting with a pen or a pencil in an hour or two a month. It uses a *cash* system as opposed to an *accrual* system, which means that you recognize income only when you receive the money and expenses only when you pay bills. This can be a small advantage if you work as a merchant and pay for merchandise before you get paid for it. At tax time your cash accounting system will show the expense but not the income for some transactions, so your tax will be slightly lower. In some states you may be required to use an accrual system if your business is incorporated.

When the business grows, you will probably want to use a computer-based accounting system such as QuickBooks Simple Start. If you have trouble setting up and learning this system, an accountant might help you free of charge in return for your agreement to use his or her services for a year. These accounting systems force you to separate business from personal expenses, so you might need two credit cards. It gets tricky when, for example, your personal TV and your business computer use the same cable service.

One role of an accountant is to help you know which expenses are deductible from your income tax. For example, trips overseas are deductible to the extent that they are for business purposes. You should get an explanation of this before you travel. If you take a business associate to lunch, only half the cost is deductible because the IRS believes that you would have eaten anyhow, with or without your associate.

As mentioned previously, with some types of business organization you pay taxes on profits only as an *individual*. You should file an estimated return each quarter, and the IRS will fine you if the amount paid with your quarterly returns is not at least 90 percent of the tax due. Ordinary corporations pay tax on profits, and then their owners pay on the dividends they receive. There also are miscellaneous small taxes on corporations that vary from state to state. In all cases, you will be much better off if you file and pay on time.

The expense of an office at home is deductible on a square foot basis. For example, if 15 percent of your residence is used as an office, you can deduct 15 percent of your rent or, if you own the house, 15 percent of what it would cost you to rent a house like it. The same percentage of your electricity and other utilities is deductible.

If you do deduct for an office at home, that space must be used only as an office. Keep your daughter's doll out of there and pay your personal bills in the kitchen. I've never heard of the IRS dropping in unannounced on someone's home office, but anything can happen. Also, if you sell your house and then buy another one, thus avoiding the capital gains tax, you will still be liable for the tax on the space that was used as an office. Your accountant might suggest that you forgo this deduction.

The deduction of travel expenses is a very attractive feature of an import or an export business. I have a friend who imported giftware from Europe and Asia for several years. Every winter he took a buying trip to some exotic land, and every summer he enjoyed selling trips to visit customers (stores) that were near beach resorts. He kept detailed records of all business meetings and was able to deduct most of the expenses. Since his wife was active in the business, her expenses were deductible as well.

Both individual and corporate profits are subject to state and local taxes, and there are some cities that tax home offices and/or levy "unincorporated business taxes." The rates are not high, but failure to file and pay can cause you problems.

When you incorporate, you will probably obtain an employer identification number (EIN) from the IRS. Just complete a form SS-4, which is available online at https://sa.www4.irs.gov/sa_vign/newFormSS4.do. This is free (hooray!) and instant. You will need this number if you have any employees. I suggest doing without them for as long as possible, to avoid getting involved in payroll and payroll taxes.

If you plan to buy merchandise for resale in any state that has a retail sales tax, you will need to contact your state tax department for a sales tax number. Also, export merchants, and importers who sell at retail, must have sales tax numbers. You can probably apply online. In Texas, for example, you can start the process at www.window.state.tx.us/taxpermit.

OBTAINING FINANCING

You should try to figure out at the beginning how much money you will need to start your business. Books on starting businesses and on business planning will tell you how to do this. If you have enough money to meet all your needs, and are willing to risk it, you will not need to look for more money. If you are short of funds, however, you will have to look for either debt or equity financing.

Debt financing means borrowing money. The cheapest and easiest ways are to borrow from a friend or a relative or to borrow against the equity in your house (or some kind relative's house). There is a large risk in this; if you lose in business, you may lose the house also.

In many areas there are government agencies or private organizations (for profit or nonprofit) that offer microloans to start-up companies. At least one organization, ACCION, has gone nationwide with microloans for which you can apply on the Internet. The site is http://accion.org/about_need_a_loan .asp. Your friendly author worked for ACCION long, long ago when its only operations were in impoverished parts of Venezuela.

You might be able to obtain a business loan from a banker if you have a solid business plan, a good credit history, and a substantial part of your total cash needs. The bank officer might suggest that the loan be guaranteed by the U.S. Small Business Administration (SBA). This will cost you around 1 percent of the loan amount but might make the difference between getting a loan and not getting one.

Credit from suppliers is common for owners of wholesale and retail businesses but not in international trade. This probably will not help you.

Financing with *equity* means that other people become part owners of your business, and you may or may not be able to find anyone who will agree to do this. It means that instead of paying interest on a loan, you will be sharing the profit. This kind of financing is usually not available to small start-ups because it tends to be complicated and expensive. *Venture capital* is a form of equity financing, but I've never heard of a start-up import or export business that could qualify for it. These investors will take large risks, but they expect large returns in just a few years.

SOURCES OF INFORMATION AND HELP

There are many books on how to get started in business, and your state, county, or city probably has a relevant publication and Web site. Some jurisdictions have enough publications and Web sites to get you thoroughly confused.

The best overall Web site for this topic might be that of *Entrepreneur* magazine, which you can find at www.entrepreneur.com. There is little information, if any, specifically about import/export businesses, but the step-by-step guide and other pages can be very helpful.

The numerous sources of information in this chapter are listed and annotated below.

- WWW.NetworkSolutions.com is a domain name registrar and lists other registered Web sites. Address: 13861 Sunrise Valley Drive, Suite 300, Herndon, VA; Phone (570) 708-8788; Fax: (703) 668-5817.

- U.S. Patent and Trademark Office is a federal agency that grants both patents and trademarks. Address: P.O. Box 1450, Alexandria, VA 22313-1450; Phone: (800) 786-9199 or (571) 272-1000; Fax: (571) 273-3245; Web site: www.uspto.gov.

- WWW.bytelevel.com benchmarks global Web sites across industries. Address: Byte Level Research, 3841 4th Avenue, #235, San Diego, CA 92103; Phone: (760) 317-2001; Fax: (253) 550-2019.

- Skype is an Internet phone company. Address: Skype Technologies, 2 Stephen Street, London, W1T 1AN, United Kingdom; Web site: www.skype.com.

- VistaPrint is a graphic design and Internet printing company. Address: VistaPrint USA, 100 Hayden Avenue, Lexington, MA 02421; Phone: (800) 961-2075; Web site: www.vistaprint.com.

- *Dome Monthly Record* is a commercially available off-the-shelf accounting and record-keeping system. It is available at most office supply stores and through www.domeproductsonline.com. Address: Dome Publishing,

10 New England Way, Warwick, RI 02886; Phone: (401) 738-7900 or (800) 432-4352; Fax: (401) 732-5377; Web site: www.domeproductsonline.com.

- *QuickBooks Simple Start* is a financial software package for tracking sales and expenses. It's available by phone at (800) 881-2079 or through www.quickbooks.com. The software is published by Intuit. Address: Intuit Corporate Headquarters, 2632 Marine Way, Mountain View, CA 94043; Phone: (650) 944-6000; Web site: www.intuit.com.

- ACCION provides microloans and business training to financially needy individuals who start their own businesses. Address: ACCION International & ACCION USA Headquarters, 56 Roland Street, Suite 300, Boston, MA 02129; Phone: (617) 625-7080; Fax: (617) 625-7020; Web site: http://accion.org/about_need_a_loan.asp.

- U.S. Small Business Administration (SBA) guarantees commercial loans to small businesses. Address: SBA Answer Desk, 6302 Fairview Road, Suite 300, Charlotte, NC 28210; Phone: (800) U-ASK-SBA; Fax: (202) 481-6190; E-mail: answerdesk@sba.gov; Web site: www.sba.gov.

4

Beginning with a Buyer

A small business owner does many things, but usually just one that brings in money: *selling*. If you can start with someone who will buy from you, you'll be miles ahead. Assuming that the buyer is honest and financially solvent and wants a product that is available, legal, and not too hard to ship, you will be in business.

WHY SOMEONE WOULD BUY FROM YOU

Everywhere in the world, buyers are more likely to do business with people whom they know and trust. This is true even in the world of high-tech products with dozens of specifications and millions of dollars on the line. This means that the quickest way to be successful is to find someone, in your country or abroad, who will invite you to supply a specific item. It may be an item that your buyer could import directly but doesn't want to deal with because the quantity would be too small. In such a case you might be able to build up a nice volume by finding other buyers for the same item or supplying other products to the same customer.

A person I once met had a good friend in the United States who purchased gloves and other items for a manufacturing plant. After some discussion, my acquaintance began to search for a company that could produce the right kind and quality of gloves and deliver them to a U.S. port. He settled on a supplier in

Pakistan, got an initial order from his friend, and began building a business. In this case the price quoted was not the lowest price the buyer received, but the gloves were slightly better quality. On a lifetime cost basis, calculated by comparing the cost with the useful life of the product, my acquaintance made a very good offer.

On the export side, thousands of foreign buyers visit trade shows in the United States to look for the products they need. At the Boston Seafood Show in 2006, I heard buyers from various countries talk about their need for more sources of good-quality frozen squid. A sharp entrepreneur could have overheard them, asked for their contact information, and tried to find a supplier. In this case the entrepreneur would probably be acting as a broker and earning a commission.

Besides friendship, people will buy from you if you can offer the best value, defined as the combination of product quality, price, and service. You don't have to have the best quality, the lowest price, and the most satisfactory service, just the appropriate combination of these factors to please your buyer. Think, for example, of the variety of shoes on the market. There are markets for every style and level of quality, at prices from about $10 to $200 or more.

WHAT VALUE MEANS TO YOUR CUSTOMERS

Your customers are most likely to be wholesalers, retailers, or distributors who buy products and resell them. To them, value is a function of volume and their gross margin. *Gross margin* is their cost for goods divided by their selling price, plus the value of any special incentives and minus expenses such as merchandise returns. You need to offer a better value than your competitors.

It will be easier if you can persuade your buyer that your product will sell quickly and profitably. You can do this with information obtained from market research. I recently worked with a group of exporters from the Dominican Republic to help them enter the U.S. market, mainly by arranging for them to meet with importing companies in Miami. Because we had done a small market study for each product, we could tell the buyers how much of the product was being imported to the United States and to the Miami area, the trend in volume, the trend in average prices, characteristics of people who used the product, and other information that helped in making sales. This knowledge helped convince the buyers to deal with the Dominican exporters.

A common way of increasing your buyer's profit is to offer better credit terms than other suppliers. If you can offer 60-day terms to someone who currently pays in 30 days, you will have an advantage. You might be able to do this by getting such terms from the manufacturer or producer.

Another important way to increase the value of your offer is to develop a *promotional package* to help your customers sell to their customers. Some buyers insist on this. A major supermarket chain in Miami reportedly asks new vendors to pay "slotting fees" of $100 per store, stock the stores free the first time, provide products for sampling, and help with special promotions. Offering these services will cost you money but can vastly increase your chances of making a sale.

ATTRACTING CUSTOMERS—SOME EXAMPLES

Note the words that are emphasized in the paragraphs that follow.

I once had a friend from Colombia who wanted to sell coffee from his country in the Washington, D.C., area but didn't know how to get into the market. Finally, he succeeded on the basis of *service* and *distribution*. He began importing coffee from Colombia and freestanding espresso machines from Italy, placed the machines in high-traffic locations, and stocked them with his Colombian coffee.

More recently, I worked with an organization in Brazil that wanted to sell frozen açaí pulp in the United States. Açaí is a "superfood" berry grown mainly in the Amazon region of Brazil and is very high in antioxidants. About the time I started working with this product, early in 1996, some firms that marketed açaí products managed to have articles published in magazines, and one company arranged to have it featured on *The Oprah Winfrey Show*. After that *publicity*, sales shot up and buyers were actually competing for the frozen pulp.

Goldman Jewelry, a company based in Israel, exports jewelry from the United States to numerous other countries. The company's secret is to make the product available everywhere by putting it on an online auction site. Because Goldman's overhead is low and its methods of promotion (eBay) and distribution (basically mail) are economical, it can offer lower *prices* than most of its competitors. It nearly always helps to have the lowest prices, although this is hard for independent exporters to do.

After the events of September 11, 2001, the demand for security equipment began expanding worldwide. A U.S. Department of Commerce study identified 44 ports, 47 airports, and other facilities that needed this kind of equipment just in the country of Spain. Large and small exporters began vying for the business, and several were successful because they had *products* that were urgently in demand. Of course, pricing was important but not nearly so much as having products that would do the job well.

At this point I should say a word about bribery, which is an all-too-common way of influencing buyers of products and services. It is so pervasive in many countries that the U.S. government has listed it as a barrier to trade. I suggest avoiding this kind of activity, even if you lose the business.

First, you may be in violation of U.S. law, depending on whom you bribe and how you do it. There is more information about antibribery legislation in the section on export regulations.

Second, if you are a beginner, you won't know how to play the game and will probably make mistakes. Anyone can ask you for money or favors and say that he or she can arrange for your offer to be accepted, but not everyone has the power or influence to make good on such a promise. I suspect there are people who make their living by offering to arrange sales in return for money or other compensation and then simply say that such and such happened and they couldn't get it done.

Third, if you pay a bribe and make a sale, you will find it very hard to avoid making similar payments on future sales to the same customer. Once you start to give something, it's hard to stop giving it. Of course, it is common in most businesses to pay commissions on sales. Unlike a bribe, a commission is usually on top of (not under) the table. Everyone knows it is being paid and accepts it as a legal and ethical cost of doing business.

FINDING BUYERS AS AN IMPORTER

In business most people start with a product, look to see who might buy it, and then adapt it as necessary to the buyer's specifications. I am suggesting that you try to work the other way. Find a buyer, get his or her specifications, and then look for a product that will meet the buyer's needs.

If you have ever been involved in direct marketing, you may have been presented with a *Whom Do You Know* booklet. This helps you find potential customers by guiding you as you think of everyone you know in all aspects of your life. You might think of someone in the United States or abroad who could need imported finished goods, parts, or ingredients.

Another technique that can pay off is informal brainstorming with friends. If you go out to dinner and cocktail parties (where it's wise to be prepared with interesting topics of conversation), why not pick people's brains for ideas of underserved markets? If you meet a baker, a painter, or whomever, ask what products used in their businesses are imported or are hard to find in the United States. If you meet a banker or an accountant, ask about clients' needs that you might be able to satisfy. Remember that one of the best-selling novelty items of all time, the Pet Rock, was supposedly conceived when men in a bar were talking about how people liked pets but didn't always like to care for them. In the six months this fad lasted, the entrepreneur became a millionaire.

You can also visit flea markets, stores, and trade show exhibits to get an idea of what kinds of people shop there and the products in which they are interested. I recently attended the Green Festival in Washington, D.C., and saw firsthand the rapid increase in buyers interested in products that will help keep them and the environment healthy. Attendance was up from 17,000 in 2005 to 25,000 in 2006, an increase of 32 percent. These people were attending lectures, eating organic foods, and actively searching for food, clothing, cosmetics, supplements, building materials, and other products that have no detrimental effects.

Suppose that fishing is your passion and you know a lot about it. You might visit tackle shops and look to see which items are imported and from which countries. By law the label on most products must include this information. See how the products compare with U.S.-made goods in regard to design, quality, packaging, and price. Finally, tell people who work in the store that you are thinking of importing fishing equipment and ask them whether they see potential in this idea, whether they can suggest any kinds of equipment or supplying countries to pursue, and, most important, whether they would be willing to look at your samples later and evaluate them.

You will probably have more luck doing this kind of research in independently owned retail stores, but your eventual customers are more likely to be chain stores or wholesalers. One way to identify wholesalers is simply to ask people who operate retail stores who they buy from. Retailers will often give you this information if you assure them that you have no plans to compete with them but simply want to add to the variety of merchandise available for them to buy and resell.

I should also mention a couple of super services, the long-established PIERS and a newer one, Zepol. You can find both on the Internet. They have more or less the same function—to provide detailed information on individual shipments arriving in the United States by sea. These services are expensive, but they let you see who is really importing the product in which you are interested. Perhaps one of these buyers will become your customer. The ones who don't become your customers are your competitors, and it may be helpful for you to know about them.

FINDING BUYERS AS AN EXPORTER

If you plan to export from the United States, there is help available from federal, state, and local government agencies. They will assist you in various ways, mostly in locating foreign buyers. You will see more information later in this book about help from government agencies.

The Internet is major source of opportunities to buy and sell. Type "trade leads" into a search engine and you'll find dozens of Web sites to look at. Some problems with this are that most of the leads are placed by sellers, not all of the listings by buyers are serious, and the listings that are serious attract too many offers. It's better to develop your own leads if you can.

If you read newspapers and magazines, which anyone involved in foreign trade should do, you may see export opportunities. Besides U.S. publications, you can find many foreign newspapers on the Internet, usually free of charge. I subscribe to an electronic newspaper from Bolivia and recently saw an article that said the government export-promotion organization, IBCE, was trying to increase exports of medicinal herbs (maybe culinary herbs also, but the article didn't mention them). This initiative surely created markets for items such as processing equipment and packaging materials, and IBCE would have the names of any potential buyers.

The same publication contained the following notice:

Argentina da $us 70 millones en créditos para adquirir
maquinaria agrícola
Santa Cruz, (Hoybolivia.com).

So, Argentina was giving Bolivia a $70 million line of credit to buy agricultural equipment. Someone would make money on that. The credit might be "tied" (restricted to paying for equipment from Argentina), but it might be open for products from anywhere, including the United States.

I have already mentioned trade shows. If there is a kind of product in which you are interested, attend a major trade show to see which specific items seem to interest foreign buyers. You can usually distinguish buyers by the colored stripes on their badges. You can't always tell which ones are from overseas, but you can guess from their appearance and language. If the trade show has an international visitors' center, you can go there and try to strike up conversations about products of interest.

If you travel overseas, have friends who do, or even have friends from other countries, you might be able to get ideas about products that are scarce or more expensive abroad. In many countries, equipment for irrigating crops is expensive, and water can be costly and scarce. Modern drip irrigation equipment was developed in Israel about the same time as a worldwide boom in export-oriented production of fruits, vegetables, and flowers. People who knew potential buyers and could locate suppliers had good opportunities to sell.

Trade statistics are another excellent source of export ideas (and import, too, for that matter). Suppose you are interested in selling to Canada. You look on a Web site such as Statcan or Strategis and find a continual increase in imports of industrial cleaning supplies to the country, or maybe to a specific province. The new imports could be going to just one buyer, but there might be an overall increase due to increased demand or problems with domestic supply. You might be able to go into a directory such as Yahoo! Canada, find distributors of this kind of product, and contact them to ask whether they are open to receive offers from the United States. Alternatively, you can find on the U.S. Department of Commerce Web site the name and e-mail address of its international trade specialist in Canada and ask him or her whether there is a trade opportunity. This contact information for all countries is available on BUYUSA's Web site at www.buyusa .gov/home/worldwide_us.html.

The same Web site will steer you to a large amount of information on each country including market data and tips for doing business there.

In fact, the U.S. Department of Commerce and numerous other federal and state agencies offer a great deal of help in finding buyers and other aspects of exporting. To see them, go to the Construction WebLink's Web site, www.constructionweblinks.com/ Organizations/International_Organizations/export_agencies.html. Click on "U.S. Government Agencies that Provide Export, International Trade Assistance," and scroll down to where the "U.S." listings begin.

On the same Web site you will find a list of all the state trade-development agencies in the United States. They can help you find buyers and provide many other kinds of assistance. Although personnel in these organizations prefer to help exporters in their own states, they will sometimes help exporters in other states to further the goal of increasing sales from the United States to the rest of the world.

Some potential buyers you find might say that you can't help them because U.S. prices on many products are higher than those of other countries, such as China and India. Sometimes you can get around this argument by engaging in barter or, better yet, *countertrade* or *buyback*. "Barter" is a simple exchange of goods—yours for theirs. "Countertrade" means that you sell and in return buy some product from your customer, probably for sale in the United States. "Buyback" means that you sell parts or ingredients and then buy the product that is made from them to sell in the United States or other countries.

Sometimes you can get around the price problem by supplying surplus merchandise. For various reasons, U.S. manufacturers often have large stocks of surplus merchandise. They don't want to sell it cheaply in the United States because such sales would undercut their domestic distributors, so they deal with exporters. Enter "surplus goods" or "surplus merchandise" in a search engine and you will see how large a business this is. You won't find the manufacturers on these sites, but you can always contact them. If you have a buyer overseas who wants, for example, computer monitors, you can find a manufacturer of this equipment and make contact to ask whether he or she has surplus monitors available. How can you find the manufacturer? One way is to look in a very large set of books called the *Thomas Register*. If you want the convenience of doing this research in your own office, you can get all the information on three CDs for, believe it or not, about $10. To get it, call (800) 699-9822; or go to www.thomasnet.com, click on "Resources" and then on "Thomas Register."

A story I heard is that not long ago executives of a major fast-food chain thought the U.S. market was ready for a spicy hamburger. They had millions of pounds of frozen patties produced, but the burgers didn't sell. All this meat became available, to be sold by companies that would promise not to associate it with the name of the fast-food chain.

Another story, published in the *Wall Street Journal* in October 2006, is of an organization named Global Vision that shipped excess stocks of clothing and accessories to major retailers outside the United States. There are several companies that trade in surplus military clothing but relatively few that trade in civilian clothing. This increases the importance of Global Vision to both its suppliers and its customers.

SOURCES OF INFORMATION AND HELP

In this chapter, I suggest that you go beyond starting with a market and actually try to start with a buyer, or more than one, if you can. Anyone who sells products, except as an agent or a broker, has to buy them or make them, and those who make products buy raw materials or components as well as production equipment, supplies, and so on. The more information you have about buyers, the better job you can do of approaching them regarding your products.

You won't find much published information precisely about this subject because it is an uncommon approach to starting a business. Web sites about finding buyers are concerned mostly with the real estate trade.

Don't underestimate the value of networking. If you go to a local chamber of commerce meeting and see 30 or 40 people, every one will buy some kind of merchandise that you might be able to supply. There are other ideas in here that will help you to have a buyer in hand when your business opens its door. The following sources of information are mentioned in this chapter.

- eBay is an online auction Web site. Address: 2145 Hamilton Avenue, San Jose, CA 95125; Phone: (408) 558-7400 or (800) 322-9266; Fax: (403) 376-6554; Web site: www.ebay.com.

- Green Festivals bring together socially and environmentally responsible buyers and sellers, and are a project of the Global Exchange and Co-op America. They are held in Chicago, San Francisco, and Washington, D.C. Web site: www.greenfestivals.org.

- Piers maintains a comprehensive database on import and export cargoes traveling through the United States, Mexico, Latin America, and Asia. Web site: www.piers.com.

- Zepol provides comprehensive data on imports. Address: Zepol Global Headquarters, 7455 France Avenue South, #409, Edina, MN 55435-4702; Phone: (612) 435-2191; Fax: (612) 435-2196; Web site: www.zepol.com.

- *IBCE* is a Bolivian electronic newspaper. Web site: www.ibce .org.bo.

- Statcan is the national statistics agency of Canada. Web site: www.statcan.ca.

- Strategis is produced by Industry Canada, a department of the Canadian federal government, to provide business and consumer information. Phone: (613) 954-5031; Web site: http://strategis.ic.gc.ca/engdoc/main.html.

- BuyUSA.gov is a service of the U.S. Department of Commerce's U.S. Commercial Service. It assists U.S. and foreign businesses with importing and exporting products and services. BuyUSA maintains offices throughout the United States and the world. Web site: www.buyusa.gov.

- Construction Weblink lists numerous federal and state organizations that provide importing and exporting assistance. Web site: www.constructionweblinks.com/Organizations/ International_Organizations/export_agencies.html.

- The *Wall Street Journal* is a daily newspaper that focuses on business. Web site: http://online.wsj.com/public/us.

5

Choosing Products
and Suppliers

If you don't have a buyer who leads you to a product line, you'll
have to go the more traditional route of beginning with a product. Then you will need to identify and select one or more suppliers and work out the terms of your relationships with them. Let's
talk first about products to import and then look at the export
side of the business.

FINDING PRODUCTS TO IMPORT

There are thousands, maybe millions, of products you can import.
It would be nice if you could find something new, different, and
desirable. If you can't do that, however, there is no reason you
can't be successful with any product. You only have to do your
purchasing and marketing better, more cheaply, or more effectively than your competitors.

The Good Old World Wide Web

Can I call the Web "old"? It isn't old, of course, but most of us use
it so much that it seems to have been around for ages.

I have already mentioned Web sites that provide trade leads.
These are also known as "import/export bulletin boards" and

perhaps by other names as well. For example, the sites www
.importleads.com and www.exportleads.com say that they provide the following.

- *Free trade leads*. You receive free trade leads from importers
  and exporters all around the world.
- *Free browsing and posting*. You receive free access to browse
  and post import and export trade leads.
- *Free matchmaking*. They will match your company to others
  with similar wants and needs.

You might click on "View and Post Leads" and then on the
product category of your choice. Import leads for "Consumer Soft
Goods" bring up a dozen advertisements, all from China and the
United States (which shows the target markets for this particular
site), but they are all for the same two or three products. I saw this
and quickly moved on.

Another site, http://trade.swissinfo.net, has a virtual exhibi-
tion center, offers to buy, offers to sell, and business opportunities.
One such opportunity was from a company named B2B Distrib,
which was looking for importers and distributors for its production
of extra virgin olive oil. There was complete contact information
and a referral to the company's Web site, www.antoniocelentano
.com, which was impressive as well as mouthwatering. It says:
"Contact us about distribution in your area" and includes a purchase order form that one can complete and send via the Internet.
Voilà! You've looked at just two sites and found what looks like a
serious exporting company with good products. If you have a way
to sell olive oil, this may be worth following up on.

Foreign Countries' Export Promotion Offices

Nearly every country in the world has one or more trade promotion offices, or TPOs. The TPOs have Web sites, of course, and
some of them have offices in the United States. One way to find
them is through the United Nations International Trade Centre
(UNITC) in Geneva, Switzerland. Go to the Web site www.intracen
.org/menus/countries.htm and select the country in which you are

interested. Select "Trade Contacts" and then "TPOs and Other Trade Support Institutions." Do this for Ethiopia, for example, and you will find nine organizations including the Ethiopian Export Promotion Agency. Select that organization and you'll get information about it as well as a link to its Web site. The Web site lists eight kinds of products and has links that presumably lead to the names of exporters, although the links don't always work.

Usually, the Web sites of these trade promotion organizations will tell you whether they have offices in the United States. If you don't see this information, try searching on a yellow pages site in major trading cities, such as New York, Miami, Dallas, Los Angeles, and San Francisco. You can also search directly. For example, if you type in a search engine "New York, KOTRA," you will instantly get information on the Korea Trade Center that covers the northeastern region of the United States. Then contact that center and ask for information about products that are available to export. If you know the type of product in which you are interested, ask for exporters' names and contact information.

Traveling

The most enjoyable way to find products to import is to go look for them. A few years ago my home away from home in Quito, Ecuador, was the beautiful Hostal Los Alpes. One morning I bought a fabulously beautiful wool sweater for 720 sucres, which was the equivalent of US$8.37. Should I have taken a few hundred to sell in the United States? Should I have at least taken a half-dozen to use as commercial samples? I could have shown them to buyers and, if I found a great deal of interest, gone back for more or perhaps tried to find an exporter to supply them to me. I could have looked for an exporter via the Internet or the national export promotion office in Quito. Of course, I would have had to look carefully at transport costs and customs duties.

Traveling to find products is more likely to pay off if you know what you are looking for and do a bit of planning. Before your trip check on U.S. import regulations for the products in which you are interested and identify companies from which you might be able to buy. Let's suppose that you plan to visit Nepal to do some mountain climbing. You look on the Web and find some interesting products from this country including clothing and carpets made from pashmina, the inner hair of mountain goats. Then you can identify companies, such as Innoxa Pashmina in Katmandu, and arrange to meet with their sales personnel.

Trade Statistics

Yet another way to find product ideas is to look at the numbers. Go on the U.S. International Trade Commission's Web site at www .usitc.gov and click on "US Imports/Export Data (DataWeb)." Don't ask me why "Imports" is plural and "Export" is singular; I have no idea. Then click on "ITC Trade DataWeb" and register. There is no charge. You will be directed to a search page on which "U.S. Imports for Consumption" is already marked. Click on "Proceed with New Query" and you'll get another search page, from which you can find details of U.S. imports of any product. You'll probably want to look at products with which you are familiar and try to find some of which imports are increasing. That will mean that demand is growing, and you might be able to account for some of that increasing volume of sales.

Although this system is very user-friendly, you will have to be familiar with HS numbers in order to use it. *HS* stands for "Harmonized System," a way of classifying and coding products in international trade that is accepted in most countries of the world. It helps greatly to clarify the nature of a product over long distances and with different languages. Start again at www.usitc.gov, but this time click on "Tariff Schedule." Then click on "Current HTSA Edition by Chapter," and you will see the table of contents. For a novice, the best way to find a specific product or product type is to start with the alphabetical index.

Here is one note of caution: there is an immense business in the world producing and selling brand-name goods without authorization from the owners of those brands. This is counterfeiting, and is illegal in most countries, although enforcement in many countries is weaker than in the United States. If a vendor overseas offers you brand-name merchandise for a low price, it may be counterfeit. If you were to import these goods, they could be confiscated by U.S. Customs, and you would not receive any compensation. Worse yet, the counterfeit goods might be faulty. They might be auto parts that will break and cause accidents, medicines that will make their users worse instead of better, and so on. Believe me, you don't want to have this kind of problem.

If you want to find other countries' trade statistics, so you can see what they are exporting and importing, try the International Trade Center at www.intracen.org. Click on "Products & Services" and then on "International Trade Statistics." Also, you can often find this kind of information on the Web sites of specific countries' ministries of economy or export promotion organizations. For agricultural products, go to www.faostat.fao.org.

GETTING PRODUCT SAMPLES

In the process of looking for products to import, you will probably find names and contact information for exporters in various countries. Some will probably have product catalogs on the Internet. In other cases, you can ask for catalogs and they will be sent to you by e-mail, airmail, or courier. At this stage, you don't have to say much about yourself or your company.

When the catalogs come, show them to some of the people to whom you might want to sell. Sometimes you can do this in small retail stores by just walking in and asking for the owner or the buyer. With larger retailers and with wholesalers and distributors, you will have to make an appointment. This can be hard to do, especially if you don't yet have product samples. Please see Appendix G for valuable tips on contacting retail stores.

When you look at the catalogs, hopefully with the help of people who are in the trade, try to find products that you can (1) transport to the United States at a reasonable cost, (2) pass through customs with little difficulty, and (3) sell in sufficient quantities that the business will be profitable. Then ask for samples.

If the items are inexpensive, you might be able to get a few samples free. Send a professional-looking e-mail message, fax, or letter explaining that you are an importer of that kind of product, have potential clients for products of the exporting firm, and would like samples for testing in the market. Say exactly which varieties or models you want and how many you want of each. You should say how you want the samples to be shipped. The usual method is via a courier service, such as DHL, but sometimes small samples come by airmail and large samples by airfreight.

If the supplier says you must pay for the samples, you should request the lowest (large-quantity) price. You can try to get the supplier to cover the shipping cost. You will probably have to pay in advance and can do so in several different ways, which are discussed later in this book.

If the amount of money is large, however you define that, you should protect against the risk of losing it. You can check the supplier's Web site to see whether it looks professional, and ask the export promotion agency or chamber of commerce in the supplier's country whether information about him or her is available. Also, you can propose to pay part of the money in advance and the remainder when you receive the products. There are other ways of protecting your money in international trade, and these will be discussed in the chapter on payment methods.

TESTING PRODUCTS IN THE U.S. MARKET

There is a very good chance that the products of which you receive samples will not be ready for the U.S. market. They may be the wrong size, shape, or color, or may not meet electrical or other specifications. The packaging may not be of the type or size that the market requires, or the label may not include the required information. Therefore, you should go through a testing process to find out whether the product will sell as it is, and if not, in which ways it will have to be changed.

To do this, think about which kinds of people would buy the product and where they would buy it. Then go to those stores, or other places, and ask a buyer in each one to take a quick look at the product that you are thinking of importing. Present your business card, of course, and try to sound like you know the product line well. For many kinds of businesses you will need appointments, and you will not always be able to get them. Most buyers are very busy, although if they deal in seasonal goods, they are more relaxed at some times of the year.

When you meet with buyers, ask them what they think of the product, whether they would recommend any changes in the product or its package or label, and whether they would be likely to buy it from you (or from a foreign exporter through you as an agent). If a buyer expresses interest, ask questions such as how many he or she would order at a time, what times of year the orders would be placed, approximately what the price should be, and how long it takes the company to pay. The question of price is critical, and you may have trouble getting honest answers. If a direct question doesn't work, try asking it this way: "For you to buy this from me, what price would I have to meet?" If that fails, ask how much the product would sell for. Later you can ask how much the markup would be. Then reach for your calculator and figure out how much the buyer would pay.

You will probably find that each buyer with whom you speak has different opinions and ideas. This is because each one has individual preferences as well as a unique group of customers to satisfy. You will have to draw conclusions about the viability of your product, modifications that should be made, the target market, the channel of distribution, and the pricing structure.

You may find, as I did with an Egyptian manufacturer of candy, that the producing firm is not willing to modify its products as required by your buyers. The firm's managers may decide that changing their product's characteristics, package, and label would require too much time and money.

As an example of this testing process, suppose you are offered some very nice rag dolls made in Colombia. They represent storybook characters such as Little Red Riding Hood, so you would have to determine whether these characters are in the public domain (not protected by patents, trademarks, or copyrights). There are actually several dolls in one. Turn Red Riding Hood upside down and she becomes the grandmother; flip over the bonnet and the grandmother becomes the big, bad wolf.

You may decide that the main customers for these dolls will not be children but grandmothers and others who purchase gifts for girls. That would make the product a gift item, not a toy. You might then decide it would sell best in high-quality gift shops. Your next step will be to identify several such stores, make appointments to see the buyers, and show them the dolls. You will be asked questions about the doll's clothing (what it's made of and whether it is flame-resistant), the buttons (whether they are toxic and how many pounds of pressure they will withstand before being pulled off), and the dolls themselves (what they are stuffed with and whether they are hand-sewn). You might be told that the dolls are too big or too little, that they are too expensive or too cheap, and that the clothing styles should be more modern, the cheeks more rosy, the hair more curly, and so on. You may be told also that they will sell better if you develop a special package and/or that the labeling should be improved.

After a few interviews you will have a good idea whether the dolls will sell, how they should be modified, how they should be packaged and labeled, to which market they should be targeted, how they should be distributed, and their selling prices at both wholesale and retail.

FINDING FOREIGN SUPPLIERS

Let's take a look at how you might find companies whose products you can sell.

Sources of Information

Suppose that one of the products you looked at passed all tests with flying colors. Your first inclination will be to procure it from the company from which you got the samples, but this may not be the best option. You should explore other options in the same country and perhaps other countries as well.

There are many directories of manufacturers, of which perhaps the best is the Kompass series. It will provide you with 23 million product and service references in 53,000 classes, 1.8 million companies in 75 countries, 750,000 trade names, and 3.6 million executives' names. That should be enough for you to start with.

Go to www.kompass.com, and you will see a product/company search page that you can use in 25 different languages. Enter the term "toilet paper," for example, and you'll find 1,381 companies in the Kompass directory that deal in this product. Click where indicated and you will see the beginning of the list of companies. Click on any company and you will see a full page of information including a link to its Web site. Amazing, is it not?

I have previously mentioned trade promotion organizations of foreign countries as sources of information about products and suppliers. You can find them on the Web or by calling a country's consulate in the United States. Many of them are listed at www .export911.com/link/link.htm#xIntl. Go to this site and click, for example, on "Romanian Foreign Trade Center." Sorry, that one doesn't always work. Try clicking on "Trade Council of Iceland." No, sorry; that one is in Icelandic and I can't find a link to an English-language version. Maybe the Hong Kong Trade Development Council? Perfect. You get a page on which you can find suppliers and a good deal of other information.

Another organization you should know about is the World Trade Centers Association, which was started in New York around 40 years ago. Go to www.wtca.org. If you click on "Search by alphabetical listing," you will see a list of hundreds of world trade centers. Click on any of these and you will find contact information. Any trade center will help you look for members who can supply the products you want.

There is a much newer system (founded in 2000) called the World Trade Point Federation (www.tradepoint.org). You can go to "Trade Point Network" on the left and find contact information for these organizations, but this part of the site is a bit awkward to use. You may be happier if you go to "ETO System" and search for specific offers of the product in which you are interested.

This book cannot include a detailed discussion of all the supply and demand matching sites on the Internet; there are simply too many. Some get their revenue from advertising, others from companies that list offers to buy or to sell, and others from commissions on business that is done. I suggest you approach any of these sites with caution. If you want to look at what appears to be one of the must successful Internet trading sites, go to www.Worldbid.com.

There you will see thousands of trade leads grouped into 44 categories, from "Aerospace" to "Travel."

If you are traveling and looking for suppliers, you can't go wrong by contacting the American Chamber of Commerce (AmCham) in each country. AmCham members are usually American companies and local companies that want to do business with the United States. You can also go to the country's directorate of foreign trade or its trade promotion organization and ask for a directory of exporters.

You may want to time your trip to coincide with a trade exhibit for the type of product in which you are interested. Want to import cookies? In a search engine, type "international bakery fair" and you will get information on such events in several countries. One of those listed is Bakery China, which is held yearly in the new international expo center in Shanghai.

Selecting Foreign Suppliers

After you identify potential suppliers, you will need to evaluate them to see which ones can best meet your needs. Here are ideas about how to do this.

When you are looking for potential suppliers, and customers, too, for that matter, you will normally want to deal with firms that are in relatively stable countries. You don't want your supply line disrupted by a revolution. Type "country risk ratings" into your search engine and you will see several companies that provide this kind of information. Most want to sell it, but some provide it free. I just subscribe to *World Trade* magazine. In June 2006, for example, it published information to the effect that one should be *very* careful in trading with Pakistan and careful with Indonesia, Argentina, the Philippines, the Ukraine, Saudi Arabia, Egypt, and Vietnam.

You will also want to deal with a country from which there is frequent transportation to the United States and whose products do not pay high duties. These topics will be discussed in other chapters. In addition, you would like a supplier located where costs of production are not rising quickly and where the value of the currency is fairly stable in relation to the dollar. In 2006, for example, the Brazilian real increased in value against the U.S. dollar. This meant that an exporter who wanted to get the same number of reals would have to increase the dollar prices to U.S. importers.

Characteristics of Suppliers

Ideally, you would like a supplier who is competent, honest, and eager to work with you. Unfortunately, these factors may be contradictory; the most competent firms may not want to work with a newcomer. They will have a wider choice of customers and may have their distribution channels well established. Ask about importing Waterford crystal from Ireland, for example, and you will probably get a nice letter saying that the exclusive importer is the company-owned facility in Wall, New Jersey.

A competent company will usually respond to your communications quickly and adequately, will have a Web site, and will be pleased to send you additional information. You would probably like to see a substantial volume of sales and experience in exporting, including exports to the United States. Prior sales to the United States indicate that the products meet U.S. legal requirements (although they may not meet all the buyer's requirements). The company will have high-quality promotional materials, in correct English, which is a big advantage. It is important to ask what kind of quality-management system is used in the manufacturing plant. A company should follow what are known as "good manufacturing practices." It may have its own customized version of them, called "standard operating procedures." For food products, the term is "standard sanitary operating procedures."

You may be told that the firm is certified to ISO 9000, a quality-management system developed by the International Organization for Standardization. There is a sister system, ISO 14000, to help companies operate in ways that are not harmful to the environment. For food products, there is yet another system, hazard analysis at critical control points, or HACCP. This method of ensuring that food products are not harmful was developed for astronauts, who somehow did not like the idea of getting stomachaches in space. It is now required for seafood, fruit juice, and cheese that are to be consumed in the United States, and it is recommended for other food products.

Try not to judge the competence of a foreign firm by the correct-
ness of the English used in its correspondence. A foreign executive
may be first-rate, except in his or her knowledge of English. On the
other hand, an executive may be mediocre, or worse, but have a sec-
retary who grew up in the United States and can write well.

Honesty is harder to evaluate. A well-established firm can usually be trusted and will not hesitate to send you references. In a
later chapter we will see how to get credit information on a foreign
company. This is important to both exporters and importers.

A good indication that a firm wants to deal with you is that
its export manager or salesperson responds promptly to your
requests for information and samples. Try contacting these people
by phone as well as by e-mail to see how they react.

A Personal Visit

If you can find the money in your budget, it can be useful to visit a
foreign supplier before you do business with him or her. This can
avert a catastrophe like having your shipment of ski boots arrive
in February or having a boot come apart on an expert slope. It is
better to make appointments in advance to avoid arriving when
the people you want to see are unavailable, even though such
warning lets them prepare to make their company look better than
it really is. The competent, honest companies don't have to make
changes to be ready for visitors. Fly-by-night operations often do.

When you get to an exporter's place of business, try to meet
with key personnel, look at the financial statements, if possible,
and tour the plant. See whether it is clean and well organized,
whether the production equipment and delivery trucks are in
good condition, and so forth. Be sure to meet the people with
whom you have been corresponding.

You would normally rather deal with a manufacturer than a
middleman, and on a personal visit you can easily tell one from
the other. Without such a visit, you can find out by asking and by
looking at your supplier's Web site and catalogs. If you receive a
catalog with your vendor's name and address on a sticker over
some other name and address, you are not dealing with a manufacturer.

However, you may be content to buy from a middleman under some conditions, for example:

- Your orders will be too small for a manufacturer to accept.
- You want small quantities of goods from each of several manufacturers.
- You are buying from a country such as Japan in which exporting is normally done by trading companies.
- You will be dealing in handmade products. Most producers of handicrafts are too small and unsophisticated to do their own exporting.

FINDING PRODUCTS TO EXPORT

Let's assume that you want to find products to export. Your interest may have been kindled by federal or state export programs or their personnel. Nearly all governments want to increase sales abroad in order to increase employment, income, and foreign exchange earnings. In fact, the United States needs your help. In 2006 the United States had a merchandise trade deficit of $235 billion, and 26 percent of that was just with one country (China).

Onetime Deals

For both importing and exporting, I strongly recommend setting up ongoing, long-term business relationships. If, however, you want to begin with individual transactions that may be repeated, you can look for closeout, surplus and liquidation merchandise. This might let you attract foreign buyers on the basis of low price. Type "closeout merchandise" into a browser, for example, and you'll find many opportunities.

You can also look at trade bulletin boards to see what people are asking to buy, but you will find many more offers to sell. Try the Baltic Import Export Bulletin Board, for example, at www .impex/lv/en. Scroll down and look on the left side for "Popular Content, Today's," and you should see current notices of interest in importing specific products. One of them says the following.

We are seriously interested in purchasing:

1) OPP, CPP, KOP, PET, LDPE, HDPE, PE/PA, Nylon, PVC post-industrial clear/white/metallized without printing irregular film roll, cutoff, film on bale, lump, floor sweep and other waste
2) PP/PE non-woven, PP diaper, PP jumbo bag
3) PET & HDPE post-consumer baled bottle, mixed plastic bottle #1-7, PET bottle flake
4) Engineering grade plastic ABS, PMMA, PS, PC, PVC, PP, PE

(Taken from www.impex.lv/en/node/198.)

If you understand these products and know where to obtain them, you may be able to do some business.

Your Own Company's Products

If you work for a company that is not exporting, you might ask people in the sales department whether they have received inquiries from other countries. Many companies receive such inquiries and ignore them because exporting seems too difficult. You can offer to try to make some sales overseas. If company managers don't like this idea, you might go ahead anyway, with approval of course, as an independent merchant. You can try to close deals in your spare time, buy from your company, and ship the products abroad.

A federal or state export promotion officer or a Department of Commerce industry specialist can give you a good idea of whether the company's products are exportable and to which countries. There will probably be a trade association for companies that deal with similar products, and it may have an export advisor with whom you can speak. You can also check trade statistics to see if similar products are being exported from the United States.

Suppose, for example, that your company makes a superior sheeter, which automatically cuts rolled materials such as vinyl into sheets. I found such an item in the New Equipment Digest at www.newequipment.com. This is a fairly common product in the category of converting equipment. You can probably get information about exporting sheeters from the Converting Equipment Manufacturers Association at www.cema-converting.org.

To see if the U.S. Department of Commerce has an industry specialist who can help you, call—yes, we're finally using the telephone instead of the computer—(800) USA-TRADE. Of course, you can do this on the Internet as well. A list of industry specialists with their names and phone numbers is available at http://web.ita.doc.gov/td/shared/tdindus.nsf/Industries. Many of the specialists have several years of experience and a very good idea of what can be sold abroad.

You might find other sources of information, about exporting converting equipment, from your state export promotion organization or perhaps the Service Corps of Retired Executives, SCORE, which is connected with the U.S. Small Business Administration. There are also world trade clubs and associations in many cities, but they are more likely to be helpful when you have your product and start doing the marketing. You might also consult specialized magazines, such as *Converting*, or attend a trade show, such as the National Prepress, Printing and Converting Machinery and Materials Showcase.

Finding Products via Research

Now let's assume that you know which country you want to sell to but not which products. Maybe you picked the country because you have traveled there, have friends there, and know the language. You can begin by looking at trade statistics at www.usitc.gov to see which products your country of interest imports from the United States. If you want to see what the country buys from other countries, you may be able to find its national import and export statistics on the Internet. You can also look at data provided by the United Nations International Trade Center in Geneva, Switzerland. Go to www.intracen.org/menus/countries.htm and select the country in which you are interested. You will see a map and, written in red on the left, the words "Trade Statistics." The data are not very detailed, but they can be helpful. I looked at Argentina, for example, and found a nice upward trend in imports of cocoa, probably as beans for its small chocolate industry.

The Food and Agriculture Organization (FAO) and other international organizations also have statistics on the World Wide Web. In addition, there are usually statistics in market studies, which are available from the U.S. Department of Commerce and from numerous private companies.

Finally, you can uncover export opportunities just from reading magazines and newspapers. On October 30, 2006, the *New York Times* reported: U.S. SAID TO FAIL IN TRACKING ARMS FOR IRAQIS. The story said that a significant number of the weapons the United States had provided to Iraqi security forces had disappeared. Maybe you knew of a source of small devices that could be hidden in something such as a gun, after the gun has been manufactured, and tracked by a global positioning or similar device. The U.S. command might be very interested in such a product (and reportedly started using one in mid-2007).

A Quick Evaluation

Do you remember when I said that most foreign products needed to be modified before they can be sold in the United States? The same is often true for U.S. products entering markets abroad. Many blunders have been committed, both technical and cultural. Your market country may not only use different voltage electricity from the United States, it may also have different-style wall sockets for plugging in appliances. Urban legend has it that a well-known cultural blunder was committed by a U.S. company that introduced baby food in an African country with a picture of a baby on the label. The people were accustomed to buying canned and bottled food with labels that depicted the contents. Imagine their reaction at the picture of a baby!

If your product of interest is a consumer good, you may want to show it to people in the United States who come from the countries in which you want to sell. They can comment on its design, size, color, and other characteristics. Some products such as cameras sell with little modification, but others such as toothpaste must cater to local tastes and cultures. I once bought shaving cream in Argentina that smelled like wet wheat. It may have done well in Buenos Aires, but it wouldn't sell in Boston.

For industrial goods, a trade association or the U.S. Department of Commerce may be able to tell you of product characteristics that should be changed. For example, Western Europe is more concerned than the United States about conserving natural resources and global warming. There are mileage standards for motor vehicles and energy efficiency standards for many kinds of equipment. In October 2006, the European Commission presented a far-reaching *Energy Efficiency Action Plan*, which affects imported products. Most industrial goods are described in detail in catalogs or product specification sheets, which you can send to potential buyers and ask for their comments.

You should not invest much money in trying to sell a product without doing research in the target market. The U.S. Commercial Service of the Department of Commerce has a collection of market studies that you can find at www.buyusainfo.net/adsearch .cfm?search_type=int&loadnav=no. For example, I searched for "health technologies" and "Croatia," and came up with several interesting documents. You can buy many market studies; the best source on the Internet is www.marketresearch.com.

If you have the expertise, time, and money, you can do your own market research overseas. Go to the market, identify potential buyers, make appointments to see them, show them the product (or product catalogs), and ask a series of questions. The U.S. Department of Commerce officer in that country will be able to give you guidance and may be able to help you hire a consultant/ guide/driver/interpreter, at your expense. Not long ago, an associate and I enjoyed a brief trip to Albania, Bosnia, Bulgaria, and Montenegro. Before going, we identified and contracted with a person in each country who made appointments for us, took us around in a car, briefed us en route about each person we were to visit, interpreted when necessary, and then gave us his or her perceptions about the meeting. This kind of local expertise is usually very valuable. I should add that if your local guide is a reckless driver or interprets only half of what is being said, by all means call it to his or her attention but in a culturally sensitive way. One of our drivers on the trip to Bosnia and other countries didn't know how to go under 90. Another got into a small accident—in a parking lot—shrugged it off, and drove away.

LINING UP SUPPLIERS

Finding U.S. suppliers of products you want to export can be surprisingly difficult. You can identify companies through the *Thomas Register of American Manufacturers* and many other directories, but many won't have exactly the products you want. Others will be uninterested in exporting, will not have products available for foreign markets, will have already made arrangements to sell overseas, or simply will not want to work with an inexperienced exporter. Of course, as you move from one company to the next, you will gain confidence and product knowledge and make a better impression. I suggest not starting with your top prospect; save that firm until you are really ready.

I once saw a buy notice on a trade bulletin board that read: "Frozen or canned avocado (New Zealand). Quantity: Refrigerated containers. Quality: Subject to market testing. Packaging: Canned. Delivery: Wants to study samples first. Quote: CIF Auckland (buyer's name and address)." Suppose you received this notice and thought you could supply the item. How would you go about it? Here is a sequence you might follow.

First, phone, e-mail, or fax the potential buyer. Tell her you are an exporter of frozen food products and have seen the notice. Then ask whether she is still looking for the product, whether she would welcome an offer from you, and whether she can give you any more information such as the quantity needed per year. Also ask how she usually pays for such shipments.

If in this process you get an impression that the buyer is not interested in receiving your quotation, you should probably move on and look for other opportunities. If, however, you receive satisfactory answers to your questions and have a good impression of the prospective buyer, you may want to go to the next step.

In major libraries, you can find a three-volume set of books called the *Thomas Food Industry Register*. You can buy it also, but the cost is around $550, and the electronic version is even more. A look in volume 1 under "avocados" will give you two companies that might be able to supply you. There may be others that are not listed in the book, but you can begin with the two you found.

The normal way to contact potential suppliers in the United States is by telephone, although many will ask for you to follow up by e-mail. Ask to speak with someone in the export department or, if there is none, the sales or marketing departments. Explain that you are an export merchant (or agent), that you have a potential customer in New Zealand for frozen or canned avocado, and that you would like a quotation on a full container load, CIF/Auckland, as requested by the buyer. The term CIF is explained in chapter 8. If the supplier will not do the work of giving you a CIF quotation, you may have to settle for a quotation delivered to a West Coast port and then add the costs to Auckland. Then you will have to add the costs of getting the container on a vessel as well as transportation and insurance. We will cover these topics in a later chapter. Your quotation will usually be in U.S. dollars. This will relieve you of any currency exchange problems and will make it easier for your customer to compare prices with those she might receive from other exporters.

Make sure to request export prices, because they may be lower than the firm's domestic prices. Also ask for the company's catalog or product list. Finally, ask if they would be willing to guarantee you a commission once a shipment has been sent and paid for. Ask how much, of course. A common figure for this kind of deal is 5 percent of the FOB/factory price.

You should be careful that the supplier and your customer do not learn each other's names until you have a promise, in writing, that your commission will be paid. Then, if the seller and the buyer both go through with the deal, you will *almost* certainly be rewarded for your efforts.

The manufacturer's price quotation may have your commission (if you're working as an agent) or markup (if as a merchant) built in. If this is not the case, you will have to add it on. You should try to add enough to make the transaction profitable but not so much that you lose the sale to a competitor. In some cases, you can increase your earnings by getting export prices with money for you built in and then charging your customers a bit extra. When you do this, it may be better to tell the manufacturer's salesperson so he or she knows that you are being honest.

Now, let's talk about the kind of written agreement you might want to have with your suppliers if you intend to work as an export agent on a long-term basis.

THE FORMAL SUPPLY AGREEMENT

Once you have found and selected a supplier, you may want a formal agreement as to how you will do business with that firm. This is to give both you and the supplier some security and to reduce the range of possible business disputes. This suggestion applies whether you plan to work as an agent or as a merchant.

A young man from Thailand who lived in California told me that he was acting, without a written agreement, as an agent for a spice exporter in his country. Apparently, he did a very good job because import brokers who were also handling the product complained to the Thai exporter. The exporter promptly told our young friend that he should not call on spice packers, the market segment with which he had done best, but should confine his efforts to compounders. He already knew from experience that compounders would not buy from him because he could not make them better offers than their established suppliers, the brokers. He was instantly put out of business.

By contrast, a neophyte export agent entered into a written agreement to be the exclusive U.S. agent for a new kind of art supply product from Japan. She spent an entire year contacting art supply dealers, wholesalers, importers, and manufacturers before making her first sale. That sale was to a manufacturer of similar products, who already had a distribution network and could easily place the item in stores throughout the country. After the first shipment was made, the agent learned later, her customer contacted the Japanese exporter and proposed that she (the agent) be cut out of the arrangement. Her services were probably no longer essential, but she had a signed agreement and the exporter honored it. Her commissions were safe for the term of her contract.

Supply agreements may be very brief or several pages long. Your supplier may have a standard agreement form that is acceptable to you (examine it carefully), or you can try to write one yourself using sample agreements in books on international commercial law. You may want to buy a copy of the *ICC Model Commercial Agency Contract* or the *ICC Model Distributorship Contract* from ICC Publishing in New York. Visit ICC on the Web at www.iccbooks .com. If, however, the stakes are high, financially or in other ways, you should seriously consider using an attorney. You can call your local bar association to find one with international business experience, or ask for a referral from your banker or the head of your local world trade club. An attorney's fees related to the contract may be $2,000 or more.

Here are some topics that international trade agreements often include. Many of these are relevant to both foreign and domestic purchasing, as well as foreign and domestic selling, whether you plan to work as an agent or as a merchant.

- *The products.* An agreement usually names the products you will handle. The supplier may, for example, give you her line of TV sets but not her computer monitors.

- *Competing products.* Some suppliers will try to restrict you from handling other companies' products that compete with theirs. Others will want you to handle several lines, so the customers can go to you instead of another agent or importer.

- *Sales targets.* Suppliers often want to have sales targets or minimums written into agreements. A target tells you how much you are supposed to sell, tells the supplier how much you are likely to sell, and gives the supplier an excuse to void the agreement if you do not perform satisfactorily.

- *The territory.* This is the geographic area in which you are authorized to sell the product and which you are supposed to cover. If you have exclusivity in the territory as a merchant, the supplier should not deal with any other importer who sells there. If you have exclusivity as an agent, you should receive a commission on every sale made to a customer in the area, whether or not you are responsible for it. As you can imagine, virtually every agent and importer would like an exclusive arrangement. Some suppliers will give it, because they feel it will encourage the agent or importer to spend time and money building up sales in the territory, but most are reluctant to do so.

- *Prices, markups, and commissions.* The principal (the foreign or domestic supplier) usually sets the price at which his agents must sell. The agreement will specify the percentage of commission to be paid as well as when it will be paid. For example, a U.S. agent for heavy equipment from Germany might receive 5 percent of the FOB/vessel value of shipments, payable when the German supplier receives a letter of credit. It is common also to have the allowable markups for import merchants included in their contracts. This is because an importer may be able to earn more by selling a small quantity for a large markup than by selling a large quantity for a small markup. In such a case, however, the supplier will not do well.

- *Payment terms.* International trade agreements usually say how the supplier wants to be paid, either by an agent's customer or by his importer. If the supplier agrees to sell on other than secure terms, orders will be subject to approval by his credit department.

- *Shipping terms.* Agreements between exporters and importers usually state how the exporter intends to ship, that is, to which point in the journey he will make shipping arrangements, retain title to the merchandise, and be responsible for loss or damage. This kind of clause is often omitted in an agency agreement.

- *Level of effort.* The exporter may want a clause that gives a minimum number of person-hours or sales calls that you, a middleman, must devote to selling the product. Often, a vague term, such as "best effort," is used, but if the supplier wants to cancel the contract and finds no other grounds for doing so, you may be accused of not putting forth your best effort.

- *Promotion.* There are often clauses in a contract that state how much promotion an importer will be responsible for and/or how much assistance the exporter will provide. For example, an importer of new canned food products may get 13 cases for every 12 she orders in the first year. The extra case is for promotional use.

- *Service and warranties.* Any product can be defective, and there should be contractual provisions that state what will happen in such instances. The exporter may agree to replace defective products at his expense, take them back for repair, or pay you for repairing them. The exporter will be very concerned about the warranty given to final buyers because, in most cases, he will end up paying the cost of repairs done under warranty.

- *Priority of orders.* Export merchants or agents will always want their orders to be given priority over the supplier's domestic orders. This decreases the possibility that a customer tires of waiting and cancels his or her order.

- *Order lead times.* This is a clause, similar to the preceding one, which specifies how soon the supplier should ship after receiving an order from you. It may say, for example, that your orders will normally be shipped within 30 days of receipt by the exporter.

- *Reporting.* The supplier may want a clause that specifies how often you should send reports. These reports may cover your sales activities, sales results, and changes in the market country including the economy, government regulations, competition, and customers.

- *Patent and trademark.* Foreign manufacturers' products may be patented or carry unique trade names or trademarks. In such a case, a manufacturer will usually apply for U.S. patents and/or register the names or marks in the United

States, or ask you to do so on *its behalf*. Both registrations are made to the Commissioner of Patents and Trademarks, Washington, D.C. 20231. Getting a patent is time-consuming and expensive. Registering a trademark, if it is truly unique, is easier. It takes a few months and costs about $250. It can be done on the Internet.

You may want to register your own trademark and have the supplier put it on the items you purchase. Then you will own it and can use it even if you change suppliers. As an option, you can have labels printed and send them to the foreign manufacturer. Under simplified rules that went into effect around 1996, you can register a U.S. trademark without having previously used it in interstate or international commerce.

Trademarks and brand names can also be registered with the U.S. Customs Service. Then, customs will try to stop imports of counterfeit goods, such as fake Rolex watches. Customs, however, will not normally enforce business agreements. If you are the exclusive U.S. importer of Beautiful You cosmetics and your supplier ships legitimate Beautiful You products to someone else in the United States, they will probably be allowed entry.

If your suppliers hold U.S. patents or trademarks, they may ask you to watch for cases of infringement. The action you must take if you hear of infringement depends on your agreements with the suppliers.

- *Relabeling and repackaging.* Sometimes manufacturers will want you to agree not to relabel or repackage their merchandise. In other cases it will be better for them to ship in bulk and have you repackage, under their labels or yours. A tasty product of the maguey cactus, tequila, is an excellent example. Most of the U.S. supply is imported from Mexico in tank trucks and bottled in the United States.

- *Legal agent.* Most supply agreements have simple statements that the agent or the importer is not a legal agent of the supplier. That is, you cannot enter into commitments that the supplier will be obliged to fulfill.

- *Assignment.* There is usually a clause that says you cannot assign the agreement to anyone else without the supplier's approval. Without this clause, the supplier would have no control over who ended up representing her.

- *Duration and termination.* There is usually a statement that sets forth the term of the contract, whether it will automatically be renewed if not canceled by either party, and how it can be canceled. Normally, the initial term of an agency or a distributorship agreement should be about two years. You don't want to work very hard for a year and have the agreement canceled just when you begin to write orders.

- *Disputes.* Finally, there is a clause that relates to the settlement of disputes. The agreement may say in which country disputes will be settled and which country's laws will apply. It is common to specify arbitration, even though international arbitration proceedings are too expensive for small-scale importers and exporters.

If you choose your suppliers carefully and deal with them competently and honestly, you should be able to resolve any disputes with neither lawsuits nor arbitration. Ultimately, a long-term business arrangement will not benefit you if it does not benefit the other party. Throughout the world, business is fueled by profit, but it is oiled by friendship and trust.

PROTECTING YOUR INTEREST

I once worked for a small firm in the Boston area that acted as an import merchant for books from Africa and an export agent for U.S. books and school supplies. We received an inquiry from a company in Haiti about desks for schools. After contacting a number of potential suppliers, we chose to quote on products of a company named Adirondack Chair. This manufacturer agreed to pay us an agent's commission. We sent the manufacturer's catalogs and prices to Haiti and, after a few phone calls and letters, the customer wrote an order to Adirondack Chair and mailed it to us. We forwarded it immediately and followed up by phone to make sure it was acceptable to the manufacturer. The goods were shipped, the importer paid, and the manufacturer promptly remitted our commission.

Unfortunately, not all export transactions go so smoothly. U.S. exporters and foreign importers may be tempted to try to save money by eliminating the intermediary, especially if there is no existing prior relationship and the transaction is large.

It is very frustrating to work on an export sale, have it fail to materialize, and then somehow find out that it was made by someone else. There are a few ways to protect yourself. First, try to deal with reputable companies. Second, obtain letters or other evidence that your commissions will be paid; when this is not possible, try to keep the exporter and the importer from identifying each other. Finally, try to make your services so valuable that they will be worth the money paid for them. Keeping the exporter and the importer from identifying each other usually works for only one transaction because the importer can identify the exporter from information on documents or the merchandise itself. (This is a problem for international trade brokers on the Internet. They find it very hard to collect fees after the first transaction between two companies.)

There is a type of payment document, a back-to-back letter of credit, that lets an intermediary use his or her customer's credit to guarantee payment to the supplier but does not identify either of them to the other (see chapter 7). This kind of letter of credit can be arranged by banks that specialize in import/export finance, but it usually requires that the intermediary be experienced in international trade and have enough collateral to cover the amount of the letter of credit. In other words, if the deal you are arranging is much larger than your bank account, you just about have to try to work as a commission agent.

SOURCES OF INFORMATION AND HELP

Two of the more important decisions you will make are the kinds of products in which to deal and the companies, domestic or foreign, from which you will obtain them. You can find information about this kind of design in various books and Web sites. One such

site, which is written for retailers but is useful anyway, is http://
retail.about.com/od/startingaretailbusiness/a/product_select
.htm. Another is from a source mentioned earlier, Entrepreneur
.com, at www.entrepreneur.com/startingabusiness/startupbasics/
article78778.html.

Most information on the Internet about selecting suppliers is
related to specific trades or product lines, but can be useful. With
practice, you can pretty well judge for yourself; you want to deal
with someone who is capable, honest, and well-financed; offers
excellent products and services; and wants to work with you.

The following sources of information are mentioned in this
chapter.

- http://trade.swissinfo.net is an import/export bulletin board
  offering trade leads.

- United Nations International Trade Centre (UNITC) in
  Geneva, Switzerland, is part of the United Nations system and
  helps developing countries to increase exports of goods and
  services. Web site: www.intracen.org/menus/countries.htm.

- U.S. International Trade Commission's Web site, www.usitc
  .gov, provides import and export data.

- Kompass maintains databases on businesses and sells business directories. Web site: www.kompass.com.

- EXPORT911.com provides lists of countries' trade promotion organizations. Address: P.O. Box 2345, Mississauga,
  ON, Canada L5B 3C8.

- World Trade Centers Association is a not-for-profit, non-
  political organization that facilitates international trade.
  Address: 420 Lexington Avenue, Suite 518, New York, NY
  10170; Phone: (212) 432-2626; Fax: (212) 488-0064; Web site:
  www.wtca.org.

- World Trade Point Federation (WTPF) is an international
  nongovernmental organization. Through its network of
  more than 120 trade information and facilitation centers, known as Trade Points, the WTPF assists small- and
  medium-size enterprises worldwide to trade internationally

through the use of electronic commerce technologies. Web site: www.tradepoint.org.

- Worldbid.com is a network of international trade market places, providing trade leads, request for proposals and tender opportunities. Address: Worldbid.com, Box 5155, Victoria, BC, Canada V8R 6N4; Phone: (250) 475-2248; Fax: (250) 475-2281.

- The American Chambers of Commerce, which are affiliated with the U.S. Chamber of Commerce, advance the interests of American business overseas. They are voluntary associations of American companies and individuals doing business in a particular country, as well as firms and individuals of that country who operate in the United States. U.S. Chamber of Commerce Phone: (202) 463-5460; Web site: www.uschamber.com/international/directory/default.htm.

- *World Trade* magazine offers international business news, information, and analysis, and is published by the Global Board of Trade Partners. Address: Corporate Office, BNP Media, 2401 West Big Beaver Road, Suite 700, Troy, MI 48084; Phone: (248) 362-3700; Fax: (248) 244-6439; Web site: www.worldtrademag.com.

- ISO 9000, a quality-management system, and ISO 14000, an environmental-management system, were developed by the International Organization for Standardization (IOS). IOS is a network of the national standards institutes of 157 countries. Address: ISO Central Secretariat: International Organization for Standardization (ISO) 1, Rue de Varembé, Case postale 56 CH-1211 Geneva 20, Switzerland; Phone: (+41) 22 749 01 11; Fax: (+41) 22 733 34 30; Web site: www.iso.org/iso/en/iso9000-14000/index.html.

- Hazard Analysis and Critical Control Point (HACCP) is a methodology for ensuring safer foods. For more information, visit the U.S. Food and Drug Administration's Web site at www.cfsan.fda.gov/~comm/haccpov.html.

- Baltic Import Export Bulletin Board is an online trade bulletin board. Web site: www.impex/lv/en.

- New Equipment Digest publishes a magazine and maintains a searchable database on new industrial and manufacturing products, equipment, suppliers, distributors, industry events, and online product demonstrations. Address: Penton Media, 1300 East 9th Street, Cleveland, OH 44114-1503; Web site: www.newequipment.com

- The Converting Equipment Manufacturers Association is a trade association for converting equipment manufacturers. Address: 201 Springs Street, Fort Mill, SC 29715; Phone: (803) 802-7820; Fax: (803) 802-7821; Web site: www .cemaconverting.org.

- U.S. Department of Commerce employs industry specialists. Phone: (800) USA-TRADE; Web site: http://web.ita.doc .gov/td/shared/tdindus.nsf/Industries.

- Service Corps of Retired Executives (SCORE) is a nonprofit organization dedicated to encouraging the formation, growth, and success of small business nationwide through counseling and mentor programs. SCORE provides consulting to clients of the Small Business Association. Address: SCORE Association, 409 3rd Street, SW, 6th Floor, Washington, DC 20024; Phone: (800) 634-0245; Web site: www .score.org.

- Food and Agriculture Organization (FAO) is a specialized agency of the United Nations that leads international efforts to defeat hunger. Numerous statistics can be found on its Web site. Address: FAO Headquarters, Viale delle Terme di Caracalla, 00100 Rome, Italy; Phone: (+39) 06 57051; Fax: (+39) 06 570 53152; Web site: www.fao.org.

- MarketResearch.com offers more than 110,000 market research reports from over 550 leading global publishers. Phone: (800) 298-5699; Fax: (212) 807-2642.

- *Thomas Food Industry Register* is a publication of Thomas Publishing. Address: 5 Penn Plaza, New York, NY 10001; Phone: (212) 695-0500; Fax: (212) 290-7362; Web site: www .thomaspublishing.com.

- The *ICC Model Commercial Agency Contract* or the *ICC Model Distributorship Contract* are both available at www .ICCbooks.com.

- Patents and trademarks can be registered with the U.S. Patent and Trademark Office. Address: P.O. Box 1450, Alexandria, VA 22313-1450; Phone: (800) 786-9199 or (571) 272-1000; Web site: www.uspto.gov.

6

Marketing in the United States and Abroad

However you start your business, with a buyer or with a product, your long-term success will depend very much on your skills in marketing. For import and export merchants the most critical business functions are purchasing and marketing, and the job of an import or export agent is almost entirely marketing.

WHAT IS MARKETING?

Traditionally, marketing is described as the group of activities required to move goods and services from producers to consumers in order to satisfy consumers' needs and wants. Consumers can be either individuals or industrial organizations including wholesalers and retailers, manufacturing companies, hospitals, restaurants, government entities, and so on. The major functions of marketing—the famous four Ps—are product, price, promotion, and place. The word "product" refers to the product and all its characteristics including its package and label. The word "price" includes the intricacies of pricing at all levels in the channel of distribution. "Promotion" includes advertising, public relations, and other ways of enticing consumers to buy the product or service, and "place" refers to the distribution system, which ends in a place where the final buyer (consumer or industrial) can obtain the product. In this age of the Internet, the place is often virtual rather than physical.

The way the four Ps are combined is referred to as the marketing mix. For example, your imported caviar might be very high in quality, which will obligate you to set a high price. Your exported razor blades might be distributed very widely, which will allow you to spend less money on promoting them. The idea is to blend the four elements in a way that will maximize your profit.

In practice, you will probably find yourself rearranging the four Ps. First, you will probably improve your product on the basis of information from potential buyers. Second, you will select one or more target markets and develop a channel of distribution to reach each of them. Third, you will set (or suggest) a price to the final buyer and work back from that, deducting expenses and markups, to calculate the price at which you will sell (assuming you can make a reasonable profit at that price). Finally, you will determine which kinds and amounts of promotion you need to do in order to sell a predetermined amount of merchandise. If your marketing plan includes selling to intermediaries, such as wholesalers or distributors, you should prepare a sell sheet (sales presentation) that you can use when you meet with them.

MARKETING IMPORTS

Here are some ideas about how you can market your products, as an agent or as a merchant, in the United States or in other countries.

Marketing Imports as an Agent

If you decide to try working as a selling agent in the United States for foreign products, you will have to select companies to represent, enter into agency agreements with them, and then find buyers in the United States who are willing and able to import and pay the shipper. Your buyers will have to place orders that are large enough to be shipped directly to them from overseas. With international package delivery services, such as

DHL, the quantities do not have to be large, but the shipping cost per unit is fairly high. Some companies, such as produce brokers, often take title to and possession of merchandise but charge fixed commissions plus expenses. This lets them sell to customers who do not want to import directly.

For several years, there has been a respectable trade in Egyptian paintings on papyrus. About 1985, the best-known supplier, Dr. Rageb's Papyrus Institute in Cairo, began by establishing an agent in the Midwest who was responsible for selling throughout the United States. Because Dr. Rageb's papyrus paintings were very high quality, this agent could contact stores that sold high-quality antiques and works of art. The number of such stores was not large, and they could be identified from trade sources or from telephone directories and yellow pages. The agent soon learned that any art dealer or museum gift shop could be a buyer. Because of the nature of the product, however, it could only be shipped in small quantities and imported by people who knew very little about importing. Later, other suppliers began selling to any company that would act as an importer and thus had no need for commission agents.

In contrast, two people who consulted me for advice decided to become import agents for a new kind of industrial floor sweeper made in northern Europe. This product could not be imported economically in small quantities. To lower transport costs per unit, several had to be brought in at a time, and each cost several thousand dollars. Because neither distributors nor the actual users were likely to buy several machines without seeing one in use, the importers had to bring in a sample, find a place to store it, and persuade potential buyers to go see it, or load it on a trailer and transport it to their places of business. They made some sales, but it was very hard until they become known in the industry. Since they did not have much money for advertising, and the foreign manufacturer would not help them with this, they had to rely on personal contact to find potential buyers.

Normally, in an agency relationship, the agent works to identify customers and obtain orders from them. Sometimes the exporting company, the principal, helps by sending leads that it has received. The agent sends the order to the principal, who will approve it if satisfied with the terms of the sale. If the terms involve extending credit, the principal must be satisfied that the customer will pay as agreed. Then the principal will ship directly to the customer, collect from the customer, and pay the agent a commission. The agent must follow up frequently to make sure the transaction is eventually made and that his or her commission is paid when it is due.

After the agent selects a product and reaches agreement with a principal, he or she faces the daunting task of finding buyers and persuading them to buy. The best list of U.S. importers is the annual *Directory of United States Importers*, published by Commonwealth Business Media. There is a companion book titled *Directory of United States Exporters*. These books are expensive but are available in major libraries. They contain useful information on thousands of companies. Unfortunately, the directory of importers omits many of the companies that import, especially manufacturers and retailers that choose to not be included. Also, like any directory, not all of the information is correct. Companies may not report all the products they handle or all the countries with which they deal, and their key personnel and their contact information can change at a moment's notice.

Commonwealth Business Media also has an electronic service for reporting information on both imports and exports, taken from steamship manifests. Note that air, road, and rail shipments are not included. Called PIERS (Port Import and Export Reporting Service), this service is expensive but is a way to find out which firms are really importing (as opposed to *saying* they import) specific kinds of products. There is comprehensive information about this service on its Web site, www.piers.com.

There are numerous other publications that either list importers or use codes to identify importing firms. These include directory issues of trade magazines, state and local industrial directories, and others such as the *Thomas Food Industry Register*, mentioned in chapter 5. There are also electronic directories on the Internet of potential customers, but I cannot vouch for their reliability.

You will probably want to determine the kinds of buyers to approach, identify companies that fall into your chosen categories, and then contact them personally. Some of the many kinds of buyers for consumer goods are the following.

- Chain restaurant operators, food service distributors, high-volume independent restaurants, cruise lines, single-unit supermarket operators, supermarket/grocery/convenience store chains, and wholesaler grocers
- Apparel specialty stores, department stores, discount and general merchandise stores, drugstore and health and beauty chains, and high-volume independent drugstores
- Automotive aftermarket suppliers, computer and consumer electronics retailers, computer value-added retailer and systems integrators, home center operators and hardware chains, home furnishings retailers, and mail-order firms.

For industrial products, you might be able to sell to factories of all kinds, hospitals, prison systems, government organizations, and so forth. If you have a small or minority-owned business, you should look into preferential buying programs of your state and local government agencies. Many private firms also have these kinds of special buying programs.

I once assisted a company in Colombia that manufactured clothing for dolls. No directories showed U.S. importers of doll clothing, but I found that nearly every U.S. doll manufacturer was importing clothing, mostly from the Far East. I had no difficulty identifying manufacturers of dolls, making appointments with them, showing them samples of the clothing, and explaining that if they imported from South America, they could save money on customs duties and forget about jet lag both during and after their buying trips. Several manufacturers gave me samples of products they were buying from Asia so the South American firm could examine them and prepare quotations.

Another Colombian firm wanted to export a canned or bottled fruit from the peach palm tree. It is known in some countries as *chontaduro* and in others as *pejivalle*. This was a Latin American specialty food that would be retailed by small food stores that catered to an ethnic clientele, but the stores themselves would not be the importers. The technique used to identify importers was to go to Hispanic areas, find small food stores, and look at the imported products they were selling. Labels on imported canned and bottled foods usually provide the importers' names and locations (in this case, cities or boroughs of New York City). A few of the importers were small firms that were not listed in telephone or electronic directories, and in these cases we got the telephone numbers from the retailers by simply asking and explaining why we needed the information.

Marketing Imports as a Merchant

As a merchant you will actually import goods from overseas, take title to them and probably (but not necessarily) possession of them, and sell and deliver them to your customers. A merchant normally invests more money and performs more functions than an agent but has the potential to make a larger profit. Because a merchant loses if he or she cannot sell, or sells but cannot collect, there is also a potential for *losing* money.

In general, an import merchant will not sell to other importers but to entities such as wholesalers, retailers, industrial distributors, and industrial users. In general, *wholesalers* are merchant firms that buy products and resell them to retailers. *Retailers* include chain stores, independent stores, mail-order and Internet retailers, flea market operators, and other kinds of businesses that sell directly to individual consumers. *Industrial distributors* are merchant firms that sell to industrial users. *Industrial users* include business, government, educational, and nonprofit organizations of all types.

Wholesalers

Wholesalers of most kinds of goods can be identified from Internet or telephone directories or from directory issues of trade magazines. One of the best sources is *Reference USA*, but unfortunately the data are available only to patrons of libraries that subscribe to this service. Your local library may. Wholesale buyers can be approached directly. They are generally very experienced and negotiate hard on prices and terms of sales. Wholesalers normally buy in quantity and pay their bills promptly but do not invest much in promotion. You will need to promote your products to retailers so they will order from the wholesalers.

The best way to persuade wholesalers to handle your product is to demonstrate that retailers will buy it and can resell it. For example, a woman interested in importing high-quality wooden furniture from France began by locating a few stores that sold products similar to hers and persuading each one to stock a few pieces. Then she could import a container load of furniture, place some in stores, and tell wholesalers that she knew the product would sell because it was already being sold.

Retailers

If you choose to sell directly to retailers, you can identify them from telephone directories or from specialized directories such as the *Salesman's Guide* series from Douglas Publications (www .douglaspublications.com). There are similar books available from other companies. These directories list the names and telephone numbers of the buyers of each kind of merchandise in major stores and store chains. You probably won't find these in libraries, so you may have to buy the one you need.

In general, the larger the store or store chain, the harder it is to get in to see a buyer. When you phone for an appointment, you may be asked to send a catalog or prices and samples. If you agree to send a catalog and do not have one, you're in luck, because new technologies have reduced the cost of preparing catalogs, and you can actually order this service on the Internet. For example, at www.printingcenterusa.com 250 copies of an eight-page, four-color catalog can cost less than $900 if you don't need accelerated printing or shipping. Alternatively, you might be able to produce your catalog on a computer if you have a good camera, the right software, and the ability to use them well. If you ask a professional photographer to take color pictures for you, 25 copies of one shot may cost about $300. Have the photograph printed on a full-size sheet of paper with the item number and name (and the dimensions and weight if relevant), and you have a catalog page. You can include the price on the same page or put it in your cover letter, or, if you have several models, you can prepare a separate list of prices. Your price list should mention your minimum order quantity, any discounts for large orders or prompt payment, and whether delivery charges are included.

A few retail stores have open buying days, when vendors can see buyers without having appointments. Some directories list these days, but you should call in advance to make sure they have not been changed. Be prepared to answer every possible question about your company and its product including its material composition and how it is made. Buyers from big stores are very professional. They do not want to take time to educate you if they doubt your product knowledge or risk buying from you if they doubt your ability to deliver.

The term *open buying* should not be confused with *open to buy*, which means that the buyer has money remaining in his or her current budget for the kind of merchandise you are selling. If you visit someone who is not currently open to buy, you will have little or no chance of making an immediate sale.

Retail buyers know pretty well what will sell and what will not and at which price each kind and quality of merchandise should be bought. They negotiate prices and specify the quantities, delivery dates, and payment terms they want. They sometimes refuse to accept merchandise even after having ordered it, and they often take longer to pay than the terms agreed upon. A store that is given terms such as "2/10, Net 30" (2 percent discount if it pays within 10 days and payment due in any case within 30 days) will often pay in 20 or 25 days and take the discount anyway.

If you choose to sell to small independent stores, such as gift shops or boutiques, you will find it easier to see buyers. Sometimes you can even walk in unannounced, ask who does the buying, and show your samples. A buyer who likes the samples and prices may place a small order, ask for immediate delivery, and write a check or even pay in cash. Cash payments may, but do not necessarily, indicate that some of the retailer's transactions are being made "off the books."

You will not, however, have time to make enough sales calls in small stores to generate a profitable volume of business. A solution to this problem is to enlist the services of manufacturers' representatives. These are agents who will book orders for your products from retail stores and send the orders to you. When you accept an order, you will ship it to the customer, request payment from the customer, and send the agent his or her commission.

You can find manufacturers' representatives on the following Web sites.

- Manufacturers Representatives of America, a national not-for-profit trade organization of multiple-line sales and marketing companies, www.mra-reps.com.
- Manufacturers' Agents National Association, with over 7,000 members and 23,000 representatives, www.manaonline.org.

There are other sites for representatives in specific industries, and there is a "play for pay" service called RepLocate that can help in your search. RepLocate is on the Web at www.replocate .com. You create an account, type in your notice, and pay by credit card.

Another approach is to ask retail buyers which agents they suggest you speak with. The buyers will probably give you the names of the agents they deal with the most. A manufacturer's representative (rep) will usually ask you for a 10 to 15 percent commission and perhaps to pay a share of his or her overhead expenses (office, etc.). You will need to supply the rep with catalogs or with product samples, price lists, and promotional literature. Thus, if you use 10 reps and they have an average of five salespersons each, you will have to supply 50 copies of your catalog. In some industries, such as automotive parts, you may be able to get by with just an online catalog.

Direct to Consumers

Selling on the *Internet* directly to consumers has become a very big business, and the cost of getting started is not high. There are many companies that will help you, including the major search engines. Type into a search engine something like "selling on the Internet," and you will find several brief how-to manuals.

Unfortunately, the ease of selling on the Net created so much competition, so quickly, that you may be more successful if you sell through an established merchant. There are many exceptions, however. I remember reading about people in a tiny Cambodian village who are selling handmade scarves to the world using a little computer, powered by a portable generator with a satellite antenna, to get them on the Net. A lady I met recently sells homemade perfumes on the Internet. One day her product was featured in a specialized e-zine, and she received so many e-mail messages that her server couldn't handle them all.

Perhaps the main difficulty in selling on the Internet is getting consumers to look at your Web site and therefore your products. There are tricks to getting placed higher on the lists of search engines, such as including technical content and putting on a few links to other sites but only those that are relevant to your type of product. You can also do more conventional advertising. For example, instead of buying a page in *Sole Collector* magazine to tell people about your shoes, you can buy a two-inch advertisement that includes a catchy headline, a carefully selected photograph or drawing, and your Web site address.

With Internet or other direct-selling techniques, you will have to set up a little "backroom" operation to perform functions such as answering questions by phone and Internet, receiving orders, packing, shipping, accounting, and processing merchandise that is returned.

Many new importers plan to sell their products by *mail order*. This is usually not as easy as it sounds. There are essentially three ways to go about it.

First, you can identify your most likely target market, buy a specialized mailing list from one of the many list dealers such as infoUSA in New Jersey (800-321-0869), prepare your mailing, and send it out. You can buy names and addresses on lists, mailing labels, three-by-five cards, magnetic tape, diskettes, and CD-ROMs. Some now include credit ratings. You should get professional help in preparing your mailing pieces or at least read books on mail-order selling. You will learn techniques such as writing "personal and confidential" on your envelope, using a postscript in your sales letter to communicate an important point, and putting a real stamp on your reply envelope. People hate to throw away stamps. For large mailings, you can save money by getting a bulk-mail permit, but many experts say the extra cost of using first-class mail is a good investment.

You should send a series of three mailings to the same addresses. Most people will throw away the first one because they have never heard of you. The second one may catch their attention, and the third one may cause them to buy from you. The rates of response in mail order are very low. A major organization that markets seminars by mail is said to be satisfied with a rate of about 0.0025, or a quarter of 1 percent. Among other things, this is because even the best mailing lists contain errors (wrong addresses, names of people who have moved, etc.) and your tiny, unknown catalog must compete for attention with the likes of Spencer Gifts and Hanover House. You will be lucky to break even in the beginning, especially when you consider the labor involved in sending the catalogs and processing the orders.

A second mail-order option is for you to advertise in newspapers or magazines (at least three issues of the same publication). You can ask respondents to order immediately or to contact you for more information. Advertising in general-interest publications is unlikely to pay off (although the *Wall Street Journal*, for example, carries ads over and over again for products that do not seem to be high-potential mail-order items, like the Poke Boat.) If you have a specialized product and can find a publication aimed precisely at your target market, this kind of marketing will work well. I once met an importer of Scottish bagpipe regalia who told me there was only one magazine for bagpipe enthusiasts in the United States. He advertised in that publication and was receiving numerous orders.

A third mail-order option is to import products and try to persuade established *mail-order houses* to include them in their catalogs. Save the catalogs that come to you and try to identify firms that sell products similar to yours. Also, you can look on the Web at sites such as www.catalogsfroma-z.com (for online catalogs) and www.buyersindex.com (for hard-copy catalogs) to identify companies that might want to handle your products. Then contact them, preferably by phone. Describe your product and say that you feel it would sell very well in their catalogs. Buyers who are interested will probably ask for a sample and prices. Your sample will not be returned unless you provide a self-addressed label and offer to accept the shipment collect from a parcel service, such as UPS, and sometimes even that will not be sufficient.

Professional mail-order firms place a high value on every square inch of every catalog page and are very selective about the products they include. Furthermore, they keep their product inventories to a minimum. They won't want to take a chance on putting an item in a catalog and getting orders for it only to find that you do not have enough in stock. Therefore, they will probably insist that you invest in a substantial inventory to keep in the United States. A few will send you mailing labels and ask you to "drop ship" directly to their customers, but this is becoming less common.

If you have an inexpensive, mass merchandise type of product, you may want to try selling it at craft shows or *flea markets* or, better yet, to flea market vendors or wholesalers. Flea markets in the United States are now an established industry with its own associations and publications, but they tend to go in and out of business quickly. Try going to flea markets in your area, speaking with dealers, and asking them which wholesalers they buy from. These same wholesalers usually also sell to street vendors, house party dealers, and other kinds of nonstore retailers.

Be warned, however, that the flea market industry works on low prices. People who shop at flea markets expect the dealers to sell cheaply. That means the dealers have to buy cheaply from the wholesalers, and the wholesalers have to buy cheaply from you. Some people consider flea marketing to be the method of selling of last resort.

Industrial Distributors

Industrial distributors are similar to wholesalers except that they buy from manufacturers or importers and sell to industrial users. To reach smaller users, there are often two levels of distributors. A familiar example is the automotive parts trade in which numerous specialized companies make virtually all parts available to a myriad of repair facilities. Industrial distributors can usually be identified through telephone directories, state industrial directories, and directory issues of trade magazines or by asking industrial users which distributors they buy from. In general, they buy in good quantities, stock merchandise, pay their bills on time, sell and do some promotion, and deliver to their customers.

Another way to find industrial distributors is to go on the Web to www.manufacturing.net and enter your product type in the space titled "Search for." You can also get useful information from the Industrial Distributors Association at www.ida-assoc.org. Both have newsletters to which you can subscribe at no cost.

I once had an acquaintance who was importing a new kind of stapler from Japan. It was small, light, inexpensive, durable, and effective. He tried to persuade distributors, such as Federal Office Products in Kansas, to stock and resell the product. Unfortunately, this business did not last long, probably because my acquaintance never put together an adequate sales presentation and didn't have the financing to offer a package of promotional assistance, which would entice users to buy the product from distributors.

Industrial Users

Industrial users include manufacturers, wholesalers, retailers, schools, libraries, hospitals, government offices, military installations, and so on. They all have people or departments in charge of purchasing, and you can usually get through to them by phone. Unfortunately, it is much harder to schedule face-to-face appointments with them. They nearly always have established suppliers of known brands, and they don't have time to deal with numerous small manufacturers and importers. If you have a new and better paper clip, don't try to sell it to IBM. Sell it instead to a distributor that sells to IBM.

You may have heard the term "significant industrial user." These are companies that are significant to the U.S. Environmental Protection Agency (EPA) because their operations cause important amounts of pollution. They are usually looking for new kinds of pollution control equipment that will help them meet EPA standards for wastewater discharge and other types of polluting activities.

A Final Note on Marketing Imports

If it sounds too hard to start an import business, you might consider buying one. Try entering in your search engine "import business for sale," and you will find a number of brokerage services and actual listings. As I write, a listing on www.us.businessesfor sale.com reads:

> Very Unique Asian Import Business for Sale.
> Asking price $140,000, Sales revenue $150,000
> Net profit $69,000, 30 years old, 1FT/1PT employee

Obviously, you have to do a careful examination of a business before you buy it, and you may want to use the services of a consultant who specializes in business valuation. Be especially wary of a business owner who says that the financial statements of the business don't reflect its true worth because there is additional income that was not recorded. This may or may not be true, and it tells you that you are dealing with a person who is not entirely honest.

Here is an example that might help you see the usefulness of a business valuation specialist. I was once peripherally involved with a person who was considering buying an import business and did now know how much he should pay for it. The importer brought into the United States an exclusive soft-goods product related to the drapery industry. She had exclusive rights to the design of the product, which was being manufactured under contract in Europe. The company imported the goods for sale to her customers.

This importer had started as a home-based business in 1988. Since then, it had grown to require a 1,200-square-foot facility, and she said it would soon require another 400 to 500 square feet.

She and her husband managed the company with one additional full-time employee and one part-time person. They handled all administration, warehousing, and shipping from the Southeastern city where they preferred to live. The distribution network consisted of about 60 independent sales representatives, who sold to approximately 3,000 dealers. The company shipped the product nationally and into Canada, usually by UPS.

The business had realized an average gross profit of 65 percent over the last four years. Average gross sales since 1973 were $298,000, and profit before interest and taxes averaged $100,000 per year. It wasn't clear whether the owners were paid salaries before the profit was calculated.

How much would it cost to purchase this business? The asking price was $250,000 for inventory and $245,000 for other assets. I made a rough estimate of the payback period, which came to about six years. Can you figure out a fair selling price? It isn't easy to do.

MARKETING EXPORTS

The July/August 2006 issue of *Hispanic Business* magazine included a list of the top 50 Hispanic exporters in the United States. Some companies on the list were quite large, but others were not. The AZF Automotive Group was exporting about $10 million per year of automotive sales and service and had only *two* employees. Kros Holdings was exporting about $6 million per year of perfume, cosmetics, food, and groceries and reported having just four employees. The A. M. Capens Company was exporting about $10 million of office and school supplies, with only 10 employees. Each of these small firms had built a line of products and was selling abroad successfully.

Foreign Market Analysis

Before you start trying to export, you should know more about the markets in which you want to sell. Through research and analysis you will obtain information to help you develop a market-entry plan including an initial marketing mix. The essential information is market characteristics that are relevant to your product.

Most market studies begin with published sources, including the Internet. This is called "desk research." Then they usually go into a second phase, which is "field research." You can probably do much or all of the desk research yourself, using other market studies and data available on the Internet. The field research is harder. You may be able to do it yourself but will have to travel to your market country, pay living expenses, and understand the culture well enough to get the information you need. The alternative is to hire a local consultant to do the research for you. Such people can often be identified through the U.S. trade attaché in each country or through a worldwide entity, such as the International Agribusiness Management Association. If you use a consultant for market research, make sure your objectives and specifications are in writing and are perfectly clear.

The final step in research is to turn the information you have obtained into a format that facilitates using it to make marketing decisions. If you do not use research results to make decisions or solve problems, you have probably wasted your money.

Suppose, for example, that you obtain the worldwide (nonmilitary) export rights for a device known as ShotSpotter. One model is the size of a coffee can and can be mounted on tops of buildings. It picks up the sound of gunfire for two miles on all sides and transmits the location instantly to a local police department. If the shooter is moving, ShotSpotter indicates the direction of travel.

You might find, on the Internet, that homicides with firearms are especially prevalent in Colombia, South Africa, Brazil, Mexico, and Estonia. You can probably look further and identify certain cities in which your product should be in use. You decide to look at Brazil first, beginning with the CIA's *World Factbook* on the Web at www.cia.gov/cia/publications/factbook. You find other sources and put them together until you have a fairly good picture of the illegal use of firearms in major Brazilian cities. You are also interested in the budgets of police departments in Brazil, and you find some relevant information on the Web. To find out if anyone is already selling a similar product, you hire a friend who is from Brazil to review major Brazilian newspapers on the Internet and to call friends in selected cities who might have information. You prepare an outline, put your information into a coherent form, and draw conclusions. For two days' work plus whatever you pay to your friend, you have a small market study.

Planning to Enter the Market

Based on the market information, you might decide to begin by targeting police departments in the cities of São Paulo and Rio de Janeiro. You estimate that minimal coverage in a high-crime area would require 100 units, so 100 per city becomes your sales forecast. You don't think the budget figures will permit buying all 100 at once, so you forecast 20 units the first year, 40 the second, and 40 the third.

The product characteristics are appropriate for the market except that you have an option of using wireless or wired sensors. Since the equipment is not likely to be moved often, and cost will be a factor, you decide to promote the wired variety. You obtain a price for translating technical information and directions into Brazilian Portuguese, and the manufacturer agrees to pay half that cost of doing so.

Your channel of distribution will be simple. You will need one very good commission agent for the country. You will have to locate and contract with such a person, train him or her, supply a unit for demonstration purposes, and remain in frequent contact.

You calculate that you can make an acceptable profit on the first 20 units (10 in each of two cities) and pay all costs including installation and your agent's commission for about $150,000 per city. This sounds very reasonable compared to the benefit, so it becomes your price. Maybe you raise it a little so you can give a discount on the first order.

You have the company's promotional literature, sales presentation, and newspaper articles translated into Brazilian Portuguese and checked for accuracy. In computing the price, you assume that transportation would be by airfreight and that payment would be made to you via a letter of credit (to be explained later), payable 30 days after the equipment reaches the customer's airport. Put all this together, and you have a brief marketing plan.

Setting Up Distribution

In the example above, your distribution channel is very straight-forward, but in other situations it might be more complicated. If the product were not ShotSpotters but intrusion alarms for private homes, you might target middle- and upper-class people in the same Brazilian cities. Your research might show that people in Latin America tend to buy this kind of product from specialty stores rather than from door-to-door salespeople or stores like Lowe's or Home Depot. Therefore, stores that specialize in security equipment would be the last link in your chain of distribution.

The specialty stores would be supplied by an importer/distributor, probably with an exclusive arrangement for the entire country. That importer would be your customer. You would have to identify potential importers, find one who was competent and honest and wanted to work with you, negotiate and sign an agreement, and provide promotional material for customers that the importer could offer to buyers in specialty stores. You may also have to help finance the initial stock of products.

Pricing, Promotion, and Sales

With the home-intrusion alarms, for example, you will probably want to work hard on the pricing. Start from your cost and add other costs and markups until you calculate a price to the consumer. Then look at a more or less average price for similar equipment in the market and see whether it is higher or lower than what you calculated. By playing with the numbers, and considering whether you want to sell on the basis of price (low), quality (high), or service (excellent), you can develop an initial price list.

You must also wrestle with the question of how to get customers to come in and ask for your product or how to get salespersons in the stores to recommend it. You probably won't be able to afford consumer-lever promotion and so will have to look at the latter approach and develop some kind of sales incentive scheme. For example, you might offer dinner in a nice restaurant to the top salesperson in each store every month. You and the importer could split the cost.

Other Approaches to Export Marketing

You may have noted that the marketing ideas above are quiet and very direct. You can also try approaches such as advertising on the Internet, advertising in foreign trade publications, participating in trade shows, and participating in organized trade missions. The U.S. and some state departments of commerce can help with these activities. The U.S. Commercial Service (USCS) of the Department of Commerce might suggest that you advertise on their showcase publication for American-made products and services, which is called *Commercial News USA*. It is widely distributed and the cost is reasonable. You can obtain information by calling (800) 581-8533 or going on the Web to www.thinkglobal.us. The USCS has several other services to help with export marketing.

A simple way to try your hand at exporting via the Internet is to go to www.worldbid.com, register for its service, and then complete a "quikpost form" to announce the product you want to sell. In the box labeled "Offer details," be specific but also promote a bit. For example, say: "Seeking importer/distributors worldwide for new line of high-quality all-natural skin creams and lotions." Carefully evaluate any replies you receive. You may hear from several people with whom you would not want to do business, but there might be a gem among that handful of stones.

SOURCES OF INFORMATION AND HELP

There is no shortage of books and other publications on marketing, and I suggest that you read at least one of them. If you plan to export, look for a book on *international* marketing. I could suggest some personal favorites, but it's probably better for you to browse in your library or bookstore and see which ones seem right for you. Look in the "small business" section; you don't want a book for a manager at General Motors. You might be able to save money by buying a used copy online, if you don't mind waiting a few days to get it.

If you want some fun reading, pick up a book on international business blunders. These mistakes, some made by important people in important companies, will both keep you laughing and warn you to be careful in working with people of cultures other than your own.

In this book there are a number of information sources that relate to marketing; these are listed below.

- *Directory of United States Importers* and *Directory of United States Exporters* is published by Commonwealth Business Media. Phone: (877) 203-5277; Web site: www.piers.com/ impexporder.

- Reference USA is an Internet-based reference service from the Library Division of InfoUSA. The Reference USA database contains, in module format, detailed information on more than 14 million U.S. businesses, 210 million U.S. residents, 855,000 U.S. health-care providers, 1.5 million Canadian businesses, and 12 million Canadian households. Address: InfoUSA Library Division, P.O. Box 27347, Omaha, NE 68127; Phone: (800) 808-1113; Web site: www .referenceusa.com.

- *Salesman's Guide* series from Douglas Publications. Address: 2807 North Parham Road, Suite 200, Richmond, VA 23294; Phone: (804) 762-9600; Fax: (804) 217-8999; Web site: www.douglaspublications.com.

- PrintingCenterUSA is an online full-service printing company. Address: 117 9th Street North, Great Falls, MT 59401; Phone: (800) 995-1555; Web site: www.printingcenterusa.com.

- Manufacturers Representatives of America is a national not-for-profit trade organization of multiple-line sales and marketing companies. Phone: (682) 518-6008; Fax: (682) 518-6476; Web site: www.mra-reps.com.

- Manufacturers' Agents National Association has more than 7,000 members and 23,000 representatives. Address: One

Spectrum Pointe, Suite 150, Lake Forest, CA 92630; Phone: (877) 626-2776; Web site: www.manaonline.org.

- RepLocate helps business to find sales representatives. Address: 1402 Liddle Lane, Hastings, MN 55033; Phone: (651) 438-3364; Web site: www.replocate.com.

- InfoUSA provides mailing lists and e-mail lists to businesses of all sizes. Address: InfoUSA, Database & Technology Center, 1020 East 1st Street, Papillion, NE, 68046; Phone (800) 321-0869; Web site: www.infousa.com.

- Catalogs From A to Z is an online directory of mail-order catalogs. Web site: www.catalogsfroma-z.com.

- Buyersindex.com features both hard-copy and Web-based catalogs. Address: Wired Markets, 1045 Via Mil Cumbres, Solana Beach, CA 92075; Phone: (858) 793-0085; Fax: (858) 793-3680.

- Manufacturing.net is a Web site featuring daily updates covering the latest news from around the globe on key topics for manufacturers. The site is operated by Advantage Business Media.

- Industrial Distributors Association has a large membership of firms and individuals. Access to its membership directory is restricted on its Web site, www.ida-assoc.org.

- *Hispanic Business* magazine is published by Hispanic Business. Address: 425 Pine Avenue, Santa Barbara, CA 93117-3709; Phone: (805) 964-4554; Fax: (805) 964-5539; Web site: www.hispanicbusiness.com/magazine.

- International Agribusiness Management Association is an association of agribusiness leaders. Address: IAMA Business Office, 333 Blocker Building, 2124 TAMU, College Station, TX 77843-2124; Phone: (979) 845-2118; Fax: (979) 862-1487; Web site: www.ifama.org.

- CIA *World Factbook* provides national-level information on countries, territories, and dependencies. The online version is updated every few weeks and is available for free on the CIA's Web site at www.cia.gov/cia/publications/

factbook. The hardback version of the *World Factbook* is updated annually and is available for sale from the following: Superintendent of Documents, P.O. Box 371954 Pittsburgh, PA 15250-7954; Phone: (202) 512-1800; Fax: (202) 512-2250; Web site: http://bookstore.gpo.gov.

- *Commercial News USA* is the U.S. Commercial Service's (USCS) showcase publication for American-made products and services. The USCS is part of the Department of Commerce. Phone: (800) 581-8533; E-mail: cnusa@thinkglobal.us.

7

Money Matters

You are in the import business. You need to place an order, and your supplier in Zurich has asked for either cash in advance or payment *at sight* in Swiss francs by a confirmed, irrevocable letter of credit with all charges for your account. Does this sound like a good deal, or will you negotiate?

Okay, now you're in the export business. You have an order from Tanzania, and the customer offers to pay in East African shillings and be billed on a 60-day open account or shipped to on 60-day SDDA (sight draft, documents against acceptance) terms. Is this acceptable, or will you negotiate?

Now that you are both importing and exporting, a firm in Malaysia offers to trade $10,000 worth of beautiful cotton blouses for industrial sewing machines of the same value. "Don't worry about duties or quotas," the manager says. "They won't apply because this is a barter deal." Will you order the blouses and send the sewing machines?

This chapter will give you ideas about how to deal with these kinds of issues. If you don't know how to deal with them, and don't have a good banker to advise you, you may have to say no to some profitable transactions. If you get involved in unique or complex deals without an understanding of how to deal with money matters, or a very good advisor, you could lose your shirt, your trousers, and more.

CREDIT DECISIONS ON SUPPLIERS AND CUSTOMERS

Whether you plan to sell domestically or to export, as a merchant you will have to decide between taking the risk of selling on credit, or losing sales by insisting on payment in cash. Your suppliers will face similar decisions about selling to you. If you work only as an agent, you will still be involved in credit decisions. You will negotiate sales for your principals and will then have to convince them that the terms of sale you have worked out with the customers are acceptable. In order to make credit decisions, you must know how to obtain and use credit information.

Bank and Trade References

The least expensive way to check on the creditworthiness of a domestic or foreign firm is to ask for bank and trade references. A company that will not give you references is not likely to be a good-paying customer.

To check a prospective customer's bank reference, give your bank (in writing) the company's name and address, its bank's name and address, and its account number. That information is not confidential; it is printed on checks. If you are verifying the status of a foreign company and want the information quickly, ask your bank to communicate with the customer's bank by e-mail or fax. You should receive a report that tells you how many years the company's account has been open, the approximate average balance, the amount of its credit line, and in general how satisfactory the account has been to the bank. This is not a great deal of data, but it will be helpful.

To check trade references, send each a letter or a fax that reads something like the one in Figure 7.1.

If you are checking on a potential supplier, the letter will be almost the same, but the questions will be something like the ones at the bottom of Figure 7.1.

Nearly all companies will answer this correspondence if it looks professional. If you send it by mail, it can help to enclose a stamped, self-addressed return envelope. It can't hurt to give your fax

Dear Sir or Madam:

The company named below has listed you as a credit reference. We will be very grateful if you will answer the questions at the bottom of this page and return this letter in the enclosed self-addressed, stamped envelope. Your prompt attention to this request will help us make an appropriate credit decision. We will be pleased to assist you in the same way if the occasion should ever arise. Thank you very much.
Sincerely,

[your signature]
_____

Name and Address of Applicant: [you will fill this in] _____
_____
_____
_____

[questions on potential customers]
Number of years you have sold to this company: _____
Highest recent balance: _____
Current outstanding balance: _____
Terms you extend this company: _____
Payment record: Discounts ( ) 30 days ( ) 60 days ( ) Over 60 ( )
Your rating of account: Excellent ( ) Good ( ) Fair ( ) Poor ( )
Additional comments: _____
_____
Your name: _____ Title: _____ Date: _____

[questions on potential suppliers]
Number of years you have dealt with this vendor: _____
Please comment on:
• Size of order supplier can fill: _____
• Adherence to shipping schedules: _____
• Accuracy in filling orders: _____
• Any problems experienced: _____
• Other comments: _____
Your name: _____ Title: _____ Date: _____

Figure 7.1 A letter requesting credit references.

number and to offer the option of replying by fax. Communication by fax may someday disappear, but so far it is holding its own.

Credit Reporting Services

How much is credit information worth to you? This depends on how much you stand to lose by making a wrong credit decision. If you make a $10,000 sale and don't get paid, a report that would have stopped your making the sale would be a good investment even if it cost $9,000. If you get paid, but a month late, at 12 percent interest, the report would be worth up to $100 ($10,000 × 0.12 × 30 / 360). If you stand to lose much importing or exporting, you should consider using the services of a credit reporting agency.

The granddaddy of this business in the United States is the Dun & Bradstreet (D&B) company. Just go on the Internet to www.dnb.com and enter the name and location of the company you want to check on. This will bring up a menu of credit reports. For companies in the United States, the range is from about $10 for a Company Profile to about $140 for a Comprehensive Insight Plus Report. When I looked up a company in Hungary, only one report was available, a Business Information Report for medium-risk credit decisions, for about $500. Of course, D&B doesn't have information on every company in the world, but it claims to cover 100 million of them.

For firms in the United States there are other options. There are small credit reporting agencies in most cities. I once called from Bolivia to such an agency in Miami, and the information it provided probably kept a Bolivian firm from losing both its merchandise and the shipping cost. Several other sources of credit information are available on the Internet, and you might want to experiment to see which gives you the most for your money. If you order and pay on the Internet, you will receive the information instantly, and this may be important to you.

Exporters might consider ordering an International Country Profile. These are available from the U.S. Department of Commerce for many companies in about 80 countries. The order must be placed through a USCS Export Assistance Center, and you can find the one nearest to you by going on the Web to www.buyusa.gov/home/export.html.

Finally, a visit to a potential vendor or customer can give you important information. If the tires on the trucks are too old, perhaps they can't afford new ones. If they still do their accounting manually, they must be too backward or too tight on money to buy accounting software and have an employee learn to use it. Finally, if they aren't willing to answer your questions or seem to be hiding something, perhaps they are.

METHODS OF PAYMENT IN INTERNATIONAL TRADE

In international trade there are several means of payment, each of which has its costs, advantages, and risks. The most important are the following:

- Open account
- Documents against acceptance
- Documents against payment
- Letter of credit
- Payment in advance

These means of payment are arrayed in order of risk, with open account being the riskiest for the exporter and payment in advance being the riskiest for the importer. Sometimes consignment is also listed as a payment term. It would go at the top of the list, because in consignment sales the risk is borne entirely by the exporter.

Terms of payment are a negotiable aspect of international trade transactions. Both parties seek a term that is favorable to themselves but still acceptable to the other. You need to understand the various methods; otherwise, you may accept a method of payment that is riskier or more expensive than can be justified by the profit on a transaction.

Open Account

How do you pay for water? It's simple: first you receive the product, and then the water company sends you a bill. Open account in international trade works the same way. First the exporter sends the shipments, and then he or she sends bills for the merchandise and related costs. The importer can pay in various ways, such as by sending a form of cashier's check or an international money order, using a bank transfer, or even paying through Pay-Pal or with a credit card. I sometimes use a service called Trancentrix, which is available through Ruesch, on the Internet at www.ruesch.com.

Payment by open account is inexpensive. It does not involve any risk for the importer, but the exporter runs the risk that the importer will not pay for the merchandise. You can pretty much forget legal remedies in case of a default. The exporter's only protection is that of the underlying contract of sale and/or the importer's word and reputation.

It may then surprise you to learn that open account is the most widely used method of payment in the import/export business. This is because the great majority of international trade, in terms of value, is between affiliated companies *or* between large firms that know and trust each other. If Toyota/Japan ships auto parts to Toyota/U.S. or to General Motors, it will not bother with costly or complex terms of payment.

As a small importer, you are unlikely to get open account terms from foreign suppliers, but through steady purchases and reliable performance you may earn this reward in a few years. As a small exporter, you will almost certainly be asked to accept payment on open account. You will probably be reluctant to agree, but if your customer is a major firm or is well known to you, you may decide to take the risk. After all, why should a foreign importer buy from you and use a risky or expensive method of payment if it is possible to get open account terms from another exporter in the United States or a third country? Marks and Spencer, for example, can probably get open account terms from any vendor in the world.

As an exporter you will want to be careful of a little game that is played by a few importers. They may start paying you on secure terms and then request open account for a small order. If you agree, their orders on open account will become progressively larger, and they will pay right on time. Then you will ship a large order, and the money will not arrive. I once tried to help a Long Island company that had fallen for this scam. When the exporter traveled to the importing country in West Africa, he found that most of his money had been invested—in houses for the importer and his relatives.

Another problem with open account shipments is that even honest buyers can take a long time to pay—reportedly around 80 days for some countries. This keeps the exporter's money tied up and weakens his cash flow.

Documentary Drafts for Collection—Against Acceptance and Against Payment

To draft a document is to write it. In international trade a draft is an unconditional order in writing, signed by the seller and addressed to a foreign buyer. It orders the buyer to pay the amount specified in the draft, either when it is presented to him or on a specified date in the future. Drafts as methods of payment are used only in international trade, and you may have heard them referred to sight drafts and documents against payment.

In brief, a draft is a simple, inexpensive means of payment that is initiated by the exporter. It works like this: Suppose I agree to sell you 10 bags of coffee for $1,300. I have my bank, Citibank, prepare a document that looks something like a bank check. It says, "Pay Citibank $1,300." Citibank sends this draft to your bank, electronically, and the cashier either calls you to come or sends it to you. You have already received the coffee, and are an honest person, so you promptly sign the draft and return it to your bank. The cashier takes the money from your account and transfers it to Citibank for my account. Technically, we wouldn't even need a sales agreement. I could select your name from a direc-tory, send you some merchandise, and have the draft sent to your bank. If you signed it, the merchandise would be yours and the money would be mine. To send merchandise without any previous agreement would, of course, be terribly risky.

This kind of draft is also called a *bill of exchange*. A bill is a piece of paper that notifies you of something, such as an exchange of merchandise for money. The exporter's bank cuts the draft, and the importer's bank presents it to her. If the importer doesn't sign it upon *first presentation*, there will later be a second presentation, and so on. When the importer writes "accepted" on the draft and signs it, she has accepted her obligation to pay the money. If the importer is supposed to pay the draft upon presentation (as soon as she sees it), it is a *sight draft*. If the agreement is that she does not have to pay immediately, but sometime after sight, the document will be called a *time draft* (even though it may say something like "60 days sight"). If payment is due by a certain date, it will be called a *date draft*.

This method of payment, as described so far, puts the risk entirely on the exporter. If the importer refuses to accept a draft for any reason, the exporter must sue the buyer to accept it, find a new buyer in the same or a different country, pay for return transportation of the goods to their point of origin, or abandon the shipment. All these options are time-consuming and expensive. If goods are abandoned, they are usually sold at customs auctions, and there is nothing to prevent the supposed importers from bidding on them. Beware of any foreign importer who wants essential parts of an item, such as axe handles and axe heads, in separate shipments with payments by sight draft. This importer is putting herself in a position to buy cheap at the customs auctions, because only she will know where to find both the handles and the heads.

There is, however, a way for the exporter to use a sight draft and still control the merchandise. It involves using a *to order bill of lading*. (See chapter 8 for a discussion of documents in international trade.) When the exporter places the goods on a ship or other vehicle for transportation, the ship's captain or his representative signs and gives the exporter a document called a *bill of lading* (an *airway bill* if the shipment is by air). This document serves, among other purposes, as title to the merchandise. The person to whom the goods are consigned on the bill of lading can claim them. If the exporter wants the importer to receive the goods without regard to payment, as in an open account shipment, he uses a *straight* bill of lading. If, however, the exporter wants to impose conditions on delivery of the goods, he uses a to order bill of lading. It is usually "to order of shipper" (the exporter). Then the shipper can *order* that the goods be delivered only under certain conditions, as when the importer has accepted the draft. In practice, the shipper usually endorses the bill of lading *in blank* on the back and trusts the banking system to give it to the buyer, endorsed to him, only when he has accepted the draft. With a properly endorsed bill of lading, the buyer can receive the merchandise.

There are restrictions on to order bills of lading with airfreight because the goods can arrive before the documents, and airlines don't want their warehouses cluttered with incoming cargo. A solution that sometimes works is to make the airway bill to order of a trusted bank in the importer's country and send the documents by courier.

With this system, the risk is not all on the exporter but is shared. If the payment document is a sight draft, the exporter still bears the risk that the importer will not pay and pick up the merchandise, but the importer bears the risk that the goods will not be as ordered. With a time or a date draft, the importer has the option of picking up the goods, examining them, and, if they are faulty, instructing her bank not to pay the draft. Then the parties to the transaction must try to negotiate a solution. Fortunately, this does not happen often.

In summary, a documentary draft is a simple payment instrument, initiated by the exporter, that goes through banking channels but is not guaranteed by the banks. It can be used for transactions of any size but is often favored for those in the range from about $500 to $4,000. There is always some risk for the exporter, and there is also risk for the importer when a sight draft is combined with a to order bill of lading, because the he or she must pay before seeing the merchandise. The cost is usually about $100 for each party per transaction, and it is common for the parties to pay their own charges.

You will find a picture and explanation of an international draft, and accompanying letter of transmittal, on the Web at www.unzco.com/basicguide/figure12.html. It is provided by UNZ & Company, a firm established in 1979. It sells international trade forms and software, and provides information and training to exporters.

The typical sequence of events with a bill of exchange transaction is as follows.

1. The exporter fills out a form online or at his or her bank.

2. The exporter sends goods and documents to the freight forwarder.

3. The freight forwarder sends the goods and gets a bill of lading signed by the carrier.

4. The freight forwarder sends the documents to the exporter's bank.

5. That bank sends the documents to the importer's bank.

6. The importer pays or accepts and gets the package of documents.

7. The importer gives the documents to the carrier and gets the merchandise.

8. The importer's bank transmits funds to the exporter's bank, which credits his or her account.

Letters of Credit

By now, or perhaps long before now, you have heard the term *letter of credit*, or LC. There are various types of LCs, but the one we will discuss here is the commercial documentary letter of credit. The word *commercial* means it is used in a business transaction, and *documentary* means it is payable upon presentation of specified documents.

You can think of a letter of credit as a letter that is written by the importer's bank to the exporter and communicated to the exporter through banking channels. Your bank (you are the importer now) is telling the exporter that when he presents specified documents containing specified information, he will be paid for a shipment.

Suppose an exporter in Somalia sells you flags from the civil war in 1991 for the sum of $40,000. The seller wants to be sure of being paid and therefore asks you for a letter of credit. If you agree, you must apply to your bank to open your LC, in favor of the exporter. This means that the bank is pledging to pay the exporter if he does exactly what the LC specifies. An LC normally specifies that an exporter provide documentary evidence that he or she has shipped the merchandise ordered, by the time and in the manner stated in the LC, including fulfilling any other specified obligations, such as purchasing insurance.

The fact that you apply to your bank for a letter of credit does not mean you will get it. Your bank will not want to take the risk of paying the exporter and then not being able to collect from you. Therefore, it will look for strong evidence of your ability to pay—such as an account with an average balance that will easily cover the credit or other evidence of financial strength and stability. In some cases, a bank will allow you to pledge assets, such as a certificate of deposit, to guarantee payment on an LC. The bottom line is that it is very hard to get an LC for a larger sum than you are able to pay. That $40,000 deal will be hard to swing with only $400 in your account.

With a letter of credit, the importer's bank is known as the *opening bank*. When it agrees to write a letter of credit, it usually transmits that document to its branch or correspondent nearest the exporter, which is known as the *advising bank* because it advises the exporter that a credit in his or her favor has been received. The banks' relationships serve, among other purposes, to protect the exporter because branches and correspondents can more easily ascertain that LCs are genuine. There have been instances, usually in developing countries, of importers using authentic-looking counterfeit LCs and LCs supposedly written by banks that did not exist. If you get the idea that I am warning you to be very careful with international payments, you are right.

An importer can specify that his or her own bank be used as the advising bank. In other cases, importers use their own banks as intermediaries between themselves and the advising banks, although this increases the cost to them because more banks are involved.

On being advised of the letter of credit and receiving a copy, an exporter should study it carefully to make sure that each of its terms and conditions can be met. Otherwise, there will be a problem. For example, the shipping date might be too early. If there are delays in production or transport to the port or the airport, of if there are no sailings or flights that have space for your cargo, you might miss the deadline. The late date of shipment will be a discrepancy and will probably cause the payment to be delayed until the discrepancy is waived or otherwise resolved.

When the exporter ships and gives the required documentary evidence to the advising bank, with no discrepancies, payment is due. With some LCs, the advising bank is also the *paying bank* and can pay the exporter very quickly. With other LCs, where the opening bank is the paying bank, there is usually a delay of a few days. Both importers and exporters often want the paying bank to be in their country because they feel it will better look out for their interests.

The letter of credit is an extremely flexible method of payment because the importer can ask her bank to make any legal stipulation. If an LC states that the exporter must personally load the baskets on the ship while wearing nothing but a flag and that this must be tied around his ankles, payment will not be made unless he presents documentary evidence of having done exactly that.

Nearly all letters of credit are *irrevocable*, which means they cannot be changed or canceled without the consent of the beneficiary. In other words, once you open an LC and the exporter is advised of it, you can't back out unless the exporter agrees to let you.

If the exporter has any doubt that the opening bank is solvent, or whether the country in which it is located will have hard (convertible) currency with which to pay, he can ask to have the LC confirmed by the advising bank or even by a different bank in the same or a third country. For example, LCs opened in some African and Middle Eastern countries are often confirmed in the United Kingdom. Confirmation means that if the opening bank is obligated to pay and for some reason will not do so, the confirming bank will pay. It usually costs the exporter less than 1 percent of the value of the LC, and gives him extra assurance of being paid. If you as an exporter receive an LC and no bank will confirm it, you should probably take this as a warning and run to the nearest exit.

There are numerous variations of letters of credit. Some operate like revolving lines of bank credit, and others permit partial payment for parts of an order. Still others allow a trading company to use its customer's credit to guarantee payment to its supplier. These are *transferable* and *back-to-back* LCs. They have advantages but are hard for a novice trader to work with. A good international banker can advise you on the appropriate kind of LC for each situation.

Many exporters customarily ask for letters of credit on all transactions, but as an importer you do not have to accept the terms that are proposed to you. Come back with a counteroffer and negotiate. Better yet, be the first to propose the method of payment and propose one that is more to your advantage. Then the other party can accept your terms or make a counteroffer.

To summarize, a letter of credit is a formal payment document opened by the importer and communicated through banking channels. The party obligated to pay the exporter is the opening bank. The cost for this service to the importer is often a fixed fee plus a percentage or a percentage with a minimum, for example, 0.25 percent (a quarter of 1 percent), with a minimum commission of $120. The exporter will pay various costs that usually come to at least $300. The total is higher if an LC is not payable at sight, if more than two banks are involved, if there are amendments or discrepancies, or if the exporter wants the credit to be confirmed.

Our friends at UNZ & Company have provided a sample of an export letter of credit on the Web at www.unzco.com/basicguide/figure13.html. If you study it, you will understand most of its terms and conditions. You can find other examples on the Web or in books about international trade procedures.

The typical sequence of events with an LC is as follows:

1. The importer applies for a letter of credit.
2. The opening bank sends the LC through its correspondent or branch, which advises the exporter that it has been received.

3. The exporter sends goods and documents to his or her freight forwarder.
4. The advising bank forwards the documents to the negotiating bank, which checks them against the LC and authorizes payment if no discrepancies are found. The importer's account is debited.
5. The importer's bank gives the importer the documents, with which he or she can claim the merchandise.

You don't necessarily have to open a letter of credit with your own bank, and, in fact, some banks have their LC applications on the Internet for all to see and complete. Go, for example, to www .commercebank.com / business / smallbusiness / international / loc .asp for the form of Commerce Bank. There is also a form here for a *standby* letter of credit, which is used to guarantee performance. For example, if you win a contract to build a concert hall in Egypt, you may be asked to open a standby LC in the name of your client. Later, if the client decides that you haven't performed as agreed, he or she will collect on your LC. As you can guess, this is an easy way to lose money.

The ways that banks deal with the hundreds of potentially unique situations and disagreements relating to international payment instruments are specified in a series of procedures called International Commercial Terms, or Incoterms. These are agreed upon internationally and change every few years. In the United States they are published by ICC Publishing in New York.

Letter of Credit–like Instruments

You may have heard of international *factoring* and/or *forfaiting*. Factoring means selling export receivables to a firm that will be responsible for collecting them. If the sale is *without recourse*, and the buyer does not pay, only the factor will lose. Of course, factors charge enough to cover their own costs, profit, risk, and interest if they must pay the exporter before receiving funds from the importer. Also, factors like to approve the importer *before* a sale is made, so plan in advance if you want to use this kind of service.

There is a similar but more complex system called *forfaiting*. This involves bank guarantees and long-term credit to the buyer, usually on sales of a quarter of a million dollars and up. It's not for everybody.

From time to time, private companies try to develop new international payment mechanisms, but most do not last long. For example, the previous edition of this book mentioned a now-extinct payment service that was run by a freight forwarding and customs brokerage firm. A bank, often your own bank, is usually the best bet.

Some companies offer international receivables management services, but these are used mainly by larger exporters. One such company is our friend Dun & Bradstreet, and there is information on the Web at www.dnb.com.au/receivables/about_receivables_management.asp. The challenges for readers of this book are to get big enough to use these kinds of services and then to carefully consider their costs and their benefits.

Payment in Advance

This is the best method if you are an exporter. Suppose you make a small sale to an importer in Africa, who has no doubts about your honesty or ability to ship. The importer may have trouble getting foreign exchange in his country but have a bank account in London or Paris. He may ask you to quote in British pounds, then just send you a check.

Or, your importer's sister in the Caribbean may ask you to find some parts that are urgently needed to keep machines in her factory running. She can't afford to have you hold up the shipment until you get paid and may simply send a check on her Miami bank account. If the importer wants you to ship without waiting for the check to clear, she can have it certified. She might prefer to send a check drawn on a bank in her country, but such a check can take several weeks to clear and many foreign currencies are not readily convertible to U.S. dollars.

As an importer, you may be asked for cash in advance in some cases. If you order a suit from Hong Kong, your supplier will probably ask for half the amount in advance. If you order a small quantity of samples, the easiest ways to pay are to use PayPal or a credit card or to buy an international money order from your bank. Of course, this means that you are taking all the risk. It is possible that the foreign exporter will simply pocket your money and not respond to your frantic e-mails, phone calls, and faxes.

Credit cards are being used now in several countries as a means of paying for small international purchases. This system usually works well and can be used with payment in advance or on open account. If you go on the Web to http://shopsite.com/cc_101_international.html, you will find links to several sites including PayPal, WorldPay, PSiGate, and Optimal Payments. There is still another, NetBanx, but as of this writing it is available only in the United Kingdom.

Consignment

Consignment is not actually a form of payment but a type of agency arrangement in which the buyer takes possession of goods but does not take title to them. Suppose, for example, that you buy a $1,000 dress, wear it once at a party, and then decide you do not want it anymore. You may take it to a high-quality used-clothing shop and leave it there on consignment. You might agree with the store owner that you are paid 75 percent of what she sells it for, but not less than $250. If and when the dress is sold, you will receive your 75 percent of the revenue. If it is not sold within a set period of time, you may reclaim it or the store owner may ask you to take it back. If it is somehow lost or damaged, you will be paid the $250 minimum.

Consignment in international trade works much the same way. It is often used for U.S. imports, especially of fresh produce and works of art. If you decide to import fresh asparagus, for example, you cannot be sure how much of what you import will be of excellent quality or what the buyers will be paying when your shipment is through customs and ready for sale. You will probably respond by seeking to import on consignment. When a shipment is about to arrive, you will make contacts to try to sell it. When it actually arrives, you will inspect it and, assuming it is of the expected condition and quality, deliver it and collect from your customers. Then you will deduct your actual expenses and perhaps a 15 percent commission and remit the remainder of the proceeds to your supplier. If you have to destroy part of the shipment because it cannot be sold, or if part of it is seized by U.S. regulatory agencies because of illegal pesticide residues or infestations, you will inform the exporter and will not pay for that part of the shipment. The exporter must trust you completely or must pay to have someone in the port of arrival verify your report of the condition and quality of the goods and the price at which they are sold.

I once heard of a Brazilian exporter of baler twine who used consignment to make sure he sold all his production every year. He shipped to a distributor in the Midwestern United States on consignment for the entire haying season. His instructions to the distributor were to keep reducing the price until every roll was sold. The distributor, by pricing to sell out and maximize his profit, automatically maximized the profit to the exporter.

In the U.S. export trade the main use of consignment is to help foreign distributors of heavy machinery and equipment. If a manufacturer of construction equipment wants to sell in Jamaica, its distributor there will need floor models and demonstrators as well as an inventory of equipment for sale. Part or all of this may be shipped to Jamaica on consignment. If and when it is sold, the distributor will pay the manufacturer.

This system of paying for merchandise definitely favors the importer. In the worst case, for example, a shipment of fresh strawberries can't be sold because the plane that was carrying it had mechanical problems and the berries turned to moldy marmalade in the interim, so the exporter will lose both the produce and the money paid for transportation. If the shipment is not insured, which is usually the case with fresh produce, the exporter may not recover any money at all.

EXPORT CREDIT AND CREDIT INSURANCE

Whenever the importer does not have to pay for merchandise upon receiving it, he or she is buying on credit. Credit terms can be even more important to an importer than the actual selling price. Why should an importer in Brazil pay cash to you when an exporter in Japan will sell equally good merchandise on 90-day terms, especially if the cost of money (the interest rate) in Brazil is high?

Exporters who provide financing normally do so from company funds or with bank loans. Eximbank, the Export-Import Bank of the United States in Washington, D.C., has a variety of programs for helping U.S. exporters obtain working capital and loans and to ensure their export receivables. For information on these programs, log on to www.exim.gov or call these numbers for small-scale exporters, (800) 565-3946 or (202) 565-3946. Yes, this organization has enough clout to get two phone numbers that are the same except for the area code. You will probably be switched to one of Eximbank's regional offices, which are as follows:

- *Northeast and Mid-Atlantic*: New York, NY: Tel, (212) 809-2650; Fax, (212) 809-2646
- *Southeast*: Miami, FL: Tel, (305) 526-7436; Fax, (305) 526-7435
- *Midwest*: Chicago, IL: Tel, (312) 353-8081; Fax, (312) 353-8098
- *Southwest*: Houston, TX: Tel, (281) 721-0465; Fax, (281) 679-0156
- *West*
  - *Orange County, CA, branch*: Tel, (949) 660-1341; Fax, (949) 660-9553
  - *San Diego branch*: Tel, (619) 557-7091; Fax, (619) 557-6176
  - *San Francisco branch*: Tel, (415) 705-2285; Fax, (415) 705-1156

Unfortunately, a small business in Eximbank terms does not include a home-based exporter's shipment worth $1,000. If you get up to shipments around $10,000, this organization is a possibility.

Eximbank has helped the U.S. Small Business Administration (SBA) to offer export credit through banks that are members of the Bankers' Association for Finance and Trade (BAFT). Information about this service is available from many banks and from SBA offices in all major U.S. cities. You may want to speak with the SBA about its trade finance programs: SBA Export Express, Export Working Capital, and International Trade Loans.

There are also several U.S. states and even some cities that can assist with financing and insurance of export shipments. Check on these through your local government's office of international business, which has different names in different states and cities. You will find them listed, with their Web sites and live links to them, at www.constructionweblinks.com/Organizations/International_Organizations/export_agencies.html.

Finally, there are private insurance companies that write export credit insurance. Euler Hermes, for example, has a variety of policies and a Web-based service through which you can apply for them online at www.eulerhermes.com/usa/en/products_services/multi-markets_policy.html?parent=products. You can complete the application in English or, *si vous voulez, en français.*

There is, of course, a significant cost involved in export credit insurance. There are some countries and many potential importers who can't be insured, and you cannot get full coverage. It is common to find insurance that covers 100 percent of loss due to political problems but only 90 to 95 percent of loss due to commercial problems. The idea is that if you make a bad credit decision, you should suffer at least some consequences.

FOREIGN CURRENCY TRANSACTIONS

Most international transactions are paid for with currency (as opposed to barter), and American traders use the U.S. dollar far more than any other nation's currency. Many Japanese and other exporters, however, prefer to be paid in the money of their countries. This has become the case in Europe as the European currency unit, the euro, has become firmly established (and has become more valuable than the dollar).

As a U.S. importer you can nearly always pay in dollars. If a foreign exporter insists on receiving some other currency, you have several choices. The best is probably to stand your ground and pay in U.S. dollars; an exporter who wants the sale will have to accept this. A second option is to agree to pay in a foreign currency, such as Swiss francs, but to get a somewhat lower price to compensate you for the risk of having to pay more dollars than you expected for the stated amount in francs. The further in the future you will be paying, the greatly the likelihood that your cost in dollars will vary significantly one way or the other.

For larger amounts you may be able to use the foreign exchange forward market. This means entering into an agreement now, with your bank, to buy the foreign currency you will need at a predetermined rate on a specified date in the future. This is a form of hedging. The more the market expects the foreign currency to rise against the dollar, the more you will have to pay for your hedge.

Large companies that have exposure in foreign currencies use other hedging techniques, such as playing the futures market. This involves buying contracts, for fixed amounts and fixed time periods, through foreign currency exchanges. International finance managers who are professionals at this earn salaries of which most of us would be very envious.

On the export side it is very common to be asked to take payment in foreign currencies. This can be dangerous, because many developing countries have currency that is not convertible or that is worth less than its official value.

If you are asked to take payment in foreign currency, check with your banker to find out the strength of the currency in question. Newspapers such as the *Wall Street Journal* report both current exchange rates and the values of futures contracts, so you can see whether the market expects the currency in question to rise or fall against the dollar. If the currency is not quoted in the *Wall Street Journal*, you probably don't want to take it. There are several Web sites that provide currency exchange rates. For example, look at www.x-rates.com/calculator.html. Remember that the converters can only give you spot rates, not future rates. No one knows exactly how many francs a dollar will buy tomorrow or next month.

If your foreign buyer wants to pay in a foreign currency and you don't want to take the risk, you may be able to negotiate other terms, for example, offering more time to pay in exchange for a letter of credit in U.S. dollars. Or perhaps you can agree to accept the foreign currency but at a rate that gives you a certain amount in dollars. That way the importer can pay in his or her national currency but may have to pay more to give you the number of dollars agreed upon. Finally, it may be worthwhile for you to use one of the hedging techniques mentioned earlier.

In brief, try to avoid dealing in foreign currencies. For importers, this is usually not a problem, but it can be. An import/export broker, Dan Casper, wrote me as follows in November 2006:

> The gold standard was getting into and on the USA market, but lately I have found the opposite. A fish processing firm in Tasmania absolutely refuses to export here regardless of the goodies I have strewn in their path. Same is true of another company domiciled in Australia that will not answer my e-mails, faxes and phone calls. Two of the European companies that I acted as agent/broker for have pulled out of our market claiming that the U.S. dollar is weak, and all in all the euro is more attractive.

Unfortunately, exporters may lose sales if they are not somewhat flexible. However, there is often a chance that you will profit from fluctuation in a rate of exchange. If you agree to take payment in Danish kroner three months in the future, and during those three months this currency rises 10 percent against the dollar, you will receive 10 percent more in dollars. If your profit on the transaction was 10 percent, you will have doubled it.

COUNTERTRADE

The term *countertrade* refers to international shipments that are not paid for entirely in cash. There are several variations, known as barter, compensation trade, buyback, counterpurchase, and offset. No one knows for sure the percentage of international transactions in which countertrade is involved, but most estimates are in the range from 10 to 25 percent.

Businesses often try to pay for merchandise with countertrade when they are in countries that are short of hard currency. This used to be the case with most Eastern European and developing countries, but the Hungarian forint, for example, is now a reasonably strong currency. El Salvador now uses the U.S. dollar. Some countries, such as Colombia and Malaysia, have passed special laws that regulate countertrade transactions.

Suppose you agree with a Peruvian businessperson that you will exchange outboard (boat) motors for alpaca sweaters. After considerable discussion, you determine how many motors, of which brand and horsepower, you will ship and how many sweaters, of which quality and sizes, your Peruvian counterpart will ship. Then you agree when and how each commodity will be shipped and who will pay for the transportation.

To put this deal in motion, the Peruvian may have to obtain government permission to ship the sweaters without receiving hard currency for them. She may also need approval to import the outboard motors. Then there will be two shipments of merchandise, either of which could be beset by problems of loss, damage, poor quality, and so on. Finally, you will have to sell the sweaters for more than your total cost, including what you paid for the motors, in order to make a profit.

The transaction just described is an example of simple barter. More often, there is a monetary value placed on each shipment, such as $20,000 worth of motors in exchange for $20,000 worth of sweaters (or $15,000 in sweaters and $5,000 in currency, etc.). Sometimes more than one country is involved in a countertrade deal, for example, engines from the United States to Peru, sweaters from Peru to Canada, and cash from Canada to the United States. This kind of triangular deal is both more expensive and more difficult to arrange. There are specialized companies, mostly in Europe but some in the United States, that specialize in arranging countertrade transactions.

With regard to the hypothetical situation at the beginning of this chapter, the fact that you pay for goods with other goods instead of with cash is of little interest to U.S. Customs. All restrictions on importation will still apply.

I once met a New York businessman who was exporting cigarettes to Romania and receiving clothing in return. He explained that the cigarettes were so valuable in Romania that he was able to make more profit than if he paid for the clothing in cash. Still, countertrade has so many pitfalls that I definitely do not recommend it to a beginner. Remember that even a simple barter deal is really two transactions instead of one. That means there are twice as many chances for something to go seriously wrong. Remember Murphy's Law; it is written in various ways, one of which is: Things will go wrong in any given situation, if you give them a chance.

SOURCES OF INFORMATION AND HELP

It is not an exaggeration to say that when you are in business, nothing is more important than getting paid. You don't want to work for nothing or for less than nothing, as can happen if you pay for merchandise and then don't collect from your buyer. Do pay a lot of attention to this topic.

I suggest you both read up on methods of payment and ask for advice. You don't want to be like the poor Taiwanese exporter of birds, who thought all American buyers were honest, and learned the hard way that he was mistaken.

Here are the sources of information and help that are mentioned in this chapter.

- Dun & Bradstreet (D&B) sells credit reports on numerous companies and offers international receivables management services. Address: D&B Corporation, 103 JFK Parkway, Short Hills, NJ 07078; Phone: (800) 234-3867; Web site: www.dnb.com.

- *International Country Profile* contains information about many companies in about 80 countries. It is published by the U.S. Department of Commerce's Export Assistance Center. Web site: www.buyusa.gov/home/export.html.

- Trancentrix is available through Ruesch International. Address: Corporate Headquarters, 700 Eleventh Street, NW, 4th Floor, Washington, DC 20001; Phone: (202) 408-1200; Fax: (202) 513-5215; Web site: www.ruesch.com.

- International draft and letter of transmittal examples can be found on UNZ & Company's site at www.unzco.com/basicguide/figure12.html.

- An export letter of credit example can be found on UNZ & Company's site at www.unzco.com/basicguide/figure13.html.

- A letter of credit example can be found on Commerce Bank's Web site at www.commercebank.com/business/smallbusiness/international/loc.asp.

- Shopsite.com offers credit card processing for international merchants. Address: ShopSite, 51 West Center, #511, Orem, UT 84057; Phone: (801) 705-4100; Fax: (801) 705-4184; Web site: http://shopsite.com/cc_101_international.html.

- Eximbank, the Export-Import Bank of the United States in Washington, D.C., has a variety of programs for helping U.S. exporters to obtain working capital and loans and to insure their export receivables. Address: 811 Vermont Avenue, NW, Washington, DC 20571; Phone: (800) 565-3946 or (202) 565-3946; Fax: (202) 565-3931; Web site: www.exim.gov.

- SBA Export Express, Export Working Capital, and International Trade Loans are loan programs available through the U.S. Small Business Administration. Address: SBA Answer Desk, 6302 Fairview Road, Suite 300, Charlotte, NC 28210; Phone: (800) U-ASK-SBA (1-800-827-5722); E-mail: answerdesk@sba.gov; Web site: www.sba.gov.

- Construction WebLinks lists numerous federal and state organizations that provide importing and exporting assistance. Web site: www.constructionweblinks.com/Organizations/International_Organizations/export_agencies.html.

- Euler Hermes is a private insurance company that writes export credit insurance policies. Web site: www.eulerhermes .com/usa/en/products_services/multimarkets_policy.html ?parent=products.
- X-Rates.com lists worldwide currency rates. Web site: www .x-rates.com/calculator.html.

8

Packing, Shipping, and Insurance

I recently helped a group of seafood exporters from West Africa to exhibit at the International Boston Seafood Show. One of the companies sent its samples at the last minute. For some reason, which I'll never know, they were sent to New York rather than to Boston. The phone number of the notify party (a customs broker in Boston) was not provided, so the broker was not notified immediately. In addition, there were errors in the documentation that made customs clearance difficult. The results, as you may have guessed, were rotten fish in New York and an empty display case at the seafood show. Time and money were lost due to shipping errors.

A few years ago a huge containership used in transatlantic voyages was caught unexpectedly in a raging storm. Fortunately, the crew and ship were able to ride out the storm and reach port safely, but to save the ship they dumped more than 30 containers off one side of the vessel and more than 70 off the other side. If your merchandise was in one of them, would you have gotten paid for it?

International transportation, moving goods from one country to another, can enhance or destroy the profitability of an import or export deal. Importers and exporters are inevitably involved in transportation functions such as packing, shipping, and insurance. If these functions are not handled properly, your goods can arrive too late, in poor condition, or not at all. The cost of shipping can sometimes be even more than the cost of the products. There are commercial organizations, like customs brokers and freight forwarders, ready and able to help you, but their charges become your costs.

PACKING FOR INTERNATIONAL SHIPMENT

You may not ever have to pack goods for shipment abroad. If you work as an import or export agent, your principal will do the packing and, if you work as an import or export merchant, your suppliers may perform this function.

You may, however, buy from U.S. suppliers who are unable or unwilling to pack for export. Yet again, you may import goods in large quantities and have to repack them in smaller units for your domestic customers. If the quantities are small, you can do the packing yourself, or you can hire a specialized firm to do it for you. Even if your principals or suppliers do the packing, you should know how they do it, and you may want to give them instructions. If the packing is inadequate to protect the goods, your risks of loss and damage will be greatly increased, and if the packing is grossly inadequate, the insurance company may cite that as justification for not paying a claim. At the other extreme, excessive packing will add weight and bulk to the shipment and thus increase your transportation cost. Finally, if your customer asks for a certain kind of packing and your principal or supplier does it differently, the shipment may be rejected, and you will lose your commission or markup.

Export packing companies and some insurance companies can often provide information on how specific kinds of goods are normally packed. There is a basic guide from UNZ & Company, in fact, it is called just that, on the Web at www.unzco.com/basicguide/c10.html. Also, there is a useful description of export packing from a company called EXPORT911, at the URL www.export911.com/e911/prod/packing.htm. This includes pictures of cartons, cases, crates, drums, bags, and barrels.

Kinds of Packing

Until a few decades ago, most products moved overseas in individual boxes or barrels. This was known as *break bulk* shipping. For the most part this has given way to containerization in the foreign commerce of the United States, but it is still common in many developing countries. Dividing a large shipment into several smaller ones is still known as breaking bulk, and there are companies that will receive a large shipment, warehouse the merchandise, and repack in smaller quantities for shipment when the owner of the goods transmits an order to them.

When several boxes are put together to make one unit, perhaps with steel straps or plastic shrink-wrap, you have *unitized cargo*. Because units can easily become too large and heavy to handle easily, they are often put on wooden or plastic platforms made so that forklift trucks can pick them up and place them in trailers. These platforms are pallets, and the cargo is said to be *palletized*. All the methods just described are known as *less than container load*, or LCL, cargo.

The real revolution in export packing came with containerization. In shipping language, a container is a large metal box that can be loaded with cargo. There are various sizes, ranging from 20 to 53 feet long. A typical 40-foot container is 8 feet wide, 8½ feet high, and 40 feet long and can hold about 2,347 cubic feet or 42,000 pounds of cargo.

The size of the container used is determined largely by the weight and size of the cargo; the availability of containers and container-handling equipment, maximum weight limitations on roads at the origin and destination points; and the ship's configuration. Containers are taken off the truck's chassis by cranes at the port of origin and fitted like Lego bricks below and on the deck of the containership. At the port of disembarkation, trucks pull up alongside the ship and the containers are lifted by cranes and fitted directly onto the chassis. This process is called lift-on lift-off, or LOLO. With a roll-on roll-off, or RORO, vessel, the trailers are rolled on board the ship together with the chassis, and both units are transported from the origin to the destination. Barges, a less common form of transport, carry break bulk cargo, trailers, and some containers. They are important, for example, on the Mississippi River and the Paraguay River.

Export shippers can own or rent containers or can use "boxes" (as they are often called) that belong to steamship companies. Typically, a container is cleaned and checked for soundness (no water leaks, etc.), packed, locked and sealed, and sent to its destination. It may move by road or rail and then by ocean and is usually not opened until it reaches the importing country or sometimes even the importer's warehouse. When sealed by the exporter, the cargo is said to move under "shipper-load-and-count," meaning the shipper (not the carrier) takes all responsibility for declaring the true cargo (products), and the weights and piece counts. Any misrepresentation of this information is considered fraud. The numbers of the seals are recorded, so that it is nearly impossible for a thief to break into a container without leaving evidence.

Containers are of major concern to port security personnel because so many arrive in the United States (and other countries), and it is impossible to know what is inside of each one. Further, containers are sometimes lost or stolen. New technologies are providing new ways of both inspecting containers (X-rays) and keeping track of them (radio frequency identification, or RIFD, tags).

There are specialized types of containers, the most common of which is the refrigerated container, or "reefer." It is used especially for carrying fresh produce, which has become very important in the U.S. import/export trade. Systems have been developed, known as controlled atmosphere (CA) and modified atmosphere (MA), to retard ripening of produce in containers. Temperature recorders are usually placed in reefers so that if produce arrives in poor condition, it will be easy to tell whether a mistake or equipment failure let it become too warm. Other types of containers have been designed to transport import/export commodities including tanks for frozen orange juice or other liquids, flatbeds for large pieces of equipment, hanging-garment vans to carry clothing on hangers, and ventilated vans for cocoa and similar products.

Containers are used also for airfreight. There are several standard sizes because of the large variation in the inside dimensions of aircraft. Exporters should check with their carrier about available container sizes and whether palletized cargo can be accepted. For fast turnaround, airlines will try to have a string of containers waiting when a plane arrives. The ideal system is to just push out one queue of metal boxes and push in another.

Many carriers have joint agreements to carry one another's freight, which lets them issue *through* airway bills when cargo must be transshipped. Some difficult air cargo issues for new as well as experienced exporters are availability of cargo space and frequency of service. There may not be enough regularly scheduled flights to meet an exporter's needs, or the connecting flights to the cargo's final destination may not be optimal, for example, leaving cargo sitting on the tarmac in the heat or missing a connection because of a delayed flight. Another issue is that with new security in place, a new exporter to the United States cannot ship cargo in the belly holds of passenger planes. He or she must find an all-cargo flight to the United States, and there are many countries from which these do not exist. I was recently in touch with an exporter from Paraguay who had that problem and was trying to solve it by transshipping in Brazil, from which all-cargo service was available.

Break Bulk Packing

If your shipments are small, they will probably be sent break bulk, or less than container load (LCL), which gives you a higher unit cost than that of larger volume shippers. Besides, your packages will be subject to the potential risks of being dropped by handlers or handling equipment, crushed by heavy cargo, or soaked in seawater. Even cargo inside waterproof boxes can get wet if the ship sails through cold areas and moisture in the air inside the box condenses. That's why in old war movies, we used to see shipments of firearms coated with grease and wrapped in waxed paper. Now shippers can shrink-wrap cargo and/or add materials to the packages that absorb moisture.

Logic tells us that heavier boxes should be loaded on the bottom and lighter ones on the top, but most steamships call at several ports. What goes in first, or what will come out last, usually ends up on the bottom. That means there may be a bulldozer resting on your Ping-Pong balls.

Finally, some kinds of packing materials may get you in trouble with regulatory authorities. One importer wanted to bring wooden bowls packed in straw to the United States from Grenada but was prohibited because straw can harbor insect pests that might harm U.S. agriculture. Even wooden pallets can harbor insects and snails, so they should be fumigated. There can be other complications. I once heard of a South American exporter who was packing fresh garlic in mahogany boxes and was fined by his country's authorities for illegally exporting precious wood.

There is a noticeable trend toward the development and use of packaging materials that are friendlier to the environment. Many countries are adopting practices pioneered by Germany, which has strict regulations with respect to use of recyclable and reusable materials, from pallets to corrugated cartons, packaging foams, and plastic crates. Shippers may even have to re-export certain materials, which, of course, adds to the cost of a transaction. It is important to know the regulations before you finalize a price.

All this means that you should pay attention to how your cargo is packed, even if you don't personally do the packing. Find out how the first few shipments from a principal or supplier are protected from hazards and, if you don't like what you see, try to get it corrected. Your Christmas ornaments packed in thin cardboard boxes may arrive intact the first time, but not the next time, when you really need them. There are several helpful sources of information on new and existing packaging, including the Institute of Packaging Professionals, whose Web site is www.IOPP.org. This organization publishes a journal and a packaging newsletter. Also, you can find the World Packaging Organization on the Web at www.worldpackaging.com.

After You Pack It, Mark It

Companies that frequently pack goods for export know how to mark them, but new exporters may have to be taught. There are several kinds of marks, which are usually printed or stenciled on boxes. In some trades, such as fresh produce, shipping boxes are printed with colorful pictures of the products they contain.

Shipping boxes are usually marked "Made in [country of origin of merchandise]." They also give the gross weight, net weight, and outside dimensions, often in both metric and English systems. A few countries have special regulations. Perhaps the most conspicuous example now is regulation by the European Union of packing boxes made of wood.

If there is more than one box in a shipment, each one is numbered. Often a box bears the exporter's name and the importer's (or his or her agent's) name, address, and order number. For cargo that is especially subject to pilferage, such as cameras and watches, there is a system of blind marks that supposedly prevents thieves from knowing the identity of the exporter or the importer or the contents of the boxes. Blind marks should be changed often because thieves have ways of learning to which shippers they belong. Fortunately, much of the cargo that thieves especially like is now shipped in sealed containers.

There are also cautionary markings on shipping boxes, sometimes in more than one language. The most common ones are "Handle with Care," "Glass," "Use No Hooks," "This Side Up," "Fragile," "Keep in Cool Place," "Keep Dry," and "Open Here."

Because cargo handlers in many ports cannot read, the same instructions are communicated with symbols. A champagne glass means "Fragile," a hook with an X across it means "Use No Hooks," and so on. Specialized books on export traffic show pictures of these symbols. I found them on the Web at www.export911 .com/e911/prod/caution.htm. Figure 8.1 shows some examples.

Finally, there is an even more extensive set of symbols for marking boxes that contain hazardous materials. If you plan to deal in any product that is (1) explosive, (2) flammable, (3) spontaneously combustible, (4) water-reactive, (5) oxidizing, (6) poisonous, (7) radioactive, or (8) corrosive, you need to be sure your packing and marking are as required by the U.S. Department of Transportation, the Coast Guard, and/or the Civil Aeronautics Board. The captain of a vessel is the final authority with regard to carrying hazardous materials. A captain who thinks a shipment is unsafe can reject it, even though it may comply with all

Figure 8.1   Symbols used in the handling of goods.

regulations. This holds true with aircraft also. Port authorities are also concerned about hazardous materials, especially since the events of 9/11, and some ports prohibit loading or unloading the more dangerous kinds.

The risk of carrying hazardous materials may translate into higher rates for shippers. An exporter once told me that one drop of mercury in a container could cause an entire 40-foot box to be considered hazardous and thus increase the shipping rate.

Shippers should consult with their carriers before sending hazardous materials, often referred to as "hazmats." The steamship line Maersk Sealand has developed information that is considered to have set much of the standard in the industry and is often a point of reference for government officials. Check with your local representative or at www.MaerskSeaLand.com for key contacts in loss prevention and claims.

INTERNATIONAL TRANSPORTATION

One of the most important decisions you will make is the method of transporting your goods. The method chosen will depend on comparative cost and other factors. This section describes the alternatives and discusses shipping rates.

Airmail

The use of international mail order, both to and from the United States, has grown tremendously, and one reason for this is the vast improvement made in many countries' post office departments. The U.S. Postal Service (USPS) deserves several prizes for the way it has improved both its domestic and international services. The maximum size, maximum weight, and other regulations vary with the country to which you are mailing. Fortunately, the USPS has nearly everything you need to know on the Internet. Look for the current edition of the *International Mail Manual* at http://pe.usps.gov/text/imm/welcome.htm, and go to the index of countries and localities.

In December 2006, a 15-pound package shipped to London from New York, using Airmail Parcel Post with the USPS, would have cost $65.35. The same package shipped via the Economy Parcel Post service (surface) would have cost $43.50, but would have taken much longer to arrive. On the high end of the scale, Global Express Mail (EMS) would be at least $72.45. There are special restrictions on shipping by EMS; for example, you can't send watches or jewelry. Insurance and registry are usually available, but indemnity limits vary by country. Customs forms are required.

You can import goods by mail to a maximum value of $2,000 per day (except most textiles, apparel, and leather goods) without having to complete a formal customs declaration. You will have to pay customs duty and a collection fee to the USPS, if there are duties on your merchandise.

Our friends at eBay provide a very good source of information on shipping overseas by mail. The Web site is http://pages.ebay.ca/help/sellerguide/shipping/index.html. You can buy your shipping and packing supplies on this site if you don't want to run to Office Depot or Staples.

An excellent example of international shipping by post is the company Isla, in San Juan, Puerto Rico. The company has a beautifully illustrated catalog and sells Puerto Rican handicrafts to customers in the United States and its territories, on military bases, and in foreign countries.

Courier Services

In mid-2007, the $65 USPS Airmail Parcel Post shipment mentioned in the previous section would have cost you $160.03 with FedEx Priority Service. What would you get for the extra money? FedEx is a $32 billion network of companies with service to most parts of the world. Customers receive free packaging materials, free shipping software, customs clearance (duties are usually paid and charged to the consignee), on-time delivery or your money back, and proof of delivery. If you can't go to any of the thousands of drop-off locations, FedEx will pick up the package for a slight extra charge. FedEx can handle large packages by air and even full container loads by sea, and there are numerous other services. Please note that I am only using FedEx as an example. There are other companies you can consider, especially DHL. There are also numerous companies set up to serve specific routes, as between Bolivia and the United States. Some of these companies, such as SkyNet, can handle shipments to and from almost any country through agreements with other courier firms.

Airfreight

The way couriers have developed, you probably wouldn't want to use airfreight for that 1-pound box. If you have a 1,500-pound box, however, you might want to contact an airfreight company. You can contact one directly or through a freight forwarder. In general, you will want to use a forwarder unless you are located near an international airport and don't mind taking your cargo there and completing an airway bill. Foreign freight forwarders and customs brokers are discussed later in this chapter.

Many airlines have 800 numbers for international cargo reservations. You can get these numbers from advertisements in international trade magazines, by calling the main number listed for your airline in a telephone directory, or on the Internet. For example, if you type "American Airlines cargo" in a search engine, you will be directed to AAcargo.com. Then click on "Customer Service," and you will find telephone numbers.

Airfreight rates are nearly always higher than ocean rates, but other costs are often so much lower that air becomes the cheaper way to ship. Figure 8.2 gives you a format for comparing air and sea to see which is less expensive overall. Note the last item, "interest on value of goods in transit." If your $100,000 export shipment arrives 10 days earlier because it was sent by air, you may get paid 10 days earlier. The value of that to you, at 12 percent interest, is $100,000 \times 10/360 \times 0.12$, or $333.

Shippers are encouraged to continue to check and double-check the rates. In one case, Guatemalan companies began exporting snow peas and shipping them by air. Ocean carriers saw this as a revenue opportunity and worked with the exporters on

Cost Item	Air	Sea
Export packing	$ 300	$ 800
Inland freight, country of origin	100	500
Freight forwarding	100	150
Shipping	3,800	2,000
Insurance	00	300
Customs clearance	80	150
Inland freight, country of destination	50	200
Interest on value of goods in transit	50	300
TOTAL COST	**$4,580**	**$4,400**

(Note: Assumes merchandise value approximately $50,000.)

Figure 8.2   Air-sea freight cost comparison.

trial shipments by sea. The results were very favorable, and ocean rates for snow peas were set low enough to take business from the air carriers. This was beneficial to nearly everyone. Because of demand for cargo space, the airlines couldn't meet all the needs, particularly as exports of refrigerated agricultural products increased. Once ocean rates were in place, exporters had both options and felt confident enough to increase their cultivation of snow peas and their volume of shipments. Ocean rates are discussed in more detail later in this chapter.

Shipping by Surface

A large part of the shipping between the United States and its partners in NAFTA (the North American Free Trade Agreement), Canada and Mexico, is done by rail and road. The rapid increase in trade with Mexico, and the terrorist attacks of September 11, 2001, have strained these methods of transportation, but systems have been put in place help traffic move more easily. One such system is the Customs-Trade Partnership Against Terrorism, or C-TPAT, a voluntary program whereby companies involved in international trade can cooperate with customs and Border Patrol on an ongoing basis.

In trade with Mexico, railcars cross the border and are subject to customs inspection, but, of course, complete inspection of every package is impossible. They are then interchanged with rail services of the other country.

NAFTA allows each country's trucks to operate, within limits, in the other countries. This system was the subject of severe protests in California, where truckers and environmentalists said that trucks from Mexico were often poorly maintained and operated by drivers with too little experience, but it is now working well. One can understand the concern of U.S. over-the-road truckers, who are proud of their overall accident rate, which is something like one accident per 2 *million* miles driven.

With most international shipments, cargo moves by road and perhaps by rail during at least part of its journey. Sometimes charges are built into a "through rate," and sometimes they are separate. Many shipments between the U.S. east coast and Asia, which formerly would have gone through the Panama Canal, now travel by double-stack train across the United States. Even though rail connections to many of our ports are antiquated and inadequate, rail is often the cheaper way to move cargo long distances on land. Deregulation of the trucking industry made road transport more competitive, but each increase in the price of diesel fuel decreases its competitiveness.

Ocean Freight

The largest weight and volume of international cargo, by far, are moved by ocean freight. The ability to handle huge weights and volumes provides a huge cost advantage. One cannot even imagine all the U.S. imports of oil and automobiles, or all the U.S. exports of wheat and gas turbines, traveling by air.

Steamship services (the word "steamship" is still used even though ships are no longer powered by steam) are either scheduled, nonscheduled, or charter. Nonscheduled lines are usually cheaper but less reliable. You can get sailing schedules from steamship lines, freight forwarders, or specialized magazines such as *American Shipper*, but the handiest and most current source is the *Journal of Commerce* newspaper. Five days a week it publishes shipping information. You can buy 52 issues per year for $175 by going online to www.joc.com and clicking on "Subscribe." Or, you can get four issues free as a trial, but then the other 48 will cost you $195. What a deal! With a subscription to the newspaper you can use their online service.

Steamship lines are classified as conference lines and independents. Lines sailing on many routes, as from the U.S. Atlantic and Gulf ports to West Africa, have banded together to form conferences. The lines in a conference compete with each other but maintain similar standards and charge the same rates. They have lower prices, known as *contract rates*, for shippers that agree to use conference carriers for most of their shipments on a given route, but even these rates can be higher than those charged by independent steamship lines.

Importers and exporters often complain about conferences and accuse them of being legalized cartels set up to keep prices high. The U.S. maritime industry is one of the few kinds of businesses that are not subject to antitrust legislation. The conference carriers reply that too much price competition would be ruinous, and that they cannot provide safe, rapid, and dependable services unless their rates are high enough to cover all their costs.

U.S. law also provides for non-vessel-owning common carriers (NVOCCs) and for shippers' associations. An NVOCC is a freight forwarder who reserves fixed amounts of space on certain vessels and then resells it to individual shippers, at lower rates than they would pay directly to the steamship line. A shippers' association is a group of shippers who pool their cargoes to make up larger quantities and therefore obtain lower rates. Freight forwarders can tell you whether either of these kinds of service is feasible for you to use.

Using charter vessels is practical only for very large quantities, although sometimes a ship charterer or broker will know of a chartered vessel that has extra space and can carry your cargo for a low rate. The downside to the lower rate may be irregular service. You should explore various avenues to find a reasonably priced service that is acceptable. Using more than one carrier gives you a ready option in case your preferred carrier has a strike or other serious problem.

Two trends affecting international shipping now are *intermodalism* and *rationalization*. Intermodalism means combining more than one mode of transport. For example, a container may be transported from the factory to the port on a truck, which is then lifted onto a vessel and taken to the destination port and finally trucked to the consignee. Some shipments add rail to this scenario so that your cargo might travel on three kinds of conveyance under one bill of lading.

Rationalization is occurring in the ocean shipping business much as in the air passenger business. Strategic alliances are formed between one or more carriers whereby space is allocated on one another's ships. While the carriers are still competitors and selling against one another, their schedules may be reduced in order to control costs. The end result is that exporters (like passengers) may find that their bill of lading indicates one carrier's name, but the cargo is actually moving on another carrier's vessel. You may have seen this kind of arrangement if you have taken a flight on X airline that was operated by Y airline. In fact, you may have almost missed a flight by waiting in line at the wrong airline's ticket counter.

Shipping Rates

Shipping rates are a controversial and often misunderstood subject. The kind of service, type of cargo, distance, the ship's route, and the amount of traffic on the route all enter into rate calculations. This is why it can cost less to bring a container of shirts to Boston from Hong Kong than from a Caribbean island. The factors that determine rates are operational costs (ships, crew, fuel, cranes, equipment, maintenance, and port charges), the characteristics of the cargo (its value, perishability, risk, and volume versus weight), and competition (number of carriers servicing a particular route and whether they are independent or belong to shipping conferences).

Both airlines and steamship lines have rate books, known as tariffs, that show the rates for different kinds of cargo between specific areas of the world. They must be made available in the public domain (e.g., on the carrier's Web site). You can obtain tariffs by calling the lines themselves, from your freight forwarder, or electronically. One electronic service, for example, is Freightquote .com. I suggest you take the service's online tour. You will see "Request for Quotation," a list of carriers with prices, and a freight tracking form.

There are general cargo rates, specific commodity rates, NES (also called NOS and FAK) rates, and container rates. The general rates are for shipments of mixed goods and are usually quite high, but fortunately, there are specific commodity rates for most kinds of cargo. If there isn't a specific rate for your goods, you can apply for one to the airline, steamship line, or shipping conference. For example, a firm in Haiti wanted to ship bars of medicinal soap to New York. Because no one had made commercial shipments of soap from Haiti to New York before, there was no rate established. The exporter completed a form for the steamship line and obtained a new special rate. This rate was then available for all companies that shipped the same product on the same route with the same steamship line, but there weren't any others.

If your cargo doesn't benefit from a specific commodity rate, it will go as not elsewhere specified (NES), not otherwise specified (NOS), or freight all kinds (FAK), depending on the tariff book you are using.

Rates are usually quoted on a weight/measure, or W/M, basis. Boxes that are large in relation to their weight are charged by the amount of space they occupy, and boxes that are heavy in relation to their size are charged according to their weight. By air, the formula is 162 cubic inches = 1 pound. If the rate is $2.00 per pound, but it takes 243 cubic inches of your product to weigh a pound, you will be charged $3.00 for each pound you ship $(243/162 \times 2)$. By sea, the formula is 40 cubic feet = 1 short ton. These numerical relationships have staying power; they have been the same for years. By the way, in 2007 the U.S. Postal Service implemented a weight/measure pricing system for packages shipped by Priority Mail.

Rates that are quoted by weight may reflect different units (e.g., pounds, kilograms, or tons). Be careful to check which of the three kinds of tons apply in your case. A short ton is 2,000 pounds; a long ton is 2,240 pounds; and a metric ton is 2,204 pounds (1,000 kilograms). Measurement cargo, which is usually bulkier or lighter weight, can be shown in the published rates by cubic feet, hundreds of cubic feet (cwt), or cubic meters.

Air container rates show a minimum price for sending each kind of container, the maximum weight that can be shipped for that price, and the charge for each kilogram above that maximum weight. By sea, you simply pay for the container, but there are often weight limits.

Each air and steamship line has a *minimum bill of lading*, which means that a minimum charge is levied on very small shipments. The minimum weight may be as low as 1 kilogram in air tariffs but is much higher by sea. About the only place you have flexibility in using shipping tariffs is with weight categories. For example, if your air shipment weighs 290 pounds, you may be able to save money by calling it 300 pounds and paying a lower rate per pound.

There are also miscellaneous charges, especially by sea. This becomes frighteningly clear with a real example (Figure 8.3)—a quotation for shipping a 40-foot, refrigerated container of chicken parts from Pompano Beach, Florida, to Santa Domingo in the Dominican Republic a few years ago.

Note that the total, $3,445, is about 25 percent higher than the base rate of $2,750. These charges do not include customs brokerage, freight forwarding, packing, and so forth, which are separate from the ocean freight quotation.

You can see other examples and even calculate freight rates on your cargo at www.freight-calculator.com. I suggest you put a bookmark on this page and save this Web site as a favorite, because this Web-based service, from a company called APX, is one you will probably want to use.

Item	Charge
Ocean freight	$ 2,750
Trucking, Pompano Beach-Port Everglades	175
Dominican Republic ITBIS (tax)	35
Shipper's Export Declaration (document)	100
Chassis recovery/wheel usage	10
Consular fee (optional)	150
Bunker surcharge (for high fuel costs)	180
Security surcharge (for extra security)	20
Consular administration	25
TOTAL COST	**$3,445**

Figure 8.3   Costs associated with ocean freight.

SHIPPING TERMS

In the early days of international trade, exporters and importers grew tired of having to negotiate all the individual conditions of every transaction. To solve this problem they developed and defined standard packages (or sets) of conditions. Once trading partners agreed on the definition of a term, such as CIF, they could sell and buy CIF without discussing so many details.

Gradually, two similar sets of terms and their definitions were developed—the American Standard Foreign Trade Definitions and the International Commercial Terms, better known as Incoterms. Most international transactions now use Incoterms, which have been revised periodically to keep up with changes in trade procedures. Still, if you want to be sure there's no confusion, you should be very specific. Tell your foreign buyer that your quotation is CIF to his or her port "according to Incoterms, 2000 revision."

The 2000 revision includes thirteen terms the definitions of which essentially specify which party makes arrangements for shipping the goods, which party has title to them at each point in their journey, and which party is responsible for loss or damage at any point. The terms are in four groups, as shown in Figure 8.4.

Group	Term	Explanation
Group E, Departure	EXW	Ex Works
Group F, Main	FCA	Free Carrier
Carriage Unpaid	FAS	Free Alongside Ship
	FOB	Free on Board
Group C, Main	CFR	Cost and Freight
Carriage Paid	CIF	Cost, Insurance, and Freight
	CPT	Carriage Paid To (location)
	CIP	Carriage and Insurance Paid To
Group D, Arrival	DAF	Delivered at Frontier
	DES	Delivered ex Ship
	DEQ	Delivered ex Quay
	DDI	Delivered Duty Unpaid
	DDP	Delivered Duty Paid

Figure 8.4   Incoterms, 2000 revision.

As you move down the list, responsibilities and title to goods change hands progressively nearer the buyer. In an ex works sale the seller need only shove the goods out the door of his or her factory. In a delivered duty paid sale, on the other extreme, the seller must actually enter the goods in the foreign country and deliver them to the buyer. Complete definitions of each term are in the publication *Incoterms 2000*, available from International Chamber of Commerce Publishing in New York.

The terms most often used when goods move by ocean are FAS, FOB, CFR, and CIF. They are sometimes written in capital letters and sometimes in lowercase letters with periods. In an FAS shipment, for example, the seller must place the goods by the side of a ship, ready to be loaded, and pay all the costs to that point. Thus, the goods are *free* of encumbrances. With FOB the seller must take care of any paperwork or expenses necessary to remove goods from his or her country and place them on an international carrier. Be careful of this term, though, because it is often used with other forms of transportation. If you buy FOB from a handicrafts exporter in the Sahara desert, and you expect the goods to be placed on board a ship, whereas he only expects to place them on board a camel outside his workshop, there will be a major problem. To confuse you more, I should explain that with airfreight, the term FOB means that the goods must be placed in the custody of an air carrier at an airport. It does not mean they must actually be loaded on a plane.

The abbreviation CFR has replaced the old C&F. It means the exporter is responsible for paying the freight bill. Ultimately, he or she will be repaid by the buyer. Once the goods are on the ship, however, the exporter is free of responsibility for subsequent loss or damage. With a CIF shipment the exporter must buy insurance. Technically, however, he or she sells the insurance policy to the importer along with the goods. Thus, if you import beer CIF and most of the bottles are broken, you will have to file a claim against insurance that was bought by the exporter. There may also be claims against that insurance by others whose cargo was damaged by the beer (yes, too much beer can be damaging).

In U.S. trade by land, especially with Mexico, DAF is used widely. For example, a shipment of bathroom fixtures from Guadalajara will be placed on the U.S. side of the international bridge in Laredo, Texas. The importer will take charge of them at that point, before they are cleared through customs.

It takes some experience to learn how to decide which shipping term to use. In the beginning, try to make it easy for yourself. Export with a group F term and import with a group C term. Later, when you are more sophisticated, you can choose terms that minimize your cost and risk and are acceptable to both parties. If you deal with a big shipper who can get lower freight rates, let him or her arrange transportation. You may want to use a term that lets you select the insurance company to make sure it's a good one, in case you have to file a claim. Some countries, however, require that import (and sometimes export) shipments be insured with their national companies.

One former client of mine was buying lovely wool sweaters from a small firm in Ireland that had no experience exporting. The solution was to buy FAS. My client arranged, through her U.S. customs broker, for a shipping agent to take charge of the goods at the Irish port.

If you have a small export shipment to a major company in Europe, the sale may well be FCA. The buyer will have several small shipments sent to a specialized firm that can consolidate them into one container for ocean shipment. Many other examples could be given.

Even experienced exporters, though, hesitate to get involved in shipping beyond CIF to developing countries. I was once asked to quote on an export shipment to be sent DDP to an importer in David, Panama. Besides being responsible for Panamanian customs clearance and duty, I would have had to arrange and pay for inland freight in the buyer's country. Although a multinational company might have agreed to that, I was willing to ship CIF and not an inch beyond. I once worked in Bolivia for an organization that had a new fax machine tied up in customs for six months. If the exporter had shipped this machine DDP, and did not receive payment in advance, he would have waited a very long time for his money.

MARINE INSURANCE

In the early days of international trade it was common for cargo to be lost when vessels ran into trouble with sandbars, storms, or pirates. Shippers would demand compensation from the steamship companies, which often lacked the resources to make restitution in full. (You may have read that pirates have become a serious problem again in the past few years, especially near East Africa and parts of Asia.)

Thus it was that ships' captains began sitting in Lloyd's coffeehouse in London, asking wealthy patrons to accept (for a small fee) the responsibility of repaying shippers when losses occurred. Finally, a patron, whom others respected, would write at the bottom of a manifest the percentage of the risk he would accept and the fee he would charge. He was the *lead underwriter*. Other patrons, underwriters, would add their percentages of risk and their signatures until the entire value of the cargo had been underwritten. From this small beginning, Lloyd's of London and the gigantic marine insurance industry were developed.

Nearly all international shipments are insured against loss and damage. A general cost guideline is 1 percent of the insured value, but this varies enormously with the type of goods, the mode of transportation, and other factors.

There are several types of limited coverage that major shippers use to save money on premiums, but most small-scale importers and exporters purchase "all risk" coverage. This covers *nearly* all risks. It does not cover loss or damage caused by war, strikes, riots, civil disobedience, or "inherent vice in the cargo." This means something in the cargo that destroys it, such as moth larvae in wool sweaters or deadly bacteria in shrimp. One can pay extra for riders (clauses) that protect against these risks.

No standard cargo insurance covers late arrival or rejection of goods by buyers or government agencies. These are insurable risks, but the rates are high and many insurance companies refuse to insure against them.

It is important for your marine insurance policy to contain a *general average* clause. This means that, for example, if the ship is in a bad storm and some heavy cargo is jettisoned to save the rest, every shipper whose cargo is on that vessel is responsible for a portion of the value of the jettisoned cargo. Even though your cargo may be safe and sound, you cannot get it until the steamship line has been assured of payment for your share of the loss.

Insurance can be port to port, warehouse to warehouse, or some combination of the two. Warehouse-to-warehouse policies cover the goods from the time they leave the exporter's premises until they are in the importer's premises. They are becoming increasingly common because it is simpler to buy one policy than to concern yourself with insurance on every carrier.

What determines who must buy the insurance? It is the shipping term that is agreed upon. The definition of each incoterm says who is responsible for insuring the cargo.

Many problems can arise. Suppose, for example, that you are exporting CFR, on open account, and the cargo is lost. The foreign importer is obligated to pay you but may not do so until he collects from his insurance company. To speed up payment, you may get involved in helping your importer settle the claim. Or suppose you are importing CIF on a letter of credit and the cargo is lost. You will have to file a claim on the insurance company from which the *exporter* purchased coverage. This will be much easier if the exporter has used a sound, reliable company that has offices in the United States.

Whenever the other party to a transaction buys insurance to protect you, and you have doubts about the adequacy of coverage, you should consider purchasing contingent insurance. This kind of coverage costs about half as much as regular insurance and pays only if there is covered loss or damage and, for some reason, the primary insurer does not pay.

Small-scale importers and exporters usually buy insurance supplied by freight forwarders under their blanket policies, or directly from airlines, whereas medium-size shippers buy through insurance brokers. Large importers and exporters have "open" policies that automatically cover all shipments of their normal merchandise in their normal trading areas. The importer or exporter simply reports each shipment to his insurance company.

It is customary to insure for the CIF value of a shipment, plus 10 percent of CIF. This means, for example, that if your goods are worth $9,000, the shipping cost is $900, and the insurance cost is $100, you should insure for $11,000 ($9,000 + $900 + 100 × 1.1). The extra 10 percent is to repay you for time and trouble, lost profit, and perhaps lost customers because you could not fulfill your obligations.

A few years ago, a friend of mine, a successful businessman, traveled to China and bought $5,000 worth of hand-carved wooden furniture to begin an import business. He had it shipped to the United States but did not tell the Chinese to insure it for CIF plus 10 percent. It was poorly packed (and the word "poorly" is the nicest way I can say it) and arrived with considerable damage. Insurance covered only part of the loss, and my friend had to absorb the rest.

You may trade for a lifetime and never have an insured loss. If you do have to file a claim, however, you will have to present the bill of lading, the insurance certificate, and a survey report with an invoice showing the amount of damage or loss. When a marine insurance company agrees that it has an obligation to pay, it usually pays from one to six months after the claim is filed.

BROKERS AND FORWARDERS

If you import a small shipment by air that has a value of $2,000 or less and doesn't include textiles, apparel, or leather goods, you can probably clear it through customs yourself. First call your carrier to verify this and ask what is needed. Then go to their cargo office at the airport, fill out a simple form (an *informal entry*), pay the duty if any is charged, and take the merchandise. Some possible complications to this scenario will be discussed in chapter 10.

If the shipment arrives by sea, is worth more than $2,000, or contains restricted products, such as textiles, apparel, or leather goods, you should probably use the services of a licensed U.S. customs broker. Customs brokers' functions are to locate your goods, fill out an entry form (a *formal entry*), and arrange for a customs inspector to clear your goods. Normally, brokers will send you one bill for both services and duty, if any is paid. Brokers usually have two weeks to pay duty to customs, so they bill the importer immediately and hope to be paid before they have to lay out cash of their own. Many now pay duties electronically.

A brokerage fee for a routine clearance is usually $100 to $150, but these fees are unregulated and vary considerably. If your product needs approval by another agency, such as the U.S. Food and Drug Administration (FDA), the broker will make the necessary arrangements. The cost of routine FDA clearance includes cartage to the FDA's office at the port or airport, the FDA fee, cartage back to customs, and a small extra broker's fee—usually around $60 all together. Any kind of special entry will cost extra. If there are problems with documents, such as a missing or incomplete commercial invoice, the broker can usually resolve them but will charge for this extra service.

When your broker fills out customs forms (see chapter 10 for details), he or she will classify each product in your shipment by its Harmonized System number and report its value. (The Harmonized System of classifying and coding merchandise in international trade is explained in chapter 10.) Because the broker is your agent, you can be fined for any error that he or she might commit. Most brokers make very few errors because they have to pass rigorous tests to become licensed and because some kinds of mistakes can be very costly to their clients.

When goods are cleared through customs, the duty that is paid is only an estimated duty. The inspectors at ports are very knowledgeable but are not product specialists. Customs has one year from the date of an entry for a product specialist to examine the paperwork and determine whether the correct duty was paid. If you paid too much, customs will send you a refund (it happened once in the year 1493). If you paid too little, customs will send you a notice and then a bill. If the product specialist wants to see a sample of the merchandise so as to determine its proper classification, customs will send you a redelivery notice. Customs can also ask for redelivery of a sample to check the labeling on your product and can do this as long as a year after your shipment has been entered.

Because importers usually receive their shipments before paying duty, customs needs a way to be sure it can collect if any duty is due. Also, there is a logical fear that an importer will bring in goods and pay too little duty, that within a year customs will try to collect the rest, and that the importer will have passed away, gone broke, or hidden in some faraway country. To reduce this risk, rules stipulate that, with few exceptions, each shipment that requires a formal entry must be covered by a bond. Provided that no approvals are required from other government agencies, such as the FDA, the usual bond is equal to the value of the cargo plus duties and taxes. If other approvals are required, the bond must be equal to triple the estimated value of the merchandise.

You can go to a bonding company yourself and purchase either a *single-entry* bond to cover just one shipment or a *term* bond to cover all your shipments for a year. Look for a company near your port of entry. A bail bond firm in Topeka, Kansas, won't know much about customs bonds. The cost will be a percentage of the value of your shipment(s), with a small minimum charge. You can get a quotation online. One site that will help you is www.traderiskguaranty.com/ImportBondLanding.aspx. Click on "Quote Calculator," select "Importer Bond," enter the amount for which you need to be bonded, and voilà!

A bonding company will protect itself by checking your income and financial position. If you use a broker to clear your shipment, however, he or she will get the bond *for* you. This may cost you as much or more but will be easier for you because bonding companies usually accept the word of a broker that an importer is honest and financially sound.

If there is a small problem with your entry, such as a missing document, the same bond will guarantee customs that the document will be submitted within 60 days.

In most ports, there are many licensed customs brokers. You should select one who will tell you clearly and honestly what the fees are and which services they cover. I once spoke with an importer in New York who had been using the same broker for several years and had never received an itemized bill. It turned out that the broker was systematically overcharging but was a good friend of the company's president.

If you have special requirements, such as rush shipments or highly perishable cargo, look for a well-established brokerage firm that can guarantee the kind of service you need. I once had an urgent shipment of product samples land at Kennedy Airport in Queens, New York, on a Saturday with everything mixed up. The shipment was consigned to the wrong party: it contained goods that were under quota and even a prohibited item; and there were no documents *at all*. My brokerage firm sent its number-one broker, a middle-aged lady about five feet tall with a voice like a Bengal tiger, and, believe it or not, the goods were out of customs and in Philadelphia by 6:00 PM on Sunday. Of course, that extra service cost me plenty.

Once your goods are cleared through customs, you can pick them up, but it will be easier to have the broker get them on a truck and delivered to your door. He or she will then be performing the function of a domestic freight forwarder. Some broker/forwarders have their own trucks for delivery, but more often they use private trucking companies. In either case, you will be billed for forwarding, trucking, and perhaps insurance if the policy in force does not cover through to your warehouse.

One importer I knew was having small shipments sent to him from Kennedy Airport by UPS. He said the charge was a fraction of what it would have been by truck. The moral: examine *all* of your options.

On the export side, air and ocean forwarders can help you in the following ways.

- Supply cost figures needed to prepare CIF quotations.
- Book space on vessels or aircraft.
- Take charge of cargo at the port or airport.
- Arrange for packing if this is needed.
- Prepare export documents.
- Make sure the cargo is loaded on the vessel.
- Collect or assemble the documents and send them to you or to your bank.
- Track shipments that do not arrive as scheduled.

These are very valuable services. For example, if you receive a letter of credit that says you must ship by July 1, and your cargo reaches the port on time but cannot be loaded because you didn't book space on the only vessel available, your payment may no longer be assured.

Freight forwarders are paid by fees from their clients (usually exporters), plus commissions from the carriers they use. Fees are not regulated and vary considerably but are usually around $100 for an air shipment and close to $200 for an ocean shipment. Commissions are around 2 to 5 percent but vary greatly, especially for ocean freight. It is illegal for forwarders to kick back any of their commissions to the shippers, but this is sometimes done, one way or another.

It *is* legal for air forwarders to charge you, the shipper, whatever rate they care to set. For example, an airline could quote a price of $2,000 for a shipment and pay the forwarders 10 percent of that as a commission. The forwarder could charge you, the shipper, only $1,900, thus effectively giving you half the commission. You may come out better than if you dealt directly with the airline.

You will want to pick a forwarder who has offices near the port or airport you use, who has experience with the kinds of cargo you will be shipping and with the destinations you will be shipping to, who has friendly, competent personnel, and is in good financial standing. This last criterion is especially important. If a forwarder handles a shipment for you and you pay for it, and then the forwarder goes out of business before paying the carrier, you will still be liable. This happened to me once, when I used a not-so-stable forwarder to airfreight a friend's dog from Boston to Jakarta. In addition, the forwarder made a mistake in the documentation and the poor dog was lost for a few days at an airport in Tokyo.

It is worth checking directly with carriers from time to time to make sure your forwarder is giving you the lowest rates to which your cargo is entitled. This can be done fairly easily by phone.

Many forwarders pick up freight at inland points of origin, and several can save you money through their roles as freight consolidators or NVOCCs. As we saw earlier, NVOCC companies reserve space on vessels and resell it to their customers. The moral, again, is to look at all of your options.

Foreign freight forwarders (and brokers as well) are listed in telephone directories, port handbooks, and some trade magazines. Many ports have online directories of local trade service companies. You can find several customs house brokers and foreign freight forwarders on the Internet and learn more about their services. Look, for example, at C. H. Robinson Worldwide's Web site at www.chrobinson.com or at Schenker's Web site at www.schenkerusa.com. You can find others without much difficulty.

If you want to see all the customs brokers in a port, go on the Internet to the U.S. Census Bureau's Web site at www.census.gov/foreign-trade/schedules/d/distname.html to get the code for the port in which you are interested. Suppose it is New York, port # 4601. Then go to the U.S. Customs and Border Protection's Web site at http://apps.cbp.gov/brokers/index.asp?portCode=4601 and enter that port code. The site will give you all the brokers that serve your port.

With increased access to information by shippers around the world, the traditional roles of customs brokers and freight forwarders have been changing. Large companies have bought smaller ones and are expanding into freight forwarding, customs clearance, warehousing, logistics, tracking shipments, and so forth. Look for more vertical integration and expansion of service in the future.

The National Customs Brokers and Forwarders Association can provide you with more information on this topic. Its home page can be found at www.ncbfaa.org. Here you can also find bonding companies and other types of firms to help you move your merchandise, quickly and safely, and, with any luck, at a reasonable cost, in or out of the United States.

SOURCES OF INFORMATION AND HELP

Packing, shipping, and insurance are topics that you might not have thought about much but are crucial to the success of your business. I recently had a client who couldn't come to terms with a buyer about shipping; the seller wanted to use FAS, the buyer preferred CFR, and neither wanted to budge.

You can read all you want on these subjects; it certainly won't hurt, but there is no substitute for professional advice about how to pack, insure, and send a shipment. Freight forwarders can be your best friends.

The sources of information and help mentioned in the chapter are as follows.

- Basic guide to shipping your product available from UNZ & Company on the Web at www.unzco.com/basicguide/c10.html.

- Description of export packing available from EXPORT911 at www.export911.com/e911/prod/packing.htm.

- Institute of Packaging Professionals is a packaging association serving the educational needs of the packaging community. The association publishes a journal and a packaging newsletter. Address: 1601 Bond Street, Suite 101, Naperville, IL 60563; Phone: (630) 544-5050; Fax: (630) 544-5055; Web site: www.IOPP.org.

- World Packaging Organization is a not-for-profit, nongovernmental, international federation of national packaging institutes, regional packaging federations, and other interested parties, including individuals, corporations, and trade associations. Address: World Packaging Organization, c/o STFI-Packforsk, Box 5604, S-114 86 Stockholm, Sweden; Phone: (+46) 8 676 70 78; Fax: (+46) 8 411 55 18; Web site: www.worldpackaging.com.

- Cautionary markings: pictorial cargo handling marks are available from EXPORT911 at www.export911.com/e911/prod/caution.htm.

- *International Mail Manual* is published by the U.S. Postal Service and available at http://pe.usps.gov/text/imm/welcome.htm.

- eBay Shipping Center is available at http://pages.ebay.ca/help/sellerguide/shipping/index.html.

- *American Shipper* magazine provides sailing schedules for steamship services. Address: American Shipper, P.O. Box 4728, Jacksonville, FL 32201; Phone: (904) 355-2601; Fax: (904) 791-8836; Web site: www.americanshipper.com.

- *Forwarder* magazine provides sailing schedules for steamship services. It is published by the Canadian International Freight Forwarders Association. Address: Canadian International Freight Forwarders Association, 170 Attwell Drive, Suite 480, Toronto, ON, Canada M9W 5Z5; Phone: (416) 234-5100; Fax: (416) 234-5152; Web site: www.ciffa.com/ newsletters_current.asp.

- *Journal of Commerce* newspaper. This is a national daily newspaper that publishes in-depth information on international trade and transportation. Address: 445 Marshall Street, Phillipsburg, NJ 08865; Phone: (908) 859-1300; Fax: (908) 454-6507; Web site: www.joc.com.

- Freightquote.com provides online tariffs at www.freightquote .com. Address: 16025 West 113th Street, Lenexa, KS 66219; Phone: (800) 323-5441.

- Freight-Calculator.com allows you to calculate your cargo's freight weight. Phone: (877) 597-0258; Fax: (877) 597-0259; Web site: www.freight-calculator.com.

- *Incoterms 2000* are internationally accepted commercial terms defining the respective roles of the buyer and seller in the arrangement of transportation. The publication is available from ICC Publishing, Inc. Address: 156 Fifth Avenue, New York, NY 10010. Phone: (212) 703-5066; Fax: (212) 944-0012; Web site: www.iccbooksusa.com.

- Trade Risk Guaranty (TRG) is an international surety agency providing customs bonds. Address: Trade Risk Guaranty Brokerage Services, 28874 West Rand Road, Suite C, Lakemoor, IL 60051; Phone: (815) 363-7220; Fax: (815) 363-7230; Web site: www.traderiskguaranty.com/ImportBondLanding.aspx.

- C. H. Robinson Worldwide is a third-party logistics company that also provides sourcing and information services. Address: 8100 Mitchell Road, Eden Prairie, MN 55344; Phone (952) 937-8500; Web site: www.chrobinson.com.

- Schenker provides integrated logistics services. Address: 150 Albany Avenue, Freeport, NY 11520; Phone: (516) 403-5416; Fax: (516) 377-3092; Web site: www.schenkerusa.com.

- The U.S. Census Bureau's Web site at www.census.gov/ foreign-trade/schedules/d/distname.html lists port codes.
- The U.S. Customs and Border Protection's (CBP) Web site at http://apps.cbp.gov lists custom brokers for specific ports.
- National Customs Brokers and Forwarders Association is an important professional association. Address: 1200 18th Street, NW, #901, Washington, DC 20036; Phone: (202) 466-0222; Fax (202) 466-0226; Web site: www.ncbfaa.org.

9

Oh, Those Lovely Documents

There is an old expression: "Trade moves on paper." In today's ever more connected age, a more accurate expression would be: "Trade moves on paper and the Internet." Either way, we are talking about documents. Their number has not diminished. Now they can be created much more quickly, and this both increases and decreases the chance of error. If someone hits the wrong key on a computer, a mistake such as "500 kings" instead of "500 rings" may be repeated on multiple documents. On the other hand, computers rarely make errors copying from one document to another or adding numbers.

Fortunately, many of the prerequisite documents, like those between airlines and the airports they fly into and out of, are never seen by the importer or the exporter. Also, most shipments are reasonably uncomplicated. If you send rubber bands from the United States to England, by airfreight on open-account terms, documents won't be much of a problem. On the other hand, if you want to ship repeating rifles to Chad, by sea freight on a letter of credit, you'd better be prepared for reams of paper.

Most international trade documents can be placed into the following categories.

- Commercial documents
- Banking documents

- Transportation and insurance documents
- Government formalities documents

In general, the purposes of all of them are to facilitate, control, and keep track of international cargo movements. We will discuss each of them in turn.

COMMERCIAL DOCUMENTS

Commercial documents are prepared by the buyer and the seller for each other. The ones to be discussed here are the following.

- Request for quotation
- Quotation
- Pro forma invoice
- Terms and conditions of sale
- Purchase order
- Order acceptance and confirmation
- Sales contract
- Commercial invoice

Buyers and sellers can exchange any number of letters, telephone calls, faxes, and e-mail messages as the initial steps of an international transaction. This will normally lead to a *request for quotation*. This can be a simple fax or other form of message that reads something like the following:

Dear Sirs:

Please send me your quotation for 50 Farm Best lawn tractors, Model number 307H. Please quote C&F Mombassa, Kenya. Payment will be by 90-day letter of credit.

Sincerely,
Seth Anjul
Monrobi Trading Company.

You, as the exporter, would logically follow with a *quotation*, which is basically the price for which you can supply the goods for the specified shipping and payment terms (although you are free to propose alternative terms). All your costs, and your profit or commission, should be included. Your quotation should reference the number on the request, if there was one, and include a date until which it is valid. Figure 9.1 shows a simple example.

You will want the quotation to be as specific as possible to avoid misunderstandings. It is often signed, and it is now possible to send e-mail messages with your signature on them (although electronic signatures are usually not accepted on contractual documents).

AGMARTRADE INTERNATIONAL
7823 Mystic Valley Parkway
Rockville, MD 20855-2275, USA
QUOTATION No. _____

This quotation is valid for 30 days from the date hereon: March 8, 2008.

Shipper: Agmartrade International, 7823 Mistic View Court, Rockville, MD 20855-2275, USA

Consignee: Monrobi Trading Company, 724 Serengetti Street, Mombasa, Kenya

50 lawn tractors, Farm Best Model 307 H as shown in the Farm Best catalog dated January 2, 2006, packed for export by the manufacturer	US$42,100
Inland freight to the Port of Baltimore	1,000
Forwarding and freight to Mombasa, Kenya, by sea	5,125
Total CFR Mombasa	US$48,225

Marine insurance to be purchased by the Consignee.

Payment by 90-day irrevocable letter of credit drawn on a first-class international bank.

Shipment to be made within 60 days after receipt of the letter of credit.

Figure 9.1   A quotation.

Sometimes an importer will want a more formal document that will help in getting an import permit or foreign exchange authorization and/or to open a letter of credit. If this is the case, the importer may go one step further and ask for a *pro forma invoice*. It looks like a regular commercial invoice (see Figure 9.4 on page 172), except that it says "Pro Forma" at the top. These words mean that the document in hand isn't the actual commercial invoice but is almost exactly what the actual invoice will look like.

Sometimes quotations and pro forma invoices are accompanied by other documents known as *standard terms and conditions of sale*. These give important information, such as "All shipments are made FOB McAllen, Texas," that is not shown on quotations or pro forma invoices. This information is analogous to the "fine print" when you open a bank account or receive a credit card.

Once satisfied with the quotation and/or pro forma invoice, the importer may place an order. This can be a simple oral or written statement such as "We hereby order as per your pro forma invoice number 627." More often, there are additional details; for example, "We hereby order 100 dozen Model R FILEMAST bicycle pumps, CIF New York, to be shipped by ocean no later than January 1, 2007, with payment by irrevocable letter of credit." An order can include other conditions such as documents that should be provided and even what should be said on the documents. Figure 9.2 is an example of an international purchase order. Note that it shows how to mark the boxes, and specifies payment by sight draft, documents against payment, and is signed.

The exporter should reply with a simple statement such as, "We accept your Purchase Order No. 387/07 dated January 8, 2007." In international trade, an order and an unconditional acceptance make a contract that theoretically can be enforced by either of the contracting parties. Chapter 10 includes some information about enforcement of contracts of sale.

In some cases importers order informally, by telephone, although this system has been partly replaced by fax, e-mail, and online Web sites. When the order is by phone, the exporter should send a *sales confirmation*, something like the one in Figure 9.3, which the importer signs and returns. This procedure creates a contract of sale.

TREICO
93 Broad Street
Syosset, NY 11791   **BANK:**   **Citibank NA**
USA   **Syosset, New York**

TO: Exporters Uribe   P.O. DATE   January 8, 2007
        77 Calle Inventada
        Rogelio, Panama   P.O. #:   387/07

                                            SHIP TO: TREICO
                                                                  93 Broad Street
                                                                  Syosset, NY, USA

NO.	MODEL	DESCRIPTION	UNIT	TOTAL PRICE
10	533	Cartons each containing 4 dozen Panama hats	$146.00	US$1,1460.00
5	529	Cartons each containing 4 dozen Panama hats	120.00	600.00
		TOTAL FOB COLON, PANAMA		US$2,060.00
		Ocean Freight		421.15
		TOTAL CFR NEW YORK		US$2,481.15
		MARKS: TREICO 387/07 Syosset, NY		
		PAYMENT: SD/DP		
		SHIPMENT: By sea, CFR New York		
		INSURANCE: TREICO will cover.		
		———————— PURCHASING DEPT.		

Figure 9.2   An international purchase order.

Good Fortune Corporation **Original for Seller**	P.O. Box xxx, Qusay, Vietnam Telephone: _____ Telefax: _____ Email: _____

Date: March 20, 2007

SALES CONFIRMATION

Ref. No. SC-563-07

Referring to (BUYER), USA	Please indicate the confirmation number on your Letter of Credit.

We confirm the following sale to you on the terms and conditions set forth below and on the other side of this document, as per your Purchase Order No. 240.

Description	Quantity	Unit Price	Amount
12 CTNS MODEL 51Q SCOOTERS, 12 PCS PER CARTON	144 PCS	**FOB Taiwan**	US$3,276.00
6 CTNS MODEL 51R SCOOTERS, 12 PCS PER CARTON	72 PCS	US$22.75	US$1,728.00
6 CTNS MODEL 53B SCOOTERS, 12 PCS PER CARTON	72 PCS	US$22.75	US$1,728.00
TOTAL	288 PCS	US$25.99	US$6,875.28

TOTAL: SIX THOUSAND EIGHT HUNDRED SEVENTY-FIVE AND 28/100 U.S. DOLLARS.

PAYMENT: By Irrevocable, confirmed Letter of Credit available against drafts drawn at sight in Favor of Seller or transferable	SHIPPING MARKS (BUYER'S NAME) NEW YORK CARTON # MADE IN VIETNAM	SIDE MARKS MODEL NO. QUANTITY ORDER NO. NET WT. GROSS WT.

SHIPMENT: Mar. 31, 2007
DESTINATION: New York
VALIDITY: 30 DAYS

Agreed and accepted by:
Buyer: (SELLER) CORPORATION

_____   _____
(Buyer's signature)   (Seller's signature)

Figure 9.3   A sales confirmation.

The Finishing Touches

With large shipments between nonaffiliated companies, there are usually more formal contracts of sale. These can run to 30 or 40 pages. If you decide to buy or sell a shipload of copper, for example, I would strongly suggest that you use the services of a good attorney, expensive though it may be.

As an exporter, once you ship you will need to supply a *commercial invoice* that says how much the importer owes you (even if he or she has already paid) and for what. Many countries have their own requirements for commercial invoices, which you can obtain from customs brokers/freight forwarders, consulates of the countries to which you are shipping, or certain publications. Foremost of these is the Dun & Bradstreet *Exporters' Encyclopedia*, which was described on the company's Web site as follows:

> *Exporters' Encyclopaedia*
> This "must have" directory has been helping global business professionals succeed in foreign trade for a century. It offers valuable insight into the trading environment of more than 220 world markets with general information on exporting and specific information on all major markets including trade regulations, documentation, key contacts, marketing information, transportation and business travel. Free, twice-monthly updates keep you abreast of late-breaking developments in this ever-changing business climate.

This book is available in major business libraries.

Some countries have special forms for commercial invoices, which you can buy from their consulates or from UNZ & Company in Jersey City, New Jersey. You may be able to see the forms or find instructions on the Internet. For example, type in your browser "Brazil, commercial invoice" and you will see information provided by various organizations. The site from the Brazilian Consulate in Miami, at www.brazilmiami.org/eng/consaff_cominv.php, provides a clear list of what should be included in the commercial invoice.

For shipments to the United States, the commercial invoice must show the following information.

- Port of entry of the merchandise.

- The date of the sale if merchandise was sold, and the date of the shipment if it is on consignment.

- Names of the seller and the buyer (usually addresses are shown as well, and these are required for some kinds of products).

- A detailed description of the merchandise, including the name and quality of each item, marks used in domestic trade in the country of origin, and marks and numbers on the export packing.

- The quantity of each item by the number of pieces, by weight and/or by volume, as specified in the product classification known as the Harmonized System.

- The purchase price of each item in the currency actually used for the transaction (if the shipment is on consignment and there is no purchase price, the value must be shown).

- Charges involved in moving the freight from FOB vessel to where the U.S. Customs inspection takes place may be shown on an attachment to the invoice, which the customs broker can prepare.

- Any rebates or similar incentives the exporter will receive from his government for having made the exportation.

- The country of origin of the merchandise.

- Any "assists," which are goods or services, usually provided by the importer to the manufacturer, that are not included in the invoice price.

The invoice should be in English or accompanied by an accurate translation and should show in detail what goods are in each individual package. This provision eliminates the need to supply another document, the packing list.

For a more detailed description of invoicing requirements, see *Importing into the United States*, published by U.S. Customs and Border Protection (CBP) and available from the superintendent of documents. You can get it free on the Internet at www.cbp.gov/linkhandler/cgov/toobox/publications/trade/iius.ctt/iius.pdf.

In the modern world, there is emphasis on reducing cost and speeding up shipments, so systems have been developed that go by the names of remote location filing (RLF) and electronic invoice processing (EIP). These are normally used by transportation companies to tell customs ahead of time what they are carrying, through the automated manifest system (AMS), and by brokers who file entries electronically using the automated broker interface

AMERICAN FOOD EXPORT CORPORATION
EXPORT DEPARTMENT
99 CROFTON STREET, 9TH FLOOR
NEW YORK, NY 10007, U.S.A.
TEL: (212) 000-0000, FAX: (212) 111-1111
	INVOICE PAGE: 1
	ORDER NO: A60273 DATE: 17 MAY 2007
	REFERENCE DATA:
	  INVOICE NO: PR 28597
	  DATE: 27 MAY 2007

BUYER: _____
ATTN: MR. _____
P.O. BOX _____
AL JAHRA, KUWAIT
	TERMS:
	  SALES: NET CFR DOHA
	  DELIVERY: NET CFR DOHA
	  PAYMENT: WIRE TRANSFER

CONSIGN TO: _____
NOTIFY: _____
ULTIMATE CONSIGNEE: _____
_____
MARKS: _____
DOHA, KUWAIT
	SHIPMENT DATA:
	  SHIP VIA: OCEAN FREIGHT
	  ARRIVES AT: DOHA
	
	THIS SHIPMENT INCLUDES
	THE ENTIRE ORDER.

ITEM	DESCRIPTION	QUANTITY	UNIT PR.	TOTAL PR.
1	240 Ctns 16 Oz. Green Beans	240	27.50	$6,600.00
2	240 Ctns 16 Oz. Pickled Beets	240	28.95	6,948.00
3	240 Ctns 16 Oz. Creamed Corn	240	28.30	6,792.00
4	180 Ctns Canned Peaches	180	32.70	5,886.00
5	180 Ctns Canned Applesauce	180	33.00	5,940.00
	All items—Stay Fresh Brand: English/Arabic labels with manufacturing and expiration dates (Shelf life—2 years)			

NET CFR DOHA $32,166.00

THESE COMMODITIES LICENSED BY U.S. FOR UNTIMATE DESTINATION KUWAIT. DIVERSION CONTRARY TO U.S. LAW IS PROHIBITED.

WE CERTIFY THAT THIS PRODUCT DOES NOT CONTAIN PORT, ALCOHOL, GELATINE, SACCHARINE OR CYCLAMATE

PER _____, TRAFFIC MANAGER

BUYER WILL INSURE

1-20′ CONTAINER NO. IEAU-284560. SEAL NO. 20382
TOTAL CARTONS: 1,080
TOTAL GR. WT.: 25,985 POUNDS/11,812 KILOS
CERTIFIED TRUE & CORRECT

_____
FOR AMERICAN FOOD EXPORT CORP.

Figure 9.4 A commercial invoice.

(ABI). I suggest not jumping into this modern world at the outset. Start with paper documents and then modernize, little by little.

Figure 9.4 shows a sample computer-generated invoice for an actual export shipment from New York to Kuwait. Note the statements made at the bottom. Since invoice requirements change often, this may not be the accepted format for future shipments to that country.

BANKING DOCUMENTS

The processes of paying and getting paid require relatively few documents. Cash in advance may be as simple as the importer's sending the exporter a check or depositing it in the exporter's bank account. It is rarely more complicated than filling out a simple form to buy a bank draft or to order an airmail or a cable transfer. Consignment, open-account, and credit card transactions are equally uncomplicated.

With payment by bill of exchange (sight or time draft), the exporter must complete a form to instruct his bank to prepare the draft and send it to the importer's bank. The first time you do this, you should sit down with your banker and go over each of the options that are presented on the form. Figure 9.5 depicts a simple bill of exchange. There is a very good explanation of this payment instrument, with a picture of a slightly different type, on the Web at www.export911.com/e911/export/bill.htm.

A letter of credit sale is somewhat more complex than other forms of international payment. There are at least four documents involved.

1. Application for letter of credit
2. Letter of credit
3. Advice of letter of credit
4. Drafts (drawn on a bank for payment)

The application for a letter of credit must be completed by the importer and given to the opening bank. It is fairly complicated and should definitely be completed the first few times with the

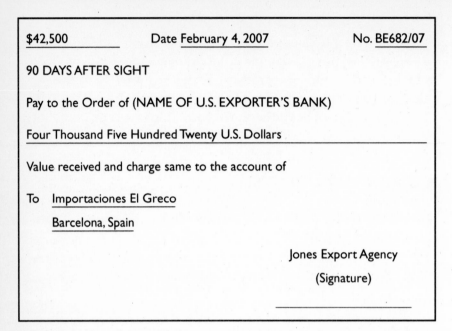

$42,500	Date February 4, 2007	No. BE682/07

90 DAYS AFTER SIGHT

Pay to the Order of (NAME OF U.S. EXPORTER'S BANK)

Four Thousand Five Hundred Twenty U.S. Dollars

Value received and charge same to the account of

To   Importaciones El Greco
     Barcelona, Spain

                                    Jones Export Agency
                                    (Signature)
                                    _____

Figure 9.5   A bill of exchange.

help of your banker. Major international banks now accept applications from established customers by computer. The importer simply fills in details on a form in his data-processing system and transmits it to his bank by modem. You can see some of the application forms on the Internet. Type "letter of credit application" into your browser and follow the link that most appeals to you. You can even complete an application online to a bank that has never heard of you, and the bank might write it for you under conditions that I'll describe a few paragraphs further on.

The actual letter of credit is transmitted by the opening bank to its branch or correspondent in the exporter's country. It tells the exporter exactly which documents to provide to get paid.

The advice of a letter of credit (see Figure 9.6) is a simple form that is sent to the exporter by a bank in its country. It says that a credit has been opened in the exporter's favor, and it is followed by the actual LC. It gives the exporting firm assurance that it "can begin preparing" the goods for shipment. The example that follows, Figure 9.6, is an advice to an exporter in New York named City Directory Company.

(NAME AND ADDRESS
OF EXPORTER'S BANK)

Their Ref. No. 68392   Our Advice LC R23259   Date 2/5/2007

TO: City Directory Company
      650 East 11th Street
      New York, New York

104-686943

Instructions
Received from: Neopolitan Bank, Florence, Italy

For Account of: Cassata Importers, Florence, Italy

Gentlemen:
    Our correspondent, named above, has instructed us to advise you that
they have opened their irrevocable credit in your favor, as designated above,
for a sum or sums not to exceed the following:

    FIFTEEN THOUSAND DOLLARS UNITED STATES CURRENCY
($15,000 USC)

Available by your draft(s):

For FULL invoice value of merchandise, to be described in your Invoice as
follows:

                GUIDEBOOKS TO MAJOR NORTH AMERICAN CITIES

Your draft(s) must be accompanied by the following:
1. Your commercial invoice, original and 3 copies
2. Your ocean bill of lading issued to order, endorsed in blank evidencing
shipment of the goods from New York to Florence.

Partial shipments are not permitted. Insurance is to be obtained by the buyers. We confirm this credit and affirm all drafts presented against it at (bank's
address) by (date) will be honored.

This credit is subject to the Uniform Customs and Practice for Documentary Credits as described in International Chamber of Commerce Publication No. 500.

                                        Yours truly,

                                        _____
                                        (Authorized Signature)

Figure 9.6   An advice of letter of credit.

Finally, the exporter must present drafts for collection to the paying or negotiating bank. For example, if you receive a letter of credit that is payable upon presentation of documentary evidence that you have shipped as instructed, you can go directly from the port to the bank, armed with a draft for collection and the required documents. More likely, you will ask your freight forwarder to do this for you. To save time, the forwarder will probably send the draft and other documents to the bank by courier (at your expense, of course).

Still other documents will be involved in more complicated LC transactions, as when partial shipments are allowed or a credit is transferred or assigned from one beneficiary to another. There are also special documents for the seller to request, and the buyer to grant, amendments to LCs.

Our friends at EXPORT911 have information about LCs on the Internet, but I prefer material from the Credit Research Foundation at www.crfonline.org/orc/cro/cro-9-1.html.

There are various specialized types of letters of credit, and one that seems to be increasingly common is the *standby* LC. It is usually used to guarantee performance, and it can be complicated. Toward the end of 2006, I heard of an importer in Canada who planned to work jointly with an exporter in South America to bring a container load of honey to the United States and sell it. The importer wasn't actually buying the product, but the exporter needed money to buy and ship it, and his bank wouldn't give him the money without a guarantee. The importer in Canada had his bank send a standby letter of credit. It essentially said to the South American bank: Give this exporter credit; if he doesn't sell the product and pay you back, you can get repaid by this standby LC. Unfortunately, there were numerous problems with the shipment, and, as of the latest report, it looked like the importer would end up losing close to $100,000.

TRANSPORTATION AND INSURANCE DOCUMENTS

The old expression "Goods move on paper" is becoming less true, but paper is still important. Goods don't move on paper, but neither do they move without some legal form of documentation. The transportation documents that will be mentioned in this section include:

- Packing list
- Delivery instructions to domestic carrier
- Inland bill of lading
- Dock receipt
- Insurance request and insurance certificate
- Shipper's letter of instructions
- Ocean bill of lading or airway bill
- Booking request
- Arrival notice
- Carrier's certificate and release order
- Delivery order and freight release

The purpose of most of these documents is to keep track of merchandise as it passes from one hand to another and to make sure it isn't delivered to someone who is not supposed to receive it. If a shipper delivers goods to a trucking company, the shipper gets a receipt to show they have been delivered (the inland bill of lading). The truck driver needs proof of delivery when the goods are delivered to the dock (a dock receipt) or to any other location. If a shipment disappears, there should be a trail of documents that will tell investigators who had custody of it at the time it was lost.

There is another important aspect to this paper trail. No one wants to be held accountable for damage to merchandise that was caused by someone else. Therefore, each party who receives goods is supposed to make a visual inspection of the boxes. If a steamship company receives a box with no apparent loss or damage, it will simply accept it and issue a bill of lading (or sign the bill of lading previously prepared by the freight forwarder). If the box is wet or badly dented, however, the steamship company will note this as an *exception* on the bill of lading. The document will then be known as a *foul* bill of lading. Letters of credit often stipulate that an exporter must present to the bank a *clean* bill of lading in order to be paid for a shipment. If a box is damaged before being loaded on the ship, and a foul bill of lading is issued, the exporter's payment will be held up until the situation is resolved.

The *packing list* is a simple document that shows how many boxes there are in a shipment, how to identify each one, and what is in each one. As I mentioned before, this document is not used for all shipments to the United States because invoices now contain the same information.

If a box is missing, one can determine from the packing list which one it is and what it contains. Or, if you should need to find something specific in a shipment, the packing list should tell you which box it is in. The sample packing list in Figure 9.7 was taken (with minor modifications) from the book *A Basic Guide to Exporting,* which used to be published by the U.S. Department of Commerce. It is now available free on the Internet from UNZ & Company. The applicable Web site is www.unzco.com/basicguide. It will give you a large amount of useful information.

You will see packing lists in many different formats. Figure 9.7 is a simplified example. Packing lists now are usually prepared electronically, as are other documents.

As an exporter, you are likely to be shipping goods by truck to seaports and airports. You must provide delivery instructions to the domestic carrier. The carrier, in turn, will provide you with a signed inland bill of lading. This document shows that the carrier has received the goods and to whom they are to be delivered. The fine print on the back makes this bill of lading also a contract of carriage.

When your trucking company delivers goods to an ocean terminal, it will obtain a *dock receipt.* This is the domestic carrier's proof of when and where it made delivery. If the exporter is responsible for insuring the shipment, he or she will fill out an insurance request and obtain an insurance certificate. If you export CIF under a letter of credit, the insurance certificate will have to be included in the package of documents you present to the bank for payment.

Assuming the exporter uses the services of an international freight forwarder, it must tell the forwarder which goods it will receive for forwarding, where and when to find them, and what to do with the goods and with the documents. This information is

PACKING LIST

OCTOBER 18, 2007

To: AUTO-ACCESSORY CO.

HAMPTON ROADS, ENGLAND

Gentlemen:

In fulfillment of your order No. 385-07, the material listed below was shipped on October 18, 2007, via truck and vessel to Hampton Roads.

BOX #	WEIGHT IN KILOS	DIMENSIONS IN CENTIMETERS	CONTENTS (ALL FOR G.M. CARS)
1 of 9	72.3	30H, 30W, 30L	Automobile spark plugs
2 of 9	15.1	32H, 48W, 48L	Fan belts model QR27
3 of 9	15.3	SAME	Fan belts model PR 74
4 of 9	16.0	SAME	Fan belts model PR 76
5 of 9	18.2	30H, 42W, 42L	Brake pads model BL 26
6 of 9	19.1	SAME	Brake pads model BL 27
7 of 9	18.6	SAME	Brake pads model BT 70
8 of 9	11.5	42H, 50W, 50L	Oil filters model 214G
9 of 9	12.1	SAME	Oil filters model 227 R

Figure 9.7   A packing list.

communicated by means of a *shipper's letter of instructions*. Figure 9.8, from an export information manual published a few years ago in Texas, is such a letter of instructions. It tells the forwarder to ship to La Paz, Bolivia, prepay the freight, insure the shipment, and present the documents to the bank. Note that the shipment is consigned to a bank in Bolivia and is probably being sent with a to order bill of lading.

EXPORT SHIPPING INSTRUCTIONS

DATE: <u>Feb. 9, 2007</u>
Shipper's ref. no. <u>78-456</u>

Ship in name of: ABC MANUFACTURING COMPANY, ANY STREET, DALLAS, TEXAS
Consign to: BANCO DE AMERICA, APTDO. 666, LA PAZ, BOLIVIA
Notify: XYZ DISTRIBUTING COMPANY, APTDO 792, LA PAZ, BOLIVIA
Port of Discharge: LA PAZ   Final Destination: LA PAZ

MARKS AND NUMBERS	NO. OF PKGS.	DESCRIPTION OF COMMODITIES	VALUE	GROSS WT. (LBS.)	MEASURE-MENT
XYX COMPANY LA PAZ P.O. 78-456 MADE IN USA CTN. #1	I CTN.	CONTAINING OIL WELL DRILLING PARTS Partes para uso en la industria petrolera 6 #2489 0 rings @ 2.89 10 #6723 gaskets @ 1.59 4 #8932 seals @ 8.79 18 #8056 bushings @ 9.30 1 #5742 shim TOTAL F.O.B. DALLAS	 $17.34 15.90 35.16 167.40 <u>12.68</u> $250.04	83	

Letter of Credit Expires: _____
Value for Customs Clearance: _____
Inland Freight to be Charged to: _____
Port Charges to be Charged to: _____
Air/Ocean Freight Prepaid or Collect: <u>PREPAID</u>
Insurance Requirements: <u>INSURE SHIPMENT</u>
Send Documents to: ___<u>BANK</u>___

Bank Documents Through: <u>BANCO DE AMERICA</u>
License No.: _____
Export Carrier: _____
Port of Origin: <u>DALLAS, TEXAS</u>
Name of Supplier: _____
Inland Routing: _____
Car No./Truck Line: _____

OTHER INSTRUCTIONS
Consular Declaration or Other: _____
_____
_____

Figure 9.8   A shipper's letter of instructions.

You may run into various types of bills of lading including "short form" and "long form," "received for shipment" and "on board," and "straight" and "to order." For example, if you ship goods by sea, FOB/vessel with payment by sight draft, you will probably use a long-form, on-board, to-order, ocean bill of lading. This sounds complicated, and it will be until you have made your first few shipments.

Figure 9.9 is an example of a short-form, intermodal bill of lading. The goods are being sent by two modes of transportation, air from Dallas to Miami and sea from Miami to La Paz, Bolivia. The bill of lading, issued by a freight forwarder, is a *forwarder's* bill of

A. FREIGHT FORWARDER, INC. DALLAS, TEXAS	SHORT FORM INTERMODAL BILL OF LADING Not Negotiable Unless Consigned "To Order"
Shipper/Exporter ABC MANUFACTURING COMPANY ANY STREET DALLAS, TEXAS	Document No.
	Exporter References: D-74896 P.O. NO. 78-456
Consignee BANCO DE AMERICA APARTADO 666 LA PAZ, BOLIVIA	Forwarding agent name and address— references A. FREIGHT FORWARDER, INC. DALLAS, TEXAS
	Goods accepted for carriage at DALLAS/FORT WORTH, TEXAS
Notify Party XYZ DISTRIBUTING COMPANY APARTADO 792 LA PAZ, BOLIVIA	Domestic routing export instructions ALSO NOTIFY: HERMANOS SOLARES APARTADO 456 La Paz, Bolivia
Pier	

Export Carrier A.N.Y. AIRLINES	Port of Lading MIAMI	Goods engaged for delivery at
Port of Discharge LA PAZ, BOLIVIA	For transshipment to	

PARTICULARS FURNISHED BY SHIPPER

MARKS AND NUMBERS	NO. OF PKGS.	DESCRIPTION OF PACKAGES AND GOODS	GROSS WEIGHT	MEASURE-MENT
XYZ COMPANY LA PAZ P.O. 78-456 MADE IN USA CTN. #1	I CTN.	CONTAINING: OIL WELL DRILLING PARTS Partes para uso en la industria petrolera 6 #2489 0 RINGS -Anillos @ 2.89 10 #6723 GASKETS -Empaques @ 1.59 4 #8932 SEALS -Sellos @8.79 18 #8056 BUSHINGS-Bujes @9.30 I #5741 SHIM -Planchas TOTAL F.O.B. DALLAS, TEXAS	83 LBS. $ 17.34 15.90 35.16 167.40 12.68 $250.04	

FREIGHT CHARGES		PREPAID COLLECT	Received by _____ for shipment by ocean vessel, from port of loading to port of discharge, and from place of acceptance and/or oncarriage to place of delivery as indicated above, the goods as specified above in apparent good order and condition unless otherwise stated. The goods to be delivered at the above mentioned port of discharge or place of delivery, whichever applies, subject to terms contained on the reverse side hereof, to which the shipper agrees by accepting this bill of lading. In witness thereof three (3) Original Bills of Lading have been signed, if not otherwise stated above, one of which to be accomplished, the others to be void.
INLAND FREIGHT DALLAS/MIAMI	XXX.XX		
OCEAN FREIGHT (MIAMI/LA PAZ)	XXX.XX		
TOTAL	XXX.XX		A. FREIGHT FORWARDER, INC. MO. DAY YEAR B/L NO.

Figure 9.9   An intermodal bill of lading.

lading. It would not be accepted for payment if the importer's letter of credit specified an "on board ocean bill of lading."

If both you and your freight forwarder are doing your jobs, the forwarder will send a *booking request* to the chosen carrier as soon as you give the information he or she needs. Then, when the goods reach their country of destination, the airline or steamship line will send an *arrival notice* to the importer or his or her customs broker. Airlines usually phone, too, to make sure the message gets through. Then the carrier will provide customs with a *carrier's certificate* and *release order*; the consignee will give his or her broker or the carrier a *release order*; and the carrier will provide the consignee with a *freight release*. More and more, this transaction is being conducted electronically between the carrier, the broker, and U.S. Customs. It is known as electronic data interchange, or EDI.

GOVERNMENT FORMALITIES DOCUMENTS

American and foreign governments all want to know which goods enter and leave their countries. They need information, which is provided by documents, both for statistical purposes and to facilitate control. A country can't limit imports of certain goods, or restrict exports to certain countries, unless it knows what is moving in and out. In many countries, import and export documentation also helps maintain employment in the bureaucracy and preserve the power of bureaucrats, including in many cases the power to extract bribes from importers and exporters.

The government control documents we will mention in this section include:

- Import license, foreign exchange authorization
- Export license application, validated license
- Certificate of origin
- Inspection report
- Commercial, special, and consular invoices
- Shipper's export declaration
- Customs entries

The United States does not use import licenses (except for a few commodities) or foreign exchange authorizations. In some countries, however, importers have to present pro forma invoices to their government authorities to get permission to import goods and/or to pay for them in hard currency. This is becoming less common as economies are liberalized. Some developing countries used to play tricks with exporters' foreign exchange earnings, such as giving them only a small percentage in hard currency and giving them the rest in local currency at artificially set exchange rates. You may still run into this now and then.

American exporters have to be sure they don't ship to importers who need licenses or authorizations before these are actually in hand, unless payment is assured whether or not the importer gets his authorizations. Sometimes importers will instruct their vendors to ship before the licenses are in hand, assuming they can obtain the required documents the correct way (or another way). If you get paid up front, and have no qualms about this kind of arrangement, it's probably all right to go ahead and make the shipment.

Some foreign countries require all their exporters to be licensed and/or to apply for a license to make each shipment. That way they can control what leaves the country and make sure that at least most of the foreign exchange is sent to the country. This system is being increasingly subverted by the huge illegal trade in guns, diamonds, people, endangered animals and species of wood, and so forth. Globalization and the liberalization of trade, which make life easier for legitimate importers and exporters, also make life easier for the people who just want to make money whichever way they can do it.

Like many foreign countries, the United States requires that all significant outgoing shipments be accompanied by export licenses. Unlike many countries, however, U.S. exporters can give themselves licenses to ship most goods to most destinations. This is explained in chapter 10 in the section on regulations for exporters.

In the instances when a validated license is required, the U.S. exporter must complete an export license application. This is obtained from and sent to the U.S. Department of Commerce. If your shipment requires a validated license, *do not try to send it* unless and until this requirement is met (see chapter 10 for more information about export licensing in the United States).

Every national government wants to know the country of origin of imported goods, and often an exporter must provide this information by means of a formal document called a *certificate of origin*. Its purpose is to make it harder for importers to falsify the country of origin in order to pay lower duties, avoid quotas, or bring merchandise from prohibited countries. Where there are prohibitions, importers are sometimes tempted to transship in third countries and use false labeling and certificates of origin, for example, cigars made in Cuba but labeled as if they were from the Dominican Republic and shipped from that country. Customs inspectors are pretty sharp, however, and those who try to deceive them often get caught.

A U.S. exporter who needs a certificate of origin can usually obtain it from the nearest large chamber of commerce by sending three copies of his commercial invoice, a letter stating that the goods are of U.S. origin, and a check (usually around $30) for the chamber's fee. The chamber will certify on the invoice that the goods are of U.S. origin, and the certified invoice then becomes a certificate of origin. In some locations, the customs brokers' association has been certified to conduct the same service. This saves the exporter both time and money. A few countries (Israel, Japan, Australia, Chile, Singapore, and Nigeria) require special forms of the certificate; these are available from UNZ & Company on the Internet at www.unzco.com/storefront/Co.html. At the same site you can order a general certificate of origin and a CAFTA certificate, used in trade with countries of the Central America Free Trade Agreement. This is described in chapter 11. Also at www.unzco.com/storefront/doc.html you will find a list of all the import/export forms that UNZ sells. It also offers import/export publications, seminars, consulting, and software.

Chambers of commerce vary in their policies toward giving certificates of origin, but most accept the declarations of exporters that their products are of U.S. origin, at least until something happens to show that a particular exporter is dishonest. Chambers usually provide better service and lower fees to companies that are members, but most will also issue certificates of origin to nonmembers.

Shipments to the United States must be accompanied by certificates of origin if they are intended to be duty-free under the preferential arrangements that are in force with Israel, Canada, Mexico, most developing countries in general, and most Caribbean and Andean countries in particular. Imports under the Generalized System of Preferences (for developing countries) and from Caribbean and Andean nations require a form A certificate of origin. This is an international form that is theoretically not available in the United States. Your foreign exporter must provide it.

Country of origin declarations are complicated by the fact that relatively few goods are produced entirely in one country. A shirt can be made with Egyptian cotton, spun and woven in England, cut in the United States, and sewn and finished in the Dominican Republic. What is the country of origin? For Generalized System of Preferences (GSP), Caribbean Basin Initiative (CBI), and Andean Trade Preference Act (ATPA) shipments, the country of origin is generally the country from which the product is shipped to the United States, provided that at least 35 percent of the value of the product was added in that country (or sometimes in a combination of eligible countries). Under CBI and ATPA rules, as much as 15 percent of the 35 percent can be U.S.-made materials or components.

Suppose, for example, that the Egyptian cotton that goes into a shirt is valued at $0.40. When the finished cloth reaches the United States for cutting, the value has increased to $1.60. After the cloth is cut into parts of a shirt and delivered to the Dominican Republic, the value has reached $2.40. The FOB country of origin value of the finished shirt is $3.60. That makes the value added in the Dominican Republic $3.60 minus $2.40/3.60, or about 33 percent. By including the value of the processing in the United States, the 35 percent rule is satisfied, and the shirt can be considered a product of the Dominican Republic.

There are many cases in which governments or importers (and sometimes exporters as well) demand *inspection reports*. Some developing countries insist on inspection of outgoing shipments to make sure their exporters are not sending illegal or low-quality merchandise. Also, some developing countries want inspection of imported goods to make sure the importers are declaring the goods they actually bring in and are not falsifying the prices paid or other costs. Finally, some importers want goods to be inspected by independent organizations as a condition for payment to be made to the exporter.

The major inspection companies in the world are SGS of Switzerland and Bureau Veritas of France, Cotecna, and Internet Group. They have offices in major U.S. cities. In some cases inspections are performed by small independent firms or by government agencies, such as the U.S. Department of Agriculture and the FDA.

Your commercial invoice, discussed previously, is a government control as well as a commercial document. Importing country authorities use it to see information such as types and quantities of goods, countries of origin, and values.

As discussed previously, some countries have special forms for commercial invoices or special requirements as to the information that must be provided on these documents. Both exporters and importers should take steps to ensure that their invoices contain all the required data.

There are a few countries that still require documents known as *consular invoices*. This is a special form that must be "legalized" by a consulate of the country to which you are shipping. It is theoretically to prevent prohibited or overpriced, or in some cases underpriced, goods from being shipped to a country, but its main function is probably to give some countries' consulates a bit of extra income.

Each commodity shipped from the United States must be accompanied by a shipper's export declaration, or SED, if it is worth more than $2,500, requires a validated export license, or is being sent to a controlled country (currently Cuba, Iraq, Iran, Libya, North Korea, and Sudan). The limit is lower for shipments that go by mail. An exception was made early in 1991 for shipments to Canada that are to *remain* in that country. A shipper's export declaration is a document on which exporters report their shipments to the U.S. Department of Commerce, both for statistical purposes and to help in enforcement of export control regulations. To complete it you need the schedule B numbers of the products you are exporting. These can be found on the Web site www.census.gov/foreign-trade/schedules/b/#search. Schedule B and Harmonized System numbers are usually the same, but there can be small differences.

The SED forms can be purchased from the superintendent of documents, from UNZ & Company, or from a good commercial stationer. Your friendly government will tell you how to complete this document on its Web site www.census.gov/foreign-trade/regulations/forms/correct-way-to-complete-the-sed.pdf. Because carriers charge extra if you use the paper version of this transaction, there is a real incentive to move to electronic filing. Nearly all freight forwarders now file this way.

Finally, there is a *customs entry*, which you or your broker must file with customs authorities when you import. There are many types of customs forms, however, the most important for you will probably be the immediate delivery entry and the entry summary. These will be discussed in chapter 10.

A FEW MORE THOUGHTS ON DOCUMENTS

Some of the information in this chapter does not apply entirely to trade with Canada and Mexico because of provisions of NAFTA, or to the Dominican Republic and Central American countries because of DR-CAFTA. These trade agreements are discussed in chapter 11.

Sometimes documents have to be translated from English to a foreign language, or vice versa. There are services that let you send your documents to them electronically and receive translations the same way, with very fast turnaround, but you should still have their work checked by a native speaker. Free translations done online or with special software are not, repeat, not good enough for international trade documents.

Most important, the computer revolution is in the process of changing radically the way documents are written and moved. The Irwin Brown Company in New Orleans, for example, is a customs broker and foreign freight forwarder that has established electronic data interchange (EDI) with its agents, customers, and import/ export service firms. They were hit hard by Hurricane Katrina but were back in operation in a few days, with the help of backup files. An exporter can flash information to Irwin Brown or a similar company, and that company can create documents to transmit electronically to steamship lines and other parties to the transaction. On the import side, the broker can receive electronic arrival notices from the steamship lines and then communicate by computer with import customers and with U.S. customs. The U.S. CBP is strongly encouraging electronic data transaction of documents through its electronic data interchange and the automated broker interface. The latter is used with a release form to allow for delivery of cargo, with an entry permit. The U.S. Customs and Border Patrol uses the Automated Clearing House (ACH) network, whereby customs duties are simply deducted from the importer's bank account. Information is available on the Web at www.cbp.gov/xp/cgov/ import/operations_support/automated_systems/ach. The disadvantage is that if for any reason too much duty is deducted, it may take quite a while for the importer to get a reimbursement.

Import/export service firms that do not keep up with the computer revolution are in danger of losing out to those that do. There are several firms that sell software, especially for importers and exporters, such as Kewill (www.tradepointsys.com) and Exit (www.exitsinc.com). Most companies that offer this kind of product will let you try it free of charge.

Are you ready to go on to the exciting world of foreign trade regulations? If so, turn to the next chapter and plunge in.

SOURCES OF INFORMATION AND HELP

To document your shipments correctly, you need information about which documents are required and how to complete them. In some cases, such as the Prior Notice under the Bioterrorism Act, you must also pay attention to *when* a document should be delivered. All this information is available in laws, but wading through them is a job for legislators and lawyers. Therefore, importers and exporters rely on information about documentation requirements that is available from secondary sources. Several of these sources are mentioned in this chapter.

- *Exporters' Encyclopedia* is a well-established and excellent publication of Dun & Bradstreet. Address: D&B Corporation, 103 JFK Parkway, Short Hills, NJ 07078; Phone: (800) 234-3867; Web site: www.dnb.com.

- Consulate General of Brazil in Miami provides the details that should be on a Brazilian commercial invoice at www.brazilmiami.org/eng/consaff_cominv.php.

- *Importing into the United States*, published by the U.S. Customs Service and available from the Superintendent of Documents, provides a detailed description of invoicing requirements. You can get it free on the Internet at www.cbp.gov/nafta/cgov/pdf/iius.pd; Phone: (866) 512-1800; Fax: (202) 512-2104.

- Bill of exchange, a simple export payment document. An example is available on EXPORT911's Web site at www.export911.com/e911/export/bill.htm.

- Letters of credit (LCs). Information about LCs is available from the Credit Research Foundation at www.crfonline.org/orc/cro/cro-91.html. Address: Credit Research Foundation, 8840 Columbia 100 Parkway, Columbia, MD 21045; Phone: (410) 740-5499; Fax: (410) 740-4620.

- *Basic Guide to Exporting*, a vital book for new exporters, is available free from UNZ & Company's Web site at www.unzco.com/basicguide.

- Special forms of certificates of origin are available free from UNZ & Company's Web site at www.unzco.com/storefront/Co.html#Israel.

- Import and export forms are available for a charge from UNZ & Company. Address: 201 Circle Drive North, Suite 104, Piscataway, NJ 08854; Phone: (800) 631-3098; Fax: (732) 868-0260; Web site: www.unzco.com/storefront/doc.html.

- Schedule B numbers of the products you are exporting can be found on the U.S. Census Bureau's Web site at www.census.gov/foreign-trade/schedules/b/#search.

- U.S. CBP's automated clearing house whereby customs duties are automatically deducted from your bank account. Web site: www.cbp.gov/xp/cgov/import/operations_support/automated_systems/ach.

- Kewill sells software specifically tailored for importers and exporters. Address: 44 Franklin Street, Nashua, NH 03064; Phone: (603) 889-3200; Fax: (603) 889-9393; Web site: www.tradepointsys.com.

- Exits., Inc. sells software specifically tailored for importers and exporters. Address: 19 Blanchard Road, Easton, CT 06612; Phone: (888) 899-0989; Fax: (203) 374-8733; Web site: www.exitsinc.com.

- The *Harmonized Tariff Schedule of the United States (t2001)* can be found on the U.S. International Trade Commission's Web site at www.usitc.gov/tata/index.htm.

- National import specialists work for the U.S. Customs and Border Patrol. They are responsible for classifying imported merchandise that enters the United States. Web site: www.cbp.gov.

10

The Regulation of Foreign Trade

Laws and regulations are a fact of life everywhere in the world. This is especially true with regard to the import/export business and is increasingly true since the events of 9/11. On the import side, laws exist in part because countries want to earn revenue from customs duties, to protect their industries from foreign competition, and to keep harmful products from entering the country. There are now special sensitivities regarding food and beverage products entering the United States and other countries. On the export side, regulations are made to increase exports, to keep some products in the country for use there, and to keep strategic materials out of the hands of foreign competitors or enemies. Note that export regulation cuts both ways because it includes both incentives and restrictions.

This chapter looks at some of the regulations on international trade, why they exist, and how to deal with them. Note that I didn't say "how to get around them." In most cases, that can't be done legally. We'll start with our friends in U.S. Customs and Border Protection, which is part of the Department of Homeland Security.

U.S. CUSTOMS AND BORDER PROTECTION

The U.S. Customs and Border Protection, or CBP, is a huge governmental department, with some 44,000 employees. It is headquartered in Washington, DC, and has offices throughout the

United States and abroad. According to the CBP Web site, on a typical day in fiscal year 2006, it processed more than 1.4 million people and nearly 70,900 truck, rail, and sea containers. On a typical day it collected more than $84 million in fees, duties, and tariffs. It made arrests for illegal conduct and seized narcotics and other contraband goods at 326 ports of entry into the United States.

Customs is responsible for enforcing laws with regard to both incoming and outgoing cargo. It can inspect part or all of any shipment and is normally not held liable for damage to products that might occur in the inspection process, although it has worked hard to develop nonintrusive ways of inspecting cargo, such as high-energy X rays that can see into a shipping container. It works closely with other U.S. government agencies and with the customs departments in foreign countries.

After September 11, 2001, CBP increased the percentage of cargo inspected and also improved its inspection procedures. This caused delays at ports and accelerated the development and use of technology to make inspections faster and more effective. It also instituted several systems to make inspections better and more efficient. The main ones are shown in Figure 10.1.

Your First Contact

To get a feel for Customs and what it's all about, you might want to log on to the Customs' Web site at www.cbp.gov. Click on "Import" or "Export" and you will see links to a large amount of information. If you don't find what you want, try the search function. To find telephone numbers, click on "Contacts," then "Field Operations Offices," and then the name of the city in which, or nearest to which, the port you want to use is located. You should get a list of offices (not people's names) and telephone numbers. You can start by calling the Public Information Office or the Customer Service Center to ask who can answer your question.

If you get the idea that Customs doesn't make it easy for you to contact someone by phone, you are right. All 44,000 employees are too busy to spend much time talking with new importers and exporters. If you get the name and phone number of someone who can and is willing to answer specific questions, *hang on to it*.

Container Security Initiative (CSI). Employed in many foreign seaports to prevent the smuggling of terrorists and weapons.

Customs-Trade Partnership Against Terrorism (C-TPAT). Participating U.S. importers and import service firms can receive expedited clearance of their shipments.

Free and Secure Trade (FAST). Allows participating U.S. importers and import service firms, which are in C-TPAT, to receive expedited clearance at land borders.

Automated Commercial Environment (ACE). Allows participating importers and import service firms to see their account information (with CBP) on the Internet.

National Targeting Center (NTC). Links various law enforcement agencies to help the CBP determine which incoming people and cargo could present risks and should therefore be inspected.

Border Release Advanced Selectivity System (BRASS). Frequent shipments of the same product across land borders can be cleared through CBP almost automatically.

Figure 10.1   Antiterrorism systems of U.S. Customs and Border Patrol.

Your concerns will probably relate to specific products that you are considering importing. For each such product, you will want to know its rate of duty and other regulations including how it should be marked. The rate of duty on a product depends on its tariff classification and Harmonized System (HS) number and its country of origin. This is discussed in the next section.

When you have the HS number for your product, you can go (on the CBP Web site) to "Imports" and click on "Duty Rates/HTS" and then on "2007 Harmonized Tariff Schedule (HTS) by Chapter." Click "OK" to leave the Customs' Web site, and you should be directed to the International Trade Commission (ITC) site and see the table of contents of the HTS. Click on the chapter you want and search for your commodity.

For complicated rulings there are national import specialists (NIS) connected with Newark/New York Seaport Customs, by phone at (646) 733-3000 and by fax at (646) 733-3250. If you call, you will get a recording that says you can leave a message but suggests you call the Customs office in your port of entry. If you leave a message and don't get a callback, try again every couple of days for a couple of weeks, or send a letter to Director, National Commodity Specialist Division, U.S. Customs Service, One Penn Plaza, New York, NY 10119. There is information about how to do this on pages 40–42 of the book *Importing into the United States*, which you can get free on the Internet.

An important task of the NIS people is to issue *binding* rulings on the classification and therefore the rate of duty on your product, which your customs broker can present to Customs at whichever port your goods come into. This is important for products that are hard to classify because they aren't exactly like any of the thousands of items in the tariff schedule. An example I ran into recently is ground coffee from Colombia, presweetened with powdered, unrefined sugar cane juice (*panela* in Spanish). To get a binding ruling, send a request in writing to the National Commodity Specialist Division, U.S. Customs and Border Protection, Attn. Classification Ruling Requests, One Penn Plaza, 11th Floor, New York, NY 10119. Please include all the information that will be needed to make a classification, including the product's composition, specifications, and perhaps a photograph. You can send a sample if you wish, but it will not be returned. If you don't hear from Customs in a few weeks, you can call the number in the preceding paragraph and leave a message that you are inquiring about the binding ruling you requested. Be sure to give your name, company name, type of product, and the date of your letter of request.

The Harmonized System

On January 1, 1989, the United States adopted a new method of classifying and coding products in international trade called the Harmonized System. This long set of definitions is very logical and has been adopted by most of the world's nations; it replaced several separate coding and classification systems that made statistical comparisons nearly impossible. It was very hard to identify the same product in different countries' statistical publications, which used different languages, descriptions, and coding systems.

The Harmonized System classifies thousands of products grouped into 21 sections and 99 chapters. Figure 10.2 is a page from the *Harmonized Tariff Schedule of the United States* (2007). This particular page, from chapter 33 of the schedule, includes "mixtures of odoriferous substances." If you follow the classification down, you will see that the category: "Of a kind used in the food or drink industries: Not containing alcohol" is HS number 3302.10.10.00. Customs' declarations should quantify the shipment in kilograms rather than some other unit of measure such as number (no.) or dozens (dz). These products are free of duty from column 1 countries and are charged at 25 percent from column 2 countries (of which there are very few). If you look at the next product, which *does* contain alcohol, you will see there is a duty based on quantity (44 cents per kilogram) in addition to the 25 percent of value. Also, according to the footnote, the product might be subject to federal excise tax.

In column 1, "general" refers to almost all countries of the world; "special" refers to countries with which the United States has some kind of special trading relationship, which usually results in lower duties. If any such relationship applies to the product, there will be symbols and sometimes duty rates in this column. In April 2007, the list of special arrangements and their symbols was as shown in Figure 10.3.

The products included and the rules for each of these trade agreements are different. An asterisk or a plus sign after a letter usually means that a country will lose its privilege of free or reduced duty on a specific product if, in any year, it exports too much of it to the United States. "Too much" is usually defined as a percent of total U.S. imports. If you are confused, be nice to your customs broker because he or she can be very helpful.

More about Customs Duties

American customs duties range from 0 to about 120 percent, and the average is probably below 3 percent. This is one of the lowest average rates in the world. Duties raise money for the federal government and also give domestic producers a little protection against products from abroad. They are negotiated in international rounds

Harmonized Tariff Schedule of the United States (2007) (Rev. 1)
Annotated for Statistical Reporting Purposes

VI
33-4

Heading/ Subheading	Stat. Suf- fix	Article Description	Unit of Quantity	Rates of Duty		
				1		2
				General	Special	
3301 (con.)		Essential oils (terpeneless or not), including concretes and absolutes; resinoids; extracted oleoresins; concentrates of essential oils in fats, in fixed oils, in waxes or the like, obtained by enfleurage or maceration; terpenic by-products of the deterpenation of essential oils; aqueous distillates and aqueous solutions of essential oils (con.):				
3301.30.00	00	Resinoids	kg	Free		Free
3301.90		Other:				
3301.90.10		Extracted oleoresins		3.8%	Free (A*,AU,BH, CA,CL,E,IL,J, JO,MA,MX, P,SG)	25%
	10	Paprika	kg			
	20	Black pepper	kg			
	50	Other	kg			
3301.90.50	00	Other	kg	Free		20%
3302		Mixtures of odoriferous substances and mixtures (including alcoholic solutions) with a basis of one or more of these substances, of a kind used as raw materials in industry; other preparations based on odoriferous substances, of a kind used for the manufacture of beverages:				
3302.10		Of a kind used in the food or drink industries:				
3302.10.10	00	Not containing alcohol	kg	Free		25%
3302.10.20	00	Containing alcohol: Containing not over 20 percent of alcohol by weight	kg	Free 1/		44¢/kg + 25% 1/
3302.10.40	00	Containing over 20 percent of alcohol by weight: Preparations requiring only the addition of ethyl alcohol or water to produce a beverage suitable for human consumption: Containing over 20 percent but not over 50 percent of alcohol by weight ...	kg	8.4¢/kg + 1.9% 1/	Free (A,AU,BH, CA,CL,E,IL,J,JO, MA,MX, P,SG) 1/	88¢/kg + 25% 1/
3302.10.50	00	Containing over 50 percent of alcohol by weight	kg	17¢/kg + 1.9% 1/	Free (A,AU,BH, CA,CL,E,IL,J,JO, MA,MX, P,SG) 1/	$1.76/kg + 25% 1/
3302.10.90	00	Other	kg	Free		50%
3302.90		Other:				
3302.90.10		Containing no alcohol or not over 10 percent of alcohol by weight		Free		88¢/kg + 50%
	10	Perfume oil mixtures and blends, consisting of products ready for use as finished perfume bases	kg			
	50	Other	kg			
3302.90.20		Containing over 10 percent of alcohol by weight ...		Free		88¢/kg + 75%
	10	Perfume oil mixtures and blends, consisting of products ready for use as finished perfume bases	kg			
	50	Other	kg			

1/ Imports under this provision may be subject to Federal Excise Tax (26 USC. 5001).

Figure 10.2   Part of a page from the *Harmonized Tariff Schedule of the United States*.

Programs Giving Special Tariff Treatment	
Preferential Program	*Symbol*
Africa Growth and Opportunity Act	D
Agreement on Trade in Civil Aircraft	C
Agreement on Trade in Pharmaceutical Products	K
Andean Trade Preference Act,	J, J* or
Andean Trade Promotion and Drug Eradication Act	J+
Automotive Products Trade Act	B
Caribbean Basin Initiative	E or E*
Dominican Republic-Central America United States Free Trade Agreement Implementation Act	P or P+
Generalized System of Preferences	A, A*, or A+
North American Free Trade Agreement, Goods of Canada under note 12 to the Tariff Schedule	CA
North American Free Trade Agreement, Goods of Mexico under note 12 to the Tariff Schedule	MX
United States-Australia Free Trade Agreement	AU
United States-Bahrain Free Trade Agreement (Implementation Act)	BH
Caribbean Basin Trade Partnership Act	L
United States-Chile Free Trade Agreement	CL
United States-Israel Free Trade Area	IL
United States-Jordan Free Trade Area Implementation Act	JO
United States-Morocco Free Trade Agreement Implementation Act	MA
United States-Singapore Free Trade Agreement	SG
Uruguay Round Concessions on Intermediate Chemicals for Dyes	L

Figure 10.3   Preferential tariff programs of the United States as of January 2007.

under the auspices of the World Trade Organization (WTO) and must be ratified by Congress. The executive branch of government likes to have "fast track authority" to negotiate trade agreements, which means that Congress can only ratify or reject an agreement as a whole. If our legislators debated tariff concessions on individual products, the talk would go on for eternity.

Nearly all duty rates are ad valorem, which means a percentage of value, but they can also be "specific" (so much per item or per kilo) or "mixed" (ad valorem plus specific). Specific duties encourage importation of better grades or qualities of an item because the incidence of duty (percentage of the value of the item that is added by tariffs) goes down as the value increases.

The United States charges duty on the first cost of an item, which is normally what you pay in the country of origin (anywhere from ex factory to FOB vessel, depending on the terms of sale). The United States does not charge duties on international transportation and insurance, although some countries do this. If you buy from an agent abroad, it may be better to use one who works for you rather than for your supplier. This is because commissions paid by a buyer (you) are not dutiable, while commissions paid by a seller are dutiable.

If there is a high duty on your product, you may want to consult a customs attorney or at least a good broker to see whether there is any way it can be reduced. The most common way is to modify the product so as to change the HS number to one that has lower rates of duty. For example, if you have a briefcase with an outer covering of cloth, made in Italy, the duty will be 20 percent. Remove the fabric, and it will drop to just 8 percent.

Marking and Labeling

In general, U.S. law requires that consumer products be marked with the country of origin in such a way that the final buyer can see and read the mark. The country name in English should be used, but additional languages are permitted as well. The type and location of the marks vary. The marks should be on a sticker glued to the bottom of a crystal ashtray, die-stamped on most metal parts, sewn in the back of the neck of shirts, and so on. You can usually find similar products in stores and see how they are marked. There is a CBP publication on marking, which you will find it on the agency's Web site at www.cbp.gov/linkhandler/cgov/toolbox/publications/trade/markingo.ctt/markingo.doc.

There are some products, such as clocks, for which separate marking of each major part is required. There are also cases of "transformation" that are not considered "substantial." For example, crude pistachio nuts from Iran that are roasted and bagged in the United States must still be identified as pistachios from Iran because they are nearly the same product.

In a few instances, containers for products must be marked separately, in case they are emptied in the United States and then sold.

Marking of raw and intermediate materials and components is done mainly for Customs and not for the consumer. Thus, if you import a keg of nails, you need to mark only the keg. If you then repackage the nails into small boxes for consumers, put your name and location on the box. The final consumer will not know the country of origin, but if anything is wrong with the nails, a lawyer who wants to know where they came from can contact you.

Proper marking is no laughing matter. If you import 100,000 candy bars, and the Swiss exporter doesn't put his country's name on them, you won't be able to sell them until they are marked properly. You might be able to get them released from Customs by posting a bond, but you cannot deliver them to a customer until you have marked them, redelivered a sample to Customs, and received approval. Sometimes Customs will even clear and release goods that are improperly marked and then (within 30 days) request redelivery. If you can't take the shipment back to Customs, you will be assessed a marking duty and a penalty.

You should also look at products on the shelf and ask a broker or an importer what other information should be on the product or its package. Some possibilities are instructions for laundering (apparel), ingredients and nutritional content (processed foods), and safety warnings (cigarettes). It is illegal to sell an imported product that lacks any of the required information.

In addition, you might ask which other federal agencies regulate the importation or sale of your product. There are several possibilities, including the Food and Drug Administration, the Consumer Product Safety Commission, and the Department of Transportation. These will be discussed later in this chapter.

You may need a license or a permit from a government agency to import any of the following products.

- Alcoholic beverages
- Animals and animal products

- Drugs (some kinds)
- Firearms and ammunition
- Fruits and nuts
- Meat and meat products
- Milk, dairy, and cheese products
- Plants and plant products
- Poultry and poultry products
- Petroleum and petroleum products
- Vegetables

There are also special restrictions on the following:

- Art materials
- Cultural property
- Electronics products (some kinds)
- Hazardous (toxic or flammable) materials
- Household appliances
- Toys and children's articles

GETTING DEEPER INTO CUSTOMS

In some cases, especially with apparel, it can be hard to correctly classify a product. Try it yourself: Are chocolate-covered cherries fruit or candy? Is a pointed piece of wire, with threads but no slot in the head, a screw or a nail? If you are in this kind of situation, try to make an appointment to show your product to a customs inspector. The inspector may not be able to look at the item and tell you the exact classification and the correct rate of duty, but in such cases, will be able to contact a national import specialist in New York. If you can't get an appointment with an inspector, perhaps your customs broker can help you figure out the correct classification. If this doesn't work, import a small quantity and have the broker guess at the classification. If the broker guesses wrong, the customs inspector will probably supply the correct

HS number. You can also use the Customs Rulings Online Search System (CROSS) to look for the correct classification of a product. Go to http://rulings.cbp.gov and click on "Downloadable Rulings."

In some cases, a customs specialist can help you by suggesting product modifications that will lead to a reduced rate of duty. For example, dry onion powder from developing countries is charged a higher rate of duty than dry onion *flakes*. Maybe your buyer will take small flakes instead of powder. There have been many interesting cases including one a few years ago, before the Harmonized System was adopted: the trademark on a shipment of blue jeans was held to be ornamental because the *e* in the mark was slanted rather than straight, and that increased the rate of duty.

Customs Procedures

When your goods arrive at a port of entry, the airline or steamship line should notify the party named on the documents. Of course, you should know, long before that, which ship or flight will be carrying your merchandise. You will want to act fast because you have only a few working days to pick up the goods before they are taken to a customs warehouse. If that happens, you will have to pay cartage to the warehouse, storage charges, cartage out, and an extra broker's fee.

As stated before, you can clear shipments worth less than $2,000 (less than $250 for most textile, leather, and a few other products from most countries of origin) with an *informal* entry form. If the value is over $2,000 or if the shipment contains textile or leather products and you try to clear it yourself, you will be asked to complete an entry/immediate delivery form 3461 and pay a duty deposit. Figure 10.4 lists the kinds of information you will need for this form.

You must also sign the following statement: "I hereby make application for entry/immediate delivery. I certify that the above information is accurate, the bond is sufficient, valid, and current, and that all requirements of 19 CFR Part 142 have been met." The CFR is the huge, huge *Code of Federal Regulations* of the United States.

Contents of an Entry/Immediate Delivery

Arrival date of the goods and entry date through Customs

Type of entry (usually "Consumption") and entry number

Port of arrival and number of your entry bond (not always needed)

Customs file numbers of the broker, consignee, and importer (whichever of these are involved in the transaction)

Name of the "importer of record"

Codes for the carrier and the ship or flight

Where the goods are when you file the entry

The U.S. port (again), carrier's manifest number, general order (GO) number, and total value

A description of the merchandise

The quantity, HS number, country of origin, and manufacturer number for each type of merchandise

---

Figure 10.4   Contents of an entry/immediate delivery form.

As you can see, this entry form is not one that you can easily fill out yourself the first time you try it, and customs employees probably will not help you. You should probably use a customs broker at least the first time, so you will have an example to follow.

After filing the entry/immediate delivery form, the broker has 10 working days to file an *entry summary* with the commercial invoice and other documents and with a check for the duty. Customs then has 30 days in which to accept or reject it. UNZ & Company sells both of the preceding forms, but their prices will frighten you. Customs offices have them as well, and you can find and complete them on the Internet at the following address: Entry/Immediate Delivery: https://forms.customs.gov/customsrf/getformharness.asp?FormName=cf-3461-form.xft and Entry Summary: https://forms.customs.gov/customsrf/getformharness.asp?FormName=cf-7501-form.xft.

The entry summary (Form 7501) asks for 40 numbered kinds of information, which can be summarized as shown in Figure 10.5. The entry summary for goods that are under quota, such as

---

Contents of an Entry Summary

Entry number, type, and date

Port code, bond number; type of bond

Manufacturer's identification number and reference number

Foreign port, mode of transportation, bill of lading, or air waybill number

Country of origin, exporting country, export date, broker or importer
number, importer name and address

Ultimate consignee name, address, and number; importing carrier, U.S. port,
import date

Merchandise commodity numbers, weights, quantities, values, duty rates, duty
amounts, taxes, other charges

Location of goods in United States

Figure 10.5   Contents of an entry summary form.

dairy products, must be filed when the goods arrive in the United
States.

In the United States, you will normally have your merchandise before the duty is paid. How does Customs know you will pay
the duty if any is due? That is one function of the bond that was
mentioned in chapter 9.

In some cases, especially when goods are highly perishable,
your broker may be able to get them precleared so they will be
released from customs as soon as they arrive in the United States.
This is becoming increasingly common, especially as more shipping lines, customs brokers, and ports begin using the automated
manifest system (AMS) and the automated broker interface (with
Customs) (ABI). You may, however, be charged a small extra fee
for this.

The final step in the entry process is called *liquidation*. This is
when a commodity specialist reviews the entry, anytime within
one year, and decides whether the proper duty was paid. When
this happens, you will receive a notice that liquidation has taken
place. If you feel that Customs has charged too much for duty, you
have 90 days from the date of liquidation to file a protest. If this

protest is denied, you have 180 days from the date of the denial in which to file a summons with the U.S. Court of International Trade. This brings you up into the big time, and you will need a big-time customs attorney. One rarely hears anyone complain that Customs charged *too little* duty.

There is also a Customs user fee charged on formal entries of goods other than those which come from Canada and Mexico under provisions of the North American Free Trade Agreement. This fee is 0.21 percent of "Customs value," with a minimum of $25 and a maximum of $485 per entry. In most cases, there are small fees (no more than $9) charged on informal entries as well.

Quotas on Imports

Most textiles and apparel, cheese, chocolate, and a few other products are subject to U.S. import quotas. They serve to protect domestic industry by limiting the supply and therefore raising the prices of foreign products to U.S. consumers, and by allocating production among supplying countries. For example, a quota on Swiss cheese from Switzerland limits that country's sales to the United States and so permits other countries to take part of the market.

Some of the quotas are *absolute* (fixed amount), and others are *tariff rate quotas*, which means that the rate of duty increases each year when a certain quantity of an item has cleared U.S. Customs. You can see a complete list of items under each type of quota at www.cbp.gov/ImageCache/cgov/content/publications/quotas_2edoc/v1/quotas.doc.

Foreign governments need systems for deciding which of their companies will be able to use their quotas in the U.S. market, and, of course, they want to get the highest possible value of exports from the allowable quantities. They use different systems to allocate quotas, including auctioning them in blocks. Holders of quotas are often allowed to sell them to other suppliers, who hope to get higher prices from their U.S. buyers.

Customs and Border Protection helps many countries enforce their quota arrangements by requiring that import shipments of quota goods be accompanied by visas issued by the designated authorities in the exporting countries. This means that if your shipment of canned tuna from Thailand reaches U.S. Customs and there is no visa among the documents, it probably cannot be entered. You can apply to the Thai consulate for a visa, but it will not be granted unless the responsible agency in Bangkok gives its approval. If you get tangled up in the Electronic Certification System (eCERT) and the Electronic Visa Information System (ELVIS), you will probably wish it were the Elvis from Graceland, not Customs.

Classification specialists in district Customs offices should know the details of quotas on the items they handle, but even they cannot always tell you the annual quota on a specific item from a specific country or how much of the year's quota is still unfilled. They can, however, translate the HS number of your product into a "Quota Category Number" and tell you where to look to find the quota level and its current status of fulfillment.

Occasionally, a product will be in a special *watched* status. In such a case, you will need a visa to import it even if it is not actually under quota. This can happen, for example, if imports of a product are increasing quickly and are suspected of harming industry in the United States.

Extra Duties

There are occasionally circumstances in which importers are charged extra duties. For example, if the U.S. government determines that a foreign country is subsidizing its exports, and that for members of the GATT (General Agreement on Tariffs and Trade), imports of the subsidized goods are hurting American producers, a *countervailing duty* can be applied to counteract the subsidy. Also, if the government determines that a country is dumping goods on the U.S. market (selling in the United States at less than the fair market value in the country of origin), a special duty may be charged.

In addition, there are sometimes extra duties or import prohibitions to try to pressure foreign countries into opening their markets to U.S. goods or protecting intellectual property (patents, copyrights, etc.) of U.S. firms. Several years ago, for example, very high duties levied on several Brazilian products had a lot to do with opening Brazil's market to U.S. computer products.

Temporary Entries

If you want to ship goods through the United States without paying duty on them, say from Brazil to Canada, you can often do so with a bond and a special kind of customs entry. The same applies to goods that are in the country temporarily for repair or to be exhibited in a trade show. Your customs broker can help you with this kind of temporary importation under bond, or TIB.

You can also use a special customs entry to bring goods into the United States and warehouse them, without paying duty, until you either reexport them or enter them into the commerce of the United States. An importer can do minor processing, such as repackaging, while goods are in a bonded warehouse. Most of these are located near seaports or major airports, and some specialize in specific kinds of merchandise.

You can also bring goods into a *foreign trade zone*, an area under Customs control in major ports and some inland cities where you can do almost any kind of processing. You can, for example, import foreign parts for small engines and combine them with U.S. parts in a foreign trade zone. If you export the engines, you never pay duty on the imported parts. If you sell them in the United States, you can pay duty on the imported parts or on the finished engines, whichever is lower. The higher the duties on your imported goods, and the larger the volume, the more likely you are to benefit from using a bonded warehouse or a foreign trade zone.

Finally, you can bring goods such as components into the United States under a *drawback* entry. If you later reexport them, even if they have been combined with U.S. components to make finished goods, you can "draw back" most of the duty that was paid. You can even draw back duty if the components you export are not the same ones you brought in with a drawback entry, as long as they are functionally identical.

There are still other types of customs entries that you can

find out about in the book *Importing into the United States*. You can download and print it at www.cbp.gov/linkhandler/.gov/ toolbox/publications/trade/iius.ctt/iius.pdf. Yes, it will cost you some ink and 211 sheets of paper (or 106 back to back), but you'll get a lot for your money.

OTHER FEDERAL REGULATIONS

There are numerous federal laws that affect both domestic and imported goods. The detailed text of each is printed in the *Code of Federal Regulations*, but importers usually get information about them from the government agencies that are responsible for enforcing them. The following is a summary of some of these laws.

Food Products

The Federal Food, Drug, and Cosmetic Act is the basic legislation governing imports of products that go into or on the body, including both human and animal bodies; and the responsible agency is the Department of Health and Human Services's Food and Drug Administration (FDA) in Rockville, Maryland. The telephone number of the Division of Import Operations and Policy is (301) 443-6553. Each FDA district is the final authority for products entering through ports in its area, so you can't get a ruling in Florida that says your canned strawberries can be imported in Oregon.

Moreover, the FDA will not analyze your product before you import it to tell you whether it will pass inspection. You should probably have it analyzed yourself by a private company that is familiar with FDA regulations on such things as microbiological and chemical substances. Otherwise, you will risk bringing in a shipment that cannot enter into the United States. One such company is Bodycote FPL in Portland, Oregon (tel. 503-253-9136). FPL is like IBM—initials of words that most people have forgotten. In this case, it stands for Food Products Laboratory.

In addition, the FDA will no longer tell you whether the label on your can, bottle, or package is satisfactory. This is important because there are numerous requirements about information on labels on food products, and they are changed periodically. A significant example is the special nutrition label, which must be on most processed foods whether produced in the United States or abroad. Very small manufacturers are generally exempt from this requirement. The rules governing food labeling are complicated. They are on the FDA's Web site at www.cfsan.fda.gov/label.html.

If you are considering importing processed foods, you may want to use the services of a specialized consultant such as Phoenix Regulatory Associates in Sterling, Virginia (tel. 703-406-0906), to make sure your product is acceptable. You could use the same kind of label information as a similar product and try it on a small shipment, but be sure to ask Customs when that shipment comes whether the label is all right. Otherwise, the inspector might overlook a technicality but stop your next (larger) shipment. Copying someone else's nutrition label would be risky because the composition of food products can vary greatly.

Some kinds of food products must meet certain criteria, known as a *statement of identity*, in order to use names such as "catsup." Requirements for "catsup," "dill pickles," and so on are spelled out in the *Code of Federal Regulations*, title 21, parts 100–169. The label should also give the net weight of the product in ounces (in the lower 30 percent of the label), the ingredients in descending order of predominance by weight, and the name and place of business of the manufacturer, packer, or distributor,

There is a category of "low acid or acidified" canned foods for which the producer must obtain a special food canning establishment, or FCE, number in order to export to the United States. I have a friend in Bolivia who made the mistake of shipping products that required an FCE number without getting one. Customs held the goods in Miami while the exporter completed the forms and sent them to the FDA. Unfortunately, the FDA continued rejecting the forms, on technicalities, until the exporter had to abandon the goods.

The FDA is keeping up with the times. In 1997, it began using the Electronic Entry Processing System (EEPS). This system requires the use of an FDA code for each commodity. For example, the product code for Chianti wine, with 12 750-milliliter bottles per case, is 32BCP02. That is derived as follows:

- **Industry:** Alcoholic beverage = 32
- **Class:** Wine = B
- **Subclass:** Glass (bottles) = C
- **PIC (process):** Cultured / cured = P
- **Product:** Wine, red (still) = 02

Your best bet is probably to ask (and pay) a customs broker to find out your product code. If you want to figure it out yourself, try the FDA's product code builder at www.accessdata.fda.gov/scripts/ora/pcb/pcb.cfm. There is a tutorial, which is very helpful.

Meat and Poultry

Fresh and frozen meat, poultry, and related products are allowed only from foreign processing plants that have been approved to export to the United States. The fears are that meat from diseased animals will be processed and shipped or that conditions in the slaughterhouse will be unsanitary. Even some industrialized Western countries cannot sell raw meat to the United States because none of their factories has the necessary certification. The occasional problems with mad cow disease and hoof-and-mouth disease have shown the importance of regulating imports of animals, meat, and hides.

The principal agencies involved with these products are the Food Safety and Inspection Service (FSIS) and the Animal and Plant Health Inspection Service (APHIS), both of the U.S. Department of Agriculture (USDA). For some kinds of poultry, such as quail, you should also consult the Fish and Wildlife Service of the Department of the Interior. Some key telephone numbers are as follows:

- FSIS, Import Inspection Division, (402) 221-7400
- APHIS, animal concerns, (301) 734-7885
- APHIS, plant concerns, (301) 734-8896
- Fish and Wildlife Service, (703) 358-2093

While I'm at it, here are some other phone numbers that you might need:

- Center for Food Safety and Applied Nutrition (CFSAN), Office of Food Labeling, (202) 205-4606
- CFSAN, Office of Seafood, (202) 418-3150

Fresh Fruits and Vegetables

Because of increased health consciousness and other factors, U.S. imports of fruits and vegetables have skyrocketed and are still growing. When fresh produce comes in counterseasonal to production in this country, consumers and intermediaries are very pleased and U.S. producers are not hurt. In fact, some U.S. farming organizations have stabilized their incomes throughout the year by importing as well as producing in the United States.

Fresh produce imports are limited to specific items from specific countries, which have been approved by APHIS, which also inspects some export shipments, such as cherries going to Japan. In both inbound and outbound trade, the main purpose is to prevent the entry of insect pests that might damage a country's agriculture. You can see lists, by country, of fresh fruits and vegetables that have been approved for import to the United States. They were listed in the USDA's *Fresh Fruits and Vegetables Import Manual* at www.aphis.usda.gov/import_export/plants/manuals/ports/downloads/fv.pdf as of May 2007, but the Web site seems to change frequently. If you want to import an item that is not on your country's list, you can apply for approval by completing form 587, an application for permit to import plants or plant products, available at www.aphis.usda.gov/ppq/forms/ppqform587.pdf. This process usually takes two years or more and often requires field-testing, under a protocol with APHIS, to show that your produce item is not a host for specified insects that can damage agriculture in the United States. Recently, APHIS has proposed speeding up the process in cases where a produce item can be treated so as to kill any harmful insects and their eggs.

There are also strict limitations on pesticide residues, established by the Environmental Protection Agency and enforced by the FDA. You can get information at the Web site, www.epa.gov/pesticides/food/viewtols.htm. Finally, several kinds of produce are subject to *marketing orders* related to quality. These are established by the Agricultural Marketing Service of USDA. Most of them pertain to fruits and vegetables, and there is information about them at www.ams.usda.gov/fv/moab.html.

Dairy Products

Many types of cheese are under quota and require import licenses. Milk and cream are regulated by both the FDA and the USDA. Milk is under a tariff rate quota, which, as you saw earlier in this chapter, means that the duty goes up after a specific quantity is imported each year. Condensed and evaporated milk, cream, and ice cream are under absolute quotas. I suggest steering clear of these products, but if you really want to look into importing one or more of them, you can look for information at the USDA's dairy programs Web site, www.ams.usda.gov/fv/moab.html.

There was a proposal in the 2007 farm bill to transfer the animal and plant health inspection service from the APHIS to the Department of Homeland Security. This proposal seemed likely to remain in the bill as it moved through Congress.

Other Food Products

There are quotas on various food products, including several species of fish, potatoes, chocolate, sugar, and peanuts. Candy containing more than 0.5 percent alcohol is prohibited entirely. Unexpected things can happen. A few years ago, a U.S. company found that it was profitable to import food products containing large amounts of sugar, extract the sugar, and sell it. This was possible because the price of sugar in the United States is maintained at more than twice the world price in order to protect beet growers in the South and the Midwest and cane growers in Hawaii. The government responded to this sugar extraction business by temporarily banning imports of a category of miscellaneous food items, some of which did not contain any sugar at all! The measure was put into effect so suddenly that quite a bit of merchandise that had been bought and shipped legally was illegal when it reached the United States.

All Food Products

To get a more complete description of rules on importing food, look at the *Food and Agricultural Import Regulations and Standards Report (FAIRS) of the United States of America* at www.fas.usda.gov/ itp/ofsts/usda.html. It is a bit out of date but still very useful.

Also, it's important to know that all imported foods are subject to the conditions of the Public Health Security and Bioterrorism Preparedness and Response Act of 2002 (the Bioterrorism Act). In brief, this law requires that nearly all organizations that handle food for consumption in the United States be registered with the FDA. There are requirements about how records should be kept and about filing prior notice of shipments of food that are to arrive in the United States. The law also specifies the rules under which the FDA can detain shipments at the port if it has any reason to suspect that biohazards are involved.

There is complete information about this law on the Web at www.fda.gov/oc/bioterrorism/bioact.html. If you plan to import food products, both you and your foreign exporter should register. This can be done on the same Web site, and there is no charge. If you plan to work as a pure agent and never see the product, which means you have no way to introduce a contaminant, you might as well register anyway. It can take as much as an hour the first time you do it, but then, if you should someday decide to store a few cases of a product in your garage, you will already be registered.

Textiles and Apparel

Textile and apparel imports are subject to numerous requirements. They must be labeled with the country of origin, fiber content, laundering instructions, and the name or trademark of the producer, importer, or marketing organization. A registered identification number, or RN, obtained from the U.S. Federal Trade Commission (FTC), can be substituted for some of this information. Questions and answers about RNs can be found at www.ftc.gov/os/statutes/textile/faq.htm. On the FTC's Web site you can also read the requirements of the Textile Fiber Identification Act and the Wool Products Labeling Act, both of which could be relevant to your products. There is also useful information on the CBP's Web site.

It's usually easier to get information about government regulations online than by any other method. Fax, mail, phone, buying publications, and even personal visits are problematic. If, however, you go to a trade show, such as Fashion Week of the Americas, and find the FTC (or other government agency) exhibiting, you will be able to ask detailed questions and pick up relevant printed information.

When the Harmonized System of tariffs and trade took effect in the United States on January 1, 1990, the soft-goods importing community expected massive confusion because of changes in the codes, classifications, and duty rates of many items. In-depth information was presented in numerous publications and seminars, and the transition was made with very little trouble. One problem that remained, and still does, is that many fabrics are blends of different materials, such as polyester and cotton. For proper classification, you need to know the relative content, by weight, of each kind of fiber.

Overlooking details can be costly. For example, the Jones Apparel Group and Tommy Hilfiger were recently assessed fines of $300,000 for violations of labeling laws related to product care. You can see a list of product-care-labeling ruling cases at http://ftc.gov-os-statutes-textile-carelblcases.htm. The violations listed are for merchandise of the United States and of foreign origin.

You should also check on regulations enforced by the Consumer Product Safety Commission, especially with regard to flammability of fabrics. The Web site is www.cpsc.gov, and the Office of Compliance and Field Operations can be reached at (301) 504-0008. In the United States and some other countries, some products cannot be imported if they burn easily. Be very careful about ordering items such as children's pajamas, especially from developing countries.

Regulations on importing textiles and apparel are liberalized periodically as part of the processes of negotiating trade agreements and pleasing America's allies. Remember the list of trade agreements in chapter 9? You are likely to find lower duties on textiles and apparel if you import from an African, Andean, Central American, or Caribbean country, but you must check the regulations carefully.

Alcoholic Beverages

You could probably guess that importing booze is harder than importing most other products. Not long ago a gentleman from Bolivia called me to ask about importing singani (unrefined grape brandy) to the United States, and I told him about the permits he needed. Apparently he didn't believe me, because a few months later, he called to say he had not gotten permits, but had ordered a load of singani, and Customs had detained it at the port. He asked what I could do to help. My help was pretty much limited to expressing sympathy on the phone and then, I confess, hanging up and chuckling.

To import any kind of alcoholic beverage, you will need an importer's basic permit (called the application for basic permit under the Federal Alcohol Administration Act) from the Bureau of Alcohol, Tobacco, Firearms and Explosives (ATF), Department of the Treasury, in Washington, D.C. The application is online at www.ttb.gov/forms/f510024.pdf. There are instructions at the end, and there is basic information about importing alcoholic beverages at www.atf.gov/alcohol/info/impreq.htm. You won't have to send money with your application, but if it is approved, you will need to pay a fee of $500 per year. Your application may not be approved if you have a criminal record or have ever declared bankruptcy.

You will also need a wholesaler's permit from the state to which you plan to import. This usually costs more than the importer's basic permit but is easier to obtain. You will need a different permit for each state in which you plan to sell, although there are fairly new exceptions for interstate shipments of wine. As always, study the regulations before you invest much money.

For wine and liquor, the bottles must be in metric sizes, and the labels must be approved in advance by the ATF. There are several label requirements, one of which is the government-dictated health warning. Another, in several states, is that the alcohol content be printed on the label. In some states, beer labels need approval also.

For liquor, you will need to buy federal stamps to place on the bottles (or have your exporter place them on the bottles). These serve as evidence that the excise tax has been paid. If you import liquor without the strips, you will have to buy them and paste them on before making deliveries. Alcoholic beverages are also subject to inspection by the FDA.

Motor Vehicles

For readers who want to import motorcars but not in large quantities, I think the best Web site to look at is that of ForeignBorn .com. You can find it at www.foreignborn.com/visas_imm/ entering_us/7importingyourcar.htm.

Basically, two kinds of laws apply to cars, trucks, and motorcycles—safety regulations and environmental regulations. You can get information about these from www.nhtsa.dot.gov or by calling (202) 366-5313. Also, all imported vehicles must meet the requirements of the Clean Air Act. Information about this is available from the Environmental Protection Agency in Washington, DC. The Web site for this is www.epa.gov/otaq/ imports, and there is an information fax-back system with a help menu at (202) 564-9240. Vehicles must be clean underneath and, if they are not new, must be fumigated by the Department of Agriculture.

Of course, you will need all the relevant documents regarding the car and your purchase of it. Do not ship it with personal items or merchandise inside. These items could be stolen, and they will definitely cause problems with Customs. I have heard that used cars exported from the United States sometimes are loaded with other items. Also, it's a good idea to check with Customs in your port before you import a car, because you may have to ship it to a registered importer. These are companies that can see if a car meets U.S. standards and, if not, can modify it as necessary. There is a list of registered automobile importers on the Web at www.nhtsa .dot.gov/cars/rules/import/web_RI_list01122006.html.

Other Products

Household appliances are subject to consumer products safety, energy efficiency, and energy labeling laws. For minimum efficiency standards, go to Energy Information Administration's web site at http://buildingsdatabook.eren.doe.gov/docs/5.10.3.xls. That should bring up a very useful table in Excel. The labeling regulations are different in different states. Check with the department of energy in your state to see what you can find out.

Electronic products that emit radiation must meet the standards of the Center for Devices and Radiological Health of the FDA in Rockville, Maryland. Their home page address is, mercifully, not as long as some others: www.fda.gov/cdrh. For electronic products that broadcast on the airwaves, contact the Federal Communications Commission, Washington, DC 20554. Its main telephone number is (888) 225-5322.

The ongoing and sometimes heated discussion about importing medicinal products is likely to continue for some time to come. Check for current regulations before you place an order. In general, drugs and cosmetics must be safe for human use and are subject to inspection and approval by the FDA. The testing period for a new product is long and the standards are strict. One result is that many remedies are much cheaper abroad than in the United States or are simply not available in this country.

Pesticides and toxic substances are regulated by the Office of Pesticides and Toxic Substances, Environmental Protection Agency, Washington, DC 20460. The telephone number of the Toxic Substances Control Act Assistance Information Service is (202) 554-1404. As of this writing you can follow the recorded instructions and get connected with a human being in an office in the United States.

Hazardous substances, such as dangerous chemicals, must meet regulations enforced by the FDA and the Consumer Product Safety Commission. Their transportation is closely regulated by the Pipeline and Hazardous Materials Safety Administration, U.S. Department of Transportation, Washington, DC 20003.

STATE AND LOCAL REGULATIONS

Government authority in the United States is fragmented among various jurisdictions, and individual states regulate some products. Toys for children, for example, can't be sold in many areas without being approved by the consumer protection offices of the state governments. With imported toys, it is usually the importer who has to apply for (and pay for) state approval.

I once worked with a Chilean company that made light switches and other simple electrical goods and was planning to export them to the United States. Federal regulations presented no difficulties, but no city or county would allow the products unless they met local standards. We had to begin by contacting Underwriters Laboratories (UL) in Northbrook, Illinois, and having both the products and the factory in Chile inspected by UL personnel (which was not inexpensive). Then, even with UL approval, we had to establish that the products met building standards in some of the cities where they were to be sold.

Counties and towns often regulate the thickness of insulation in houses, the color of trash cans, the size of mailboxes, and so on. If you import 1-inch-high street numbers for houses, and a new county law specifies 2-inch numbers, you'll have to find a new supplier or get your existing supplier to retool in a hurry.

How do you find out about these kinds of regulations? First, look carefully at products like yours in stores to see whether there is any mark or label on them that you don't understand. If there is, find out what it is and why it is there. Second, ask people in the trade as well as local government authorities. In 2007 and beyond, look especially for new security and environmental regulations.

At the same time, keep your eyes open for new ordinances that are about to be enacted. If your town is debating a dog litter law, there may be a market for leashes and pooper-scoopers. If it is about to start a complete trash-recycling program, every house will need containers for glass and tin, newspaper, wet garbage, and miscellaneous trash (but the type and size may be specified by a local ordinance).

REGULATION OF EXPORTS

A lawyer specializing in international trade could probably list a hundred laws that affect export operations. In Washington, DC, the international trade association counts many attorneys as members, and they all seem to be busy. In this book, however, I will mention just those laws that are most likely to be encountered by small-scale exporters. They are the Trading with the Enemy Act, the Business Practices and Records Act, the antiboycott laws, and those involving tax incentives.

Trading with the Enemy Act

The Trading with the Enemy Act is the authority behind most U.S. export control regulations. These regulations are to prevent harm to the U.S. national interest caused by exporting products that are in scarce supply at home (there are very few in this category) or that should be kept in the United States in order to maintain this country's military and industrial positions. As you can imagine, both the number of controlled products and the level of enforcement have increased in the past few years. In general, the less friendly a country is with the United States, the fewer products can be exported with no license required (NLR). NLR is for nonrestricted products and requires only that the exporter write those initials in the appropriate box in a document known as a shipper's export declaration.

If a product is restricted, you will need a license to send it abroad, and the less friendly a country is with the United States, the harder it will be to get a license. Since it is easy for a foreign company to order a product shipped to one country and then send it on to another, some products require licenses to be shipped *anywhere*. In some cases the U.S. government requires a signed statement to the effect that the items will remain in the country of destination. If they don't remain there, no matter what the reason, the signer of the statement will be in violation of export control laws.

The U.S. Department of State regulates military technologies; the Department of Energy regulates trade in nuclear technology; and the Department of the Treasury restricts exports to countries that are subject to U.S. embargoes, boycotts, or trade sanctions. The Department of Commerce regulates so-called dual use technologies. This gets complicated, because virtually any product can have both civilian and military applications. A person can use boots to hike for pleasure or to participate in a military maneuver—sometimes the same person in the same day.

The first step in complying with export control legislation is to find your product on the Department of Commerce Commerce Control List (CCL). There is an overview of the process at www .bis.doc.gov/licensing/exportingbasics.htm. You can also look at www.access.gpo.gov/bis/ear/ear_data.html#ccl. The list is divided into categories, as follows:

0 = Nuclear Materials, Facilities and Equipment and Miscellaneous Items

1 = Materials, Chemicals, Microorganisms, and Toxins

2 = Materials Processing

3 = Electronics

4 = Computers

5 = Telecommunications and Information Security

6 = Sensors and Lasers

7 = Navigation and Avionics

8 = Marine

9 = Propulsion Systems, Space Vehicles and Related Equipment

When you find your product on the list, it will fall into one of five product groups, as follows:

A. Equipment, Assemblies and Components

B. Test, Inspection and Production Equipment

C. Materials

D. Software

E. Technology

Also on the list you will see a four-digit Export Control Classification Number (ECCN) and a letter that indicates the country groups for which your product requires a validated license. Next, you must look at the Commerce Country Chart, which is available on the Web site www.gpo.gov/bis/ear/pdf/738spir.pdf. You can, theoretically, cross-reference your ECCN with the country to which you want to ship and determine whether an export license is needed. If it is, you need to get a rather complicated form and submit it to the Department of Commerce for approval of your export shipment. You will have to write in, among other things, the recipient of your goods and the use to which they will be put. Some recipients and some uses may be prohibited for your goods. On the other hand, you may not need a license because of an *exception*, such as a shipment of low value.

Applications for export licenses are supposed to be approved within two weeks, unless they have to be reviewed by more than one government department. Then it can take much longer. Sometimes requests even go to Congress, as when Pakistan places a major order for military equipment with a U.S. firm.

There are some special types of export licenses, and there are often requirements that applications be accompanied by special statements or certificates. As mentioned before, you may have to state on your bill of lading or airway bill that the product cannot be diverted to a third country without authorization from the U.S. government, and your buyer may have to provide a written statement that the product will not be diverted. Every shipment that requires a license, no matter what its value or destination, also requires a shippers' export declaration.

If you want to find out what is happening to your application for a license, you can call STELA. Her full name is the system for tracking export license applications, and her telephone number is (202) 482-2752. Just give STELA your application control number, and she'll tell you everything she knows.

Your chance of going through this process correctly the first time is about the same as your chance of swimming over Niagara Falls upstream. You may be able to get help from your freight forwarder, your nearest field office of the U.S. Department of Commerce, or USDC contact numbers on the Web sites.

Business Practices and Records Act

You may have heard that in June 2007, the U.S. government began to investigate BAE Systems for a possible violation of the Business Practices and Records Act. This law replaced the Anti-Foreign Corrupt Practices Act, which was commonly known as the anti-bribery law. The intent is to enhance the image of the United States, and reduce the cost of doing business by reducing bribery by U.S. exporting companies. The primary means of enforcement is by the record-keeping requirements that are built into the law.

Essentially, this law makes it illegal for U.S. exporters to bribe foreign officials to do something that is not one of their normal functions. Of course, the definitions of *bribe, foreign official,* and other terms are critical. It is legal to give a small payment to a foreign customs inspector to get your shipment cleared expeditiously. The small payment would not be considered a bribe, the customs inspector would not be considered a foreign official (not high enough in the hierarchy), and clearing your shipment expeditiously is a normal function for inspectors. It is *not* legal to give the brother of the minister of health several thousand dollars to bring about the purchase of your line of antibiotics. If your foreign sales agent pays a bribe and you didn't know about it, you can be held accountable if the Department of Justice believes that you *should* have known about it.

Most U.S. government officials have understood that not being able to offer bribes puts U.S. firms at a competitive disadvantage with regard to firms of other countries. Therefore, the law has not been enforced very diligently (and it is a hard one to enforce anyway). Still, there have been major convictions with regard to, for example, selling aircraft to the Netherlands and selling petroleum equipment to Mexico. Other countries have been joining the United States in trying to reduce corruption. This has been a subject of interest in international trade agreements for the past 60 years (see chapter 11).

In 1998, the Anti-Bribery and Fair Competition Act was passed. Essentially, it directs the U.S. government to try to reduce the amount of corruption on a worldwide basis. The more successful this effort is, the less need there will be for American companies to engage in corrupt practices. This will be good for nearly everyone except those who have been receiving the bribes.

Antiboycott Laws

Talk about a law that has teeth in it! The fines imposed on people who violate the antiboycott laws can be high enough to really hurt! This legislation was designed to counter the Arab boycott of Israel, but it applies to any foreign boycott that the U.S. government does not support.

You may, for example, be asked by a buyer in Syria to certify that your goods are not of Israeli origin, were not made by an Israeli-owned company, and will not be shipped on Israeli vessels. If you make such a statement, you will be in violation of U.S. law. You can usually make a positive statement, such as certifying that the goods are a product of the United States. It's better to check with an expert, such as a freight forwarder or an official of the Department of Commerce's International Trade Administration, to make sure you are on safe legal ground.

If you receive a boycott request, it should be reported to the Office of AntiBoycott Compliance of the USDC in Washington, DC. Call (202) 482-5914 or (202) 482-2381 and speak with a specialist for the specific geographic area in which your boycott requests originated. Also, a specialized attorney can advise you as to what you can and cannot do.

If you receive a letter of credit that contains boycott provisions, your bank will probably refuse to handle it, so you will probably not be able to make the shipment.

DISCs and FISCs

You may have heard of tax incentives known as DISCs and FISCs, perhaps because U.S. exporters would like to make them more useful whereas other countries' exporters would like to see them abolished. The former is a domestic international sales corporation, and the latter is a foreign sales corporation. Both are legal devices to reduce the tax burden on U.S. exporters. The most common type now is probably the IC-DISC, where *IC* stands for "interest charge." There is a very good explanation of this device on the Web at www.irs.gov/pub/irs-soi/00icdisc.pdf.

The DISC law allows U.S. exporters to channel their exports through shell corporations, on their own premises if they wish, and to postpone payment of income tax on part of the export profits. When the GATT (the father of the World Trade Organization) ruled that this was a subsidy, the rules of DISCs were changed, effective January 1, 1985, to make them less attractive, and FISCs were created. Later the IC-DISC was created to make DISCs more palatable to the other members of the GATT.

There is at least one company that specializes in helping American companies set up IC-DISCS—Export Subsidy Services. It is on the Web at www.exportfsc.com.

A FISC must be a separate corporation, which is set up offshore in an approved country and which has personnel to handle export paperwork. Export transactions (not actual merchandise) are routed through the FISC, and income taxes on a portion of the profits are waived. Your company alone may be too small to own its own FISC, but the law allows trade groups and associations to set up FISCs that serve all their members. If you become a substantial exporter, these tax incentives will probably be worth looking into.

Foreign Import Regulations

Remember that in addition to U.S. regulations on exports you will have to consider foreign countries' import regulations. These vary considerably and can be quite stringent; help is available from several sources, including your foreign buyers, the U.S. Department of Commerce, and consulates of the countries to which you are selling. The U.S. government is always watching for foreign country import controls that may act as unfair barriers to U.S. sales abroad, and often takes action to try to remove them.

For example, exporters of foods, food additives, dietary supplements, cosmetics, and a few other products, such as animal feed, must sometimes provide what is known as a certificate of free sale. For dietary supplements, infant formula, and "medical foods," there are the *Guidelines for Certificate of Free Sale* at www.ag.state

.co.us/Mkt/CertificateofFreeSale.pdf. The cost of a certificate is just $10, and there is a sample at http://agr.wa.gov/Food Animal/Links-Doc/SC%20Example%204.pdf. You may be able to save $10 because some trade associations and state governments issue these certificates free to their members or constituents.

SOURCES OF INFORMATION AND HELP

Laws and regulations that affect international trade are extensive and dynamic. Laws are fairly constant, but regulations that deal with implementation of laws can sometimes be changed on short notice. If in or after 2002 you had planned to import from an Islamic country and transfer your payment through a money transfer system known as a ḥawāla, you might have had your payment held up or stopped and might have been questioned about possible links to possible terrorists.

To keep up to date with laws and regulations, you can network with other importers or exporters through the World Trade Club and can subscribe to a magazine such as *World Trade*. It is available from BNP Media in Troy, Michigan, phone: (248) 262-3700. You can subscribe on the Internet at www.worldtrademag.com.

In chapter 10, you have seen references to many sources of information and help, as follows:

- Quotas: a complete list of quotas on merchandise for import to the United States is available from the U.S. Customs and Border Patrol's Web site at www.cbp.gov/ImageCache/cgov/content/publications/quotas_2edoc/v1/quotas.doc.
- Electronic Visa Information System (ELVIS) is an "electronic program developed by U.S. CBP for information, particularly visa stamps, normally found on commercial invoices." Web site: www.cbp.gov/xp/cgov/import/textiles_and_quotas/elvis/elvis.xml.
- Electronic Certification System (eCERT) is an "electronic government-to-government system developed by the U.S. CBP for transmitting a certificate, like an export license/

certificate or a certificate of eligibility, used for importation into the United States for specific commodities as a requirement to qualify for in-quota or tariff preference rates of duty." Web site: www.cbp.gov/xp/cgov/import/textiles_and_quotas/ecert.

- The Federal Food, Drug, and Cosmetic Act is enforced by the U.S. Food and Drug Administration (FDA) in Rockville, Maryland. Phone: (301) 443-6553; Web site: www.fda.gov/opacom/laws/fdcact/fdctoc.htm.

- Bodycote FPL (Food Products Laboratory) is a food testing laboratory. Address: 12003 Northeast Ainsworth Circle, Suite 105, Portland, OR 97220; Phone: (503) 253-9136; Fax: (503) 253-9019; Web site: www.fplabs.com/main.htm.

- Food labeling laws are available on the FDA's Web site at www.cfsan.fda.gov/~dms/sbel.html.

- Phoenix Regulatory Associates provides assistance in meeting regulations of the FDA. Address: 21525 Ridgetop Circle, # 240, Sterling, VA 20166; Phone: (703) 406-0906; Web site: www.phoenixrising.com.

- Electronic Entry Processing System (EEPS) is a way of facilitating trade, administered by the FDA.

- FDA product code builder helps in determining FDA product codes for specific goods. Web site: www.accessdata.fda.gov/scripts/ora/pcb/pcb.cfm.

- Food Safety and Inspection Service (FSIS) is the public health agency in the U.S. Department of Agriculture and is responsible for ensuring that the nation's commercial supply of meat, poultry, and egg products is safe, wholesome, and correctly labeled and packaged. FSIS, Import Inspection Division, Phone: (402) 221-7400; Web site: www.fsis.usda.gov.

- Animal and Plant Health Inspection Service (APHIS) is responsible for protecting and promoting U.S. agricultural health, administering the Animal Welfare Act, and carrying out wildlife damage management activities. Plant concerns, Phone: (301) 734-8896; Web site: www.aphis.usda.gov.

- Fish and Wildlife Service of the U.S. Department of Interior is responsible for conserving, protecting, and enhancing fish, wildlife, plants and their habitats. Phone: (703) 358-2093; Web site: www.fws.gov.

- Consumer Product Safety Commission (CPSC) is committed to protecting consumers from products that pose a fire, electrical, chemical, or mechanical hazard or can injure children. CPSC's Office of Compliance's can be reached at (301) 504-0608; Web site: www.cpsc.gov.

- Application for basic permit under the Federal Alcohol Administration Act is granted by the Bureau of Alcohol, Tobacco, Firearms and Explosives, a law enforcement agency within the U.S. Department of Justice. Web site: www.atf.gov/forms/pdfs/f510024.pdf.

- Foreignborn.com provides various kinds of information including that on importing a motor vehicle into the United States. Web site: www.foreignborn.com/visas_imm/entering_us/7importingyourcar.htm.

- National Highway Transportation Safety Administration (NHTSA) establishes and enforces safety performance standards for motor vehicles. Phone: (202) 366-5313; Web site: www.nhtsa.dot.gov. NHTSA's Web site lists registered automobile importers at www.nhtsa.dot.gov/cars/rules/import/web_RI_list01122006.html.

- Environmental Protection Agency (EPA) is responsible for enforcing the Clean Air Act. Imported motor vehicles must adhere to this act. Information fax-back system with a help menu available at (202) 564-9240. Web site: www.epa.gov/otaq/imports.

- Energy Information Administration is a statistical agency of the U.S. Department of Energy. It has energy efficiency standards for household appliances at www.eia.doe.gov/emeu/efficiency/appliance_standards.html.

- Center for Devices and Radiological Health is part of the FDA, responsible for ensuring the safety and effectiveness of medical devices and eliminating unnecessary human exposure to man-made radiation from medical, occupational, and consumer products. Address: 1350 Piccard Drive, Rockville, MD 20850; Phone: (800) 638-2041 or (240) 276-3103; Web site: www.fda.gov/cdrh/index.html.

- The Federal Communications Commission is charged with regulating interstate and international communications by radio, television, wire, satellite, and cable. Address: 445 12th Street, SW, Washington, DC 20554; Phone: (888) 225-5322; Web site: www.fcc.gov.

- Toxic Substances Control Act (TSCA) Hotline provides technical assistance and information about programs implemented under TSCA. Phone: (202) 554-1404; Fax: (202) 554-5603.

- The Pipeline and Hazardous Materials Safety Administration oversees compliance with numerous regulations pertaining to transportation of hazardous substances. Address: U.S. Department of Transportation, 400 7th Street, SW, Washington, DC 20590; Web site: www.hazmat.dot.gov.

- Underwriters Laboratories is an independent, not-for-profit product-safety testing and certification organization. Address: 333 Pfingsten Road, Northbrook, IL 60062-2096; Phone: (847) 272-8800; Fax: (847) 272-8129; Web site: www.ul.com.

- Department of Commerce export controls are available on the Bureau of Industry and Security's Web site at www.bis.doc.gov/licensing/exportingbasics.htm. The Web site is designed to give people who are new to exporting and, in particular, new to export controls a general understanding of the regulations and how to use them.

- The Commerce Country Chart is important in knowing whether export control regulations apply to your outgoing shipment. It is available at www.gpo.gov/bis/ear/pdf/738spir.pdf.

- Antiboycott compliance: the U.S. Department of Commerce's Bureau of Industry and Security is responsible for enforcing antiboycott laws. Phone: (202) 482-2381; Web site: www.bis.doc.gov/complianceandenforcement/AntiboycottCompliance.htm.

• Interest-Charge Domestic International Sales Corporations (IC-DISC's) are domestic corporations formed to export U.S. products. More information about IC-DISCs can be found on the Internal Revenue Service's Web site: www.irs.gov/pub/irs-soi/00icdisc.pdf.

• Export Subsidy Services specializes in assisting American companies set up IC-DISCs. Address: 8132 Camino Del Sol, La Jolla, CA 92037; Phone: (800) 243-1372; Fax: (858) 459-6999; Web site: www.exportfsc.com.

• Guidelines for certificate of free sale: these requests provide assurance to foreign importers that products offered for entry into their country comply with the U.S. laws for distribution in our domestic commerce. More information is available at www.ag.state.co.us/Mkt/CertificateofFreeSale.pdf.

11

NAFTA, GATT, and Other Trade Pacts

You may remember, from chapter 10, the trade agreements and preferential program listed in Figure 11.1. They all represent agreements between the United States and one or more other countries, or unilateral concessions that the United States has offered. An essential difference between the two is that a trade agreement is bilateral and intended to be permanent, while a preferential program is unilateral and can be revoked at any time. That makes it risky to invest much time and money in producing products for export to the United States, because if the preference is revoked, your duties will increase.

You should have at least a rudimentary understanding of how international trade is affected by trade agreements and concessions, partly because they make excellent subjects for dinner conversations, but, more important, because they can have major effects on your business. Here is a brief rundown on some of the agreements and concessionary programs.

TRADE AGREEMENTS

The following is an introduction to the complex and controversial subject of international trade agreements.

Trade Agreement or Preferential Program

African Growth and Opportunity Act
Agreement on Trade in Civil Aircraft
Agreement on Trade in Pharmaceutical Products
Andean Trade Preference Act, Andean Trade Promotion and Drug
   Eradication Act
Automotive Products Trade Act
Caribbean Basin Initiative
Dominican Republic-Central America United States Free Trade Agreement
   Implementation Act
Generalized System of Preferences
North American Free Trade Agreement
United States-Australia Free Trade Agreement
United States-Bahrain Free Trade Agreement Implementation Act
United States-Caribbean Basin Trade Partnership Act
United States-Chile Free Trade Agreement
United States-Israel Free Trade Area
United States-Jordan Free Trade Area Implementation Act
United States-Morocco Free Trade Agreement Implementation Act
United States-Singapore Free Trade Agreement
Uruguay Round Concessions on Intermediate Chemicals for Dyes

Figure 11.1   Harmonized Tariff Schedule: the United States' trade agreements
and preferential programs as of mid-2007.

What Are Trade Agreements, Anyway?

Historically, countries have restricted imports for the reasons
already mentioned in this book. For the law of international comparative advantage to work, by increasing specialization according to the different countries' natural endowments, barriers to
trade must be low. In most cases, however, countries have not
wanted to lower their import barriers unilaterally. Rather, they
have negotiated with one or more other countries to lower barriers simultaneously. The resulting agreements are normally catego-
rized as follows:

- *Free trade areas.* Member countries eliminate most or all of
  their tariff and quota barriers to trade with each other, but
  each keeps its own barriers to the rest of the world. The

countries must then agree on *rules of origin* to prevent foreign products from coming into the country that has the lowest duty and then moving freely to the other member countries. The Free Trade Area of the Americas (FTAA) is one of these.

- *Customs unions.* Member countries eliminate most or all of their tariff and quota barriers to trade with each other and agree on a common *external tariff* to the rest of the world. The South African Customs Union (SACU) is one of these.
- *Common markets.* Customs unions that reduce or eliminate barriers on the movement of labor and capital. The European Union (EU) is an example.

These simple concepts become complicated in practice because traded goods and services affect and are affected by many elements of a country's economy and society. Regulations to preserve and protect the environment, for example, vary greatly from one country to another. If country X establishes free trade with country Y, must it accept merchandise whose production hurts the environment in country Y? Must it accept merchandise that is legal in country Y but whose *use* might hurt the environment in country X? Should it try to impose its environmental or labor standards and regulations on country Y, which may be at a lower stage of development and unable to afford them? Alternatively, should it accept country Y's lower standards to make the trade agreement work smoothly? There are thousands of these kinds of questions that must be faced in the implementation of a trade agreement.

The more countries that are involved in a trade agreement, the harder it is to negotiate and implement. That is why the European Union, formerly the European Community and before that other names, has developed slowly over many years and has such a large and costly bureaucracy. Nonetheless, comparative advantage is much greater and more useful when applied to several countries with diverse economies. Joining two countries that produce apples in autumn is not nearly as helpful as joining two that produce apples in different seasons or one that grows apples (South Korea) and another that grows bananas (Taiwan).

By the way, the theory of *comparative* advantage has in large part given way to the newer theory of *competitive* advantage. "Comparative" advantage says that a country will export things it can produce the cheapest, relative to its trading partners, based on natural endowments such as land, minerals, and labor. "Competitive" advantage recognizes the importance of policies, skills, and so forth. For example, a country will be less competitive if it has a tax on exports and more competitive if its government helps its businesses with market research or promotion.

Opposition to Free Trade

While freer trade is nearly always good for consumers, not everyone is a winner. In each country, the industries that are high-cost producers are often injured, and since they can predict this in advance, they often lobby hard against new trade agreements. On the other hand, industries that are low-cost producers profit because the size of their potential market increases. One excellent example is the exportation of chicken meat from the United States to Mexico. The North American Free Trade Agreement resulted in lower Mexican duties, but Mexican negotiators obtained safeguards to prevent U.S. exports from increasing too fast and driving their poultry producers out of business. The safeguards were scheduled to diminish gradually, and each reduction has been protested in Mexico and cheered in the United States. One argument used in Mexico (and a pretty good one) is that the competition is not fair because the United States subsidizes producers of feed grains, which keeps the price of chicken feed artificially low. Feed is the largest cost in producing chickens.

The United States is no exception with regard to opposition to trade agreements. The first attempt to form a world trade organization, after the Second World War, failed because the U.S. Congress would not ratify it. In its place, 23 nations signed a simpler document, the General Agreement on Tariffs and Trade, which became known as the GATT and was expanded through the years. Almost 40 years later, the secretariat of the GATT became the World Trade Organization, or WTO.

The United States has its share of ultranationalists and other people who are against trade agreements because of fears that they will cost U.S. jobs. Studies have shown that when the United States enters into a trade agreement, there is usually a net job *gain*. Unfortunately, the word *net* means only that there are more winners than losers. If new exports create 100 new high-paying jobs, while new imports cause a smaller number of lower-paying jobs to be lost, the country as a whole will be better off. It is, however, quite logical that the people whose jobs are lost will be bitter and will complain.

Another reason for opposition to free trade is that it can limit the ability of the United States to regulate commerce. For example, there are fears that we might have to accept tuna that was caught in nets that also caught dolphins, or charge interest on tax payments that companies postpone because they are operating domestic international sales corporations (DISCs). These arguments, too, have some validity, not just for the United States but also for all countries that enter into trade agreements.

The GATT and the WTO

The GATT is the world's most far-reaching global trade arrangement. After its formation in 1947, the GATT developed into an international forum and organization devoted to increasing international trade to improve standards of living and to promote peace (by making countries more dependent on one another). It did this mainly by bringing trading nations together in meetings called *rounds* to negotiate reductions in their import duties. Each round lasted several years. Members were to give equal treatment, known as nondiscrimination, to all member countries, except that they could discriminate in *favor of* less-developed countries by giving them special privileges such as the Generalized System of Preferences, which is explained later. Also, member countries could enter into trade agreements, such as free trade areas, and give preferential treatment to their partners in these agreements.

The GATT also provided a forum for discussion and settlement of trade disputes. After much discussion and negotiation, it could even authorize a country to retaliate by raising trade barriers against a nation that was violating GATT rules by keeping its products out.

The coverage of GATT agreements has extended to most

manufactured goods traded by about 150 countries. Trade in agricultural products was not included until recently, at least in part because many developed countries did not want an agreement by which they would have to reduce their subsidies to farmers. Trade in services has also been a difficult issue because developing countries are weak as service providers. They fear that an agreement in this area will lead to dominance in their markets by banks, insurance companies, and the like from the United States, Western Europe, and Japan.

The GATT may have looked like an organization but technically it wasn't one. It was an agreement with a secretariat to help implement it. Proponents of freer trade had long believed that an entity with more legal standing was needed to advance the process of trade liberalization and to help keep nations from sliding back into protectionism. On April 15, 1995, in Marrakech, Morocco, this was achieved. Article I of the Agreement Establishing the World Trade Organization says simply: "The World Trade Organization (hereinafter referred to as 'the WTO') is hereby established."

The scope of the WTO is, among other things, to "provide the common institutional framework for the conduct of trade relations among its members." In general, its functions are to facilitate the implementation of trade agreements, to provide a forum for future trade negotiations, to administer the Understanding on Rules and Procedures Governing the Settlement of Disputes and the Trade Policy Review Mechanism, and "to further greater coherence in global economic policy-making."

This organization is headquartered in Geneva, Switzerland, and has a permanent staff of 635 people, whose salaries are ultimately paid by the taxpayers of member countries. Its main tasks are to administer WTO trade agreements, provide a forum for trade negotiations, handle trade disputes, monitor national trade policies, and provide technical assistance and training for developing countries. It does this in cooperation with other international organizations.

The WTO's latest worldwide round of negotiations, the Doha (Qatar) round, more or less collapsed in July 2006. One of the reasons for this was dissatisfaction among developing countries with the speed at which most developed countries were willing to reduce their subsidies to agriculture. Another, according to some reports, was that countries such as Brazil and India didn't see a need for more overall reductions in their import duties while they were enjoying preferential access (low duties on their products) to the major market countries. The collapse of the Doha round gave new impulse to the formation of smaller (two or a few countries) trade agreements, of which there are now around 400 in the world.

NAFTA

International economists said for years that free trade in North America would be a boon to all the countries, but few people actually thought it could happen. In the early 1990s, Mexico was progressing and there were pro-trade governments in all three North American countries. An agreement was negotiated and signed in December 1992. Despite political battles in all three countries, the agreement was ratified in all three and went into effect on January 1, 1994. To a large extent, it was an expansion of the U.S.-Canada Free Trade Agreement, which had taken effect five years earlier.

The institution of NAFTA was intended to enhance prosperity in its member countries by increasing trilateral trade and investment, through elimination of both tariff and nontariff barriers. It eliminated some tariffs at the outset, and others have been reduced to naught over a period of years (a maximum of 15 years for the most sensitive products). There are complex rules of origin to determine whether an item is indeed a product of one or a combination of the three member countries. These rules are especially complex in the case of textile and apparel products. The basic rule is called *yarn forward*. Essentially, this means that for an item to be considered a NAFTA product, all processes, beginning with weaving of the yarn, should be done in one or a combination of the three countries.

There is a special certificate of origin form that must be used for shipments for which NAFTA duty rates are requested, available at https://forms.customs.gov/customsrf/getformharness.asp ?formNone=cf-434-form.xft. This must be completed and signed by the *exporter*. On the form there are several preference criteria, or ways that a good can qualify as a NAFTA product. There are also special rules on marking the country of origin on products.

The agreement also covers trade in services, investment, protection of intellectual property rights, and settlement of disputes. There are supplemental agreements relating to labor standards and environmental issues, although the effectiveness of these is still being debated.

In the first year of NAFTA, two-way trade between the United States and Mexico increased by a phenomenal 23 percent. The early winners were U.S. exporters, but soon the Mexican peso was "cut loose" and allowed to find its value in the marketplace. This resulted in a sharp devaluation, which benefited Mexican exporters. Since about 1996, growth in trade has been more balanced among the member countries.

There are many sources of information about NAFTA on the Internet, but the best starting point is the Web site of the U.S. government's Office of NAFTA and Inter-American Affairs at www .mac.doc.gov/nafta. The main phone number is (202) 482-0393. You can also go to ExportZone's Web site at www.exportzone.com and click on the listings under "NAFTA Assistance." This Web site can guide you to a great deal of other information for exporters.

The FTAA

In June 1994, when the heads of state of nearly every country in the Western Hemisphere agreed to create a Free Trade Area of the Americas (FTAA) in 10 years, it seemed that the obstacles could all be overcome. NAFTA already included three of the principal countries. Chile was expected to be the next to join; Trinidad was lobbying to be one of the first; and other countries were defining their positions.

But that was in June 1994. Shortly thereafter, problems in Mexico and the U.S. congressional elections disrupted the process. Early accession for Chile was forgotten, and the Latin American and Caribbean nations began expanding their own trade areas. There are more than 20 of them, including the Southern Common Market (MERCOSUR), the Andean Community of Nations

(CAN), the Central American Common Market (MCCA), and the Caribbean Community and Common Market (CARICOM). These various groups of countries could later merge into a larger trade area, although this would be complicated by differences in rules on valuation of goods, country of origin labeling, sanitary and phytosanitary procedures, and so forth. Some efforts have been made to harmonize decisions in these areas, but it is understandably hard for any country group to adopt the procedures followed by another group.

The trade ministers of participating countries are supposed to meet once a year and to invite ideas and information from the business community. Starting with the meeting in Colombia in March 1996, there is an Americas Business Forum immediately before the meetings of ministers. Incredible as it sounds, the Colombian hosts succeeded in publishing a report of the forum, in two languages, just hours after it ended. The Toronto ministerial meeting in 2001 produced a number of declarations that were designed to keep the process moving. The last meeting in Miami in 2003 produced recommendations in the areas of agriculture, competition policy, dispute settlement, government procurement, institutional issues, intellectual property rights, investment, market access, services, smaller economies, subsidies, antidumping, and countervailing duties.

I predicted early and often that the proponents of FTAA were wildly optimistic, and apparently they were. A third draft agreement was produced near the end of 2003, and negotiations and technical work have continued, but we're a long way from having free trade in the Americas. Also, President Chavez in Venezuela is promoting an agreement that he sees as an alternative to the FTAA. You can read more about the FTAA on the Web site www.ftaa-alca.org/alca_e.asp.

DR-CAFTA

In recent years, the United States has given more attention to the Dominican Republic-Central America Free Trade Agreement, DR-CAFTA (also written CAFTA-DR). It has been negotiated and is being ratified, country by country, including by the United

States in July 2005. There are many similarities between NAFTA and CAFTA, and there are differences of opinion about it. An April 2005 article on the *St. Petersburg Times* Web site describes CAFTA as "NAFTA's ugly stepsister" (www.sptimes.com/2005/04/11/Business/DR_CAFTA_NAFTA_s_ugl.shtml).

It's a gross understatement to say that the United States will dominate its partners in this deal, but then it has had great influence on them for many years. With DR-CAFTA the United States is helping its partners in several ways to improve their products, transportation systems, and so forth, and this will put the Mesoamerican nations in a better position to compete in free international markets.

Most products imported to the United States from CAFTA countries have been free of duty for years, under a system of preferences, but now the duty-free treatment is being extended to more products and made permanent. Also, exports from the United States to CAFTA countries will gradually be free of duties and other restrictions on trade. There will be winners and losers, as with any trade agreement, but importers and exporters like you will clearly be among the winners.

There are several sites on the Web for more information about DR-CAFTA. Start with Wikipedia if you want, and then go to www.ustr.gov/Trade_Agreements/Bilateral/CAFTA/Section_Index.html.

Other Trade Agreements

The United States also has bilateral free trade or trade promotion agreements with the following countries: Australia, Bahrain, Chile, Israel, Jordan, Malaysia, Morocco, Korea, Singapore, the South African Customs Union, and the United Arab Emirates. In addition, agreements have been negotiated with Colombia, Panama, and Peru, but as of September 2007 their ratification by the U.S. Congress was being delayed and was not assured. While they follow a similar pattern, each has unique features and follows a different schedule for reduction of duties. The most important point for you is that your trade, especially import trade, with these countries is likely to move with low or no duties and few other barriers. It means, for example, that you might be better off buying a product from Chile and not from Argentina, because there is an agreement in effect with Chile.

The United States has bilateral investment agreements with numerous countries and trade and investment framework agreements with many other nations and groups of nations, especially in eastern Europe, the Middle East, and Africa. A trade and investment framework agreement is a formal arrangement under which the United States and another country, or bloc of countries, can discuss issues related to trade and investment. These agreements won't be of much use to you unless you become a large-scale exporter and have some kind of problem with a country that has signed one with the United States. The agreement will provide a framework within which the U.S. government can try to help you resolve the problem.

PREFERENTIAL ARRANGEMENTS

Trade agreements are negotiated by two or more countries and affect both U.S. importers and exporters, in numerous ways. Trade *preferences*, on the other hand, are unilateral, affect only importers, and deal almost entirely with U.S. customs duties. In theory, the United States could prefer (offer lower duties on) products from a country, say, Poland, without consulting with Polish government or businesspeople. Such preferences are usually offered by developed countries to developing countries to make it easier for them to export. What is given, however, can be taken away. Developed countries usually review their preferential schemes every few years and do not have to renew them (although they are nearly always renewed, sometimes with minor changes). These arrangements can be used as a lever to help enforce policies. For example, the United States might tell Bolivia that if it cuts back on efforts to reduce cultivation of coca, the U.S. duty on its products might go back up to normal levels.

For many years, the United States has had a Generalized System of Preferences that applies to most products of nearly all developing countries. More recently, it has enacted laws designed to sweeten the deals for African, Andean, and Caribbean Basin countries. Suppose, then, that you are importing pears from Peru, with which a free trade agreement has been negotiated. They will be able to enter the United States under the following arrangements:

- The Most Favored Nation rule of GATT, and be charged normal duties;
- The Generalized System of Preferences, and probably pay low or no duties;
- The Andean Trade Preference Act, and probably pay no duties;
- The U.S.-Peru Free Trade Agreement, and almost certainly pay no duties.

The importer or the customs broker must choose the duty regime under which the products are being imported, and so state on the customs declaration. It will usually be the regime that results in the lowest levels of duties and "red tape."

Generalized System of Preferences

Shortly after 1971, when the GATT allowed member countries to discriminate *in favor of* the less developed nations, virtually all developed countries enacted their own GSP systems. The U.S. Generalized System of Preferences (GSP) gives free or reduced duties, on almost all products, to almost all developing countries. As you know from chapter 10, an A in the special column of the tariff schedule shows that the product in question is covered by the GSP. Almost all products are covered, with a few exceptions, such as most textiles and apparel, footwear and parts of footwear, watches and watch parts, and canned tuna. Also, some countries have lost their GSP privilege for specific products by exporting too much of them to the United States in a given year.

Since most items are really products of more than one country, there must be a rule for determining whether an item is eligible for the GSP. The normal rule is that at least 35 percent of the value of a good must be in raw materials, parts, or labor of the exporting country. Imported raw materials and parts can count toward the

35 percent if they are from other beneficiary countries. There are other rules, of course. Be sure you understand them if you plan to import under this preferential scheme.

The Office of the United States Trade Representative has a GSP information center at phone (202) 395-6971, or e-mail contact usa@ustr.eopo.gov. There is a GSP guidebook online at www.ustr .gov/assets/Trade_Development/Preference_Programs/GSP/ asset_upload_file890_8359.pdf.

African Growth and Opportunity Act

The GSP focuses mostly on customs duties and exempts some items that developing countries want to export, especially apparel and footwear. Therefore, the U.S. Congress passed and, in 2004, extended, the African Growth and Opportunity Act (AGOA). It covers nearly all products, but there are still exemptions for some apparel items. If you go to www.agoa.gov/eligibility/product_ eligibility.html, you will see links to "Country Eligibility," "Product Eligibility," and "Apparel Eligibility."

In addition, AGOA includes U.S. assistance to African exporters through four *trade hubs*, one each for East and Central Africa (in Kenya), West Africa (in Senegal and Ghana), and Southern Africa (in Botswana). These are operated by companies under contract with the United States Agency for International Development (USAID) in cooperation with other organizations.

The official site for information about this trade preference scheme is www.agoa.gov, although you will have to dig some to find useful information. Much of the site is devoted to success stories and reports about the glories of AGOA. Presumably the proponents have to show it is worthwhile, to keep the detractors from doing away with it.

Andean Trade Preference Act

The Andean Trade Preference Act (ATPA) dates back to 1991 and pertains to Bolivia, Colombia, Ecuador, and Peru. The main Web site for information is www.ustr.gov/Trade_Development/ Preference_Programs/ATPA/Section_Index.html. Actually, the name was changed in October 2002 to the expanded Andean

Trade Promotion and Drug Eradication Act (ATPDEA), which tells you one of its purposes. The thinking is something like "If Colombia sells more cocoa, it will sell less coca." You and I know that without outstanding law enforcement that doesn't make much sense; Colombia can sell more cocoa without affecting its coca industry, but, as far as I'm concerned, that's not a serious criticism of this preferential arrangement. If the law helps the people and companies that produce and process cocoa and make lovely chocolates and other products, I'm all for it.

Under ATPDEA, apparel assembled in the Andean region from U.S. fabric or fabric components, or from components knit-to-shape in the United States, may enter the United States duty-free. There is no quantity limit. Apparel assembled in the Andean region from Andean fabric or components knit-to-shape in the region may enter duty-free but with a limit, which started at 2 percent of total U.S. apparel imports and is being increased very gradually. The act also provides for duty-free imports of tuna in pouches, leather products, footwear, petroleum and petroleum products, and watches and watch parts, if the president determines that the imports are not "sensitive." In trade talk, this means that they will not harm U.S. producers.

Caribbean Basin Initiative

Two laws together, the Caribbean Basin Economic Recovery Act (CBERA) and the United States-Caribbean Basin Trade Partnership Act (CBTPA), are known as the Caribbean Basin Initiative. The former dates back to 1983, and the latter, which expanded the benefits, went into effect in 2001. Twenty-four countries are included, including the nations in DR-CAFTA. The benefits are roughly the same as those of ATPDEA, which is described above. Two of the 24 countries, the Dominican Republic and Costa Rica, have accounted for more than half of all exports to the United States under CBERA.

The main effect of these laws for you is duty-free treatment for almost all imports from Antigua and Barbuda, Aruba, the Bahamas, Barbados, Belize, the British Virgin Islands, Costa Rica, Dominica, the Dominican Republic, El Salvador, Grenada, Guatemala, Guyana, Haiti, Honduras, Jamaica, Montserrat, the Netherlands Antilles, Nicaragua, Panama, St. Kitts and Nevis, St. Lucia, St. Vincent and the Grenadines, and Trinidad and Tobago. There are still a few restrictions, however, so check the Harmonized System and ask your customs broker about them before you place an order.

SOURCES OF INFORMATION AND HELP

The importance of trade agreements and preferences is increasing steadily as the United States enters into new pacts with other countries or offers tariff concessions unilaterally. You should at least know the basics of the arrangements that apply to the countries with which you are trading. A little research might save you trouble, money, or both.

There is probably no comprehensive source of information on all trade agreements and preferential offers; if there were, it would be too big to carry. The best starting point is probably www.export .gov, where you can search for a "Country Commercial Guide" on the country in which you are interested. For example, the guide on Yemen is 48 pages long and is found at www.export.gov/ middleeast/country_information/yemen/CCG04.pdf.

This chapter contains numerous sources of information on trade agreements and preferences:

- World Trade Organization (WTO) is the global international organization dealing with the rules of trade between nations and administers the General Agreement on Tariffs and Trade (GATT). Address: Centre William Rappard, Rue de Lausanne 154, CH-1211 Geneva 21, Switzerland; Phone: (41-22) 739 51 11; Fax: (41-22) 731 42 06; Web site: www .wto.org.

- The North American Free Trade Agreement (NAFTA) establishes free trade among the United States, Mexico, and Canada. For information, contact the U.S. International Trade Administration's Office of NAFTA and Inter-

American Affairs. Address: 14th Street and Constitution Avenue NW, Suite 3024, Washington, DC 20230; Phone: (202) 482-0393; Fax: (202) 482-5865; Web site: www.mac.doc .gov/nafta.

- ExportZone's Web site can provide further information concerning NAFTA. It is at www.exportzone.com.

- Free Trade Areas of the Americas (FTAA) is the ongoing effort to unite the economies of the Americas into a single free-trade area. For further information, consult the following Web site: www.ftaa-alca.org/alca_e.asp.

- The Dominican Republic-Central America Free Trade Agreement (DR-CAFTA or CAFTA-DR) is a trade deal that will erase tariffs between the U.S. and the Dominican Republic as well as Central America. There is information in many places, including the Web site of the *St. Petersburg Times* at www.sptimes.com/2005/04/11/Business/DR_ CAFTA_NAFTA_s_ugl.shtml and that of the Office of the U.S. Trade Representative at www.ustr.gov/Trade_ Agreements/Bilateral/CAFTA/Section_Index.html.

- Generalized System of Preferences (GSP), a program designed to promote economic growth in the developing world, provides preferential duty-free entry for more than 4,650 prod-ucts from 144 designated beneficiary countries and territories. For assistance, you can contact the Office of the U.S. Trade Representative, USTR Annex, Room F-220, 1724 F Street, NW, Washington, DC 20508; Phone: (202) 395-6971; Fax: (202) 395-9481; GSP guidebook Web site: www.ustr .gov/assets/Trade_Development/Preference_Programs/ GSP/asset_upload_file890_8359.pdf.

- The African Growth and Opportunity Act (AGOA) assists the economies of sub-Saharan Africa and seeks to improve economic relations between the United States and the region. For further information, consult the Web site www .agoa.gov.

- The Andean Trade Preference Act (ATPA) permits apparel assembled in the Andean region (Bolivia, Colombia,

Ecuador, and Peru) from U.S. fabric or fabric components, or from components knit-to-shape in the United States, to enter the United States duty-free. For further information, consult the Office of the U.S. Trade Representative's Web site at www.ustr.gov/Trade_Development/Preference_ Programs/ATPA/Section_Index.html.

- The Caribbean Basin Initiative is aimed at providing several tariff and trade benefits to many Central American and Caribbean countries. For further information, consult the Office of the U.S. Trade Representative's Web site at www.ustr .gov/Trade_Development/Preference_Programs/CBI/ Section_Index.htm

Epilogue

In mid-2007, there were serious problems with several kinds of merchandise imported to the United States, mostly from China. Pet food ingredients and millions of tires, toys, and other products were recalled by their sellers, including giant companies such as Hasbro and Mattel. Consumers screamed for protection from unsafe products.

This sort of thing had happened before but on a smaller scale. There are basically four remedies to avoid this problem: (1) the U.S. government increases the enforcement of existing laws and enacts new ones, (2) importing companies increase inspections of their foreign suppliers and incoming products, (3) governments of exporting countries improve their legislation and law enforcement, and (4) foreign manufacturers improve their operations and form associations that can guarantee the safety of exported products.

When the news of these recalls broke in 2007, at least three of the remedies began to come into play. New laws were introduced in the U.S. Congress, and there was talk of increasing the budget of the Consumer Products Safety Commission (CPSC). Importing companies, some of which were faced with lawsuits because of the unsafe products, gave clearer instructions to their foreign suppliers and increased inspection and testing of products. The Chinese government told its exporters to clean up their act and even took action against the former head of its food and drug agency.

It is hard to predict the outcome of this situation or its effect on small-scale importers to the United States. It seems likely that Congress will become occupied with more pressing issues and will not pass new product safety laws. Nor does it seem likely that the CPSC's budget will be increased, at least not until the new Congress assembles in 2009. The Chinese government has tried to partly shift blame to U.S. importers for the unsafe products, and there are no signs that the export sector in China is organizing to police itself. So, by default, U.S. importers will be the main actors in this product safety drama. It appears that a few key companies, such as Colgate Palmolive and Wal-Mart, will take the lead.

The optimistic forecast is that as buyers force their suppliers to pay more attention to product safety, most companies that export to the United States will follow along. The pessimistic view is that as low-quality suppliers become unable to sell to major importers in the United States, they will shift their sights to smaller importers in the United States and other countries as well. The lesson here is to be especially careful about what you import, and from whom. American wholesalers, retailers, and consumers have surely become more alert, and they do not want anyone to supply them with products that may cause injury or illness.

Sample Market Study Outline

Most small businesses are started with inadequate market studies or with none at all. Yet a market study is almost the only way to support your income (sales) projections and your marketing plan. In February 2007, I finished a study for a proposed factory in El Salvador that was going to make four products from the same raw material and export them to the United States. Unfortunately, the two most important products had very low market potential. If the entrepreneur had equipped his plant before finding this out, he would have had a major problem. The other two products had fairly high market potential, and because of the study, he knew how to market them and to whom to sell them.

The following is a topical outline for a report on the market for any product being exported from one country to another. If you can produce or buy this kind of information before you begin, you might decide to try another product or another market. If you decide to go ahead, your chances of success will be increased considerably. Moreover, a solid market study looks very good to potential investors and lenders.

Basic Information

- Product name and HS number
- Country of origin, exporting country, importing country

Regulations

- Exporting country controls and taxes
- Importing country controls and taxes

- Import restrictions, quotas, and so forth
- Import duties
- Marketing and labeling laws
- Other regulations

Supply and Demand

- Availability of supply in the exporting country
- Domestic production less imports in the importing country (five years' statistics with trend calculation)
- Imports for consumption (five years' statistics with trend calculation)
- Percent of product for consumption that is imported
- Industry experts' perception of current and future supply and demand in the importing country
- Selected buyers' perceptions of same

Competition

- Survey of producers in the importing country
- Description of selected producers
- Sources of imports (countries), with import market share of each
- Average FAS and CIF prices from each country

Target Markets

- The market and market segments
- Characteristics of important market segments
- Kinds of industrial users
- Main industrial users and a brief description of each

Product Description

- Main types/varieties of the product
- Required or desired product characteristics
- Required or desired packaging and labeling

Distribution

- Normal distribution system in the importing country
- Principal importers and wholesalers
- Principal industrial distributors

Pricing

- Representative prices and markups at each level in the channel
- Price trends
- Discounts used in the trade

Promotion

- Methods of promotion used in the trade
- Promotional assistance usually expected of exporters
- Approximate costs of this assistance

Logistics

- Steamship lines and airlines serving the route
- Usual method of shipping this product
- Availability of vessels (planes) and cost of shipping
- Shipping term normally used
- Payment term normally used

Other Considerations

- Local laws on the product, label, distribution, pricing, promotion

- Distributors' and consumers' openness to new suppliers
- Image of exporting country in the importing country

Sources of Industry Information

- Industry experts including consultants
- Associations and trade publications
- Trade exhibits
- "Off-the-shelf" market study reports
- Government organizations
- Other information sources

Appendix B

Guidelines for Business Planning

It is very important to have a solid business plan before you start your company. Such a plan will help you plan your business better and determine whether it is likely to be profitable. Advice on preparing business plans is available from the U.S. Small Business Administration and from small business development centers, books, software, and the Internet.

If you plan to borrow money to start your business, be sure to ask if your potential lender has a special business plan format. The U.S. Small Business Administration's format is frighteningly long and detailed, but it will remind you of many details that you should consider.

The following is a suggested outline for an import/export business plan, with some annotation. You can find other outlines in books on business planning and on the Internet.

Cover Page

Table of Contents

Executive Summary (This should give the highlight of each of the sections that follows. Most people who read business plans look through the summary and then read other sections only as needed for clarification or additional details.)

Narrative Section (This section of the plan describes in words, with graphs if you wish, how your business will be set up and operated. It can be from 12 to 15 pages in length.)

- Type of trade and products
    Whether you plan to import or export and your sources

of supply, types of products, and product characteristics including packages, labels, and brands.

- Potential markets, market segments, and competition

   A description of the likely consumers of your product, the channels of distribution through which you will reach them, and your main competitors.

- Promotion and sales plan

   Your anticipated strategy with regard to pricing, promotion and selling, that is, how you actually cause your customers to buy your product.

- Organization and personnel

   A description of the company's managers, employees, and sources of assistance, such as your advisors, accountant, banker, and attorney.

- Import/export logistics

   How you expect to handle the functions of packing, shipping, insurance, documentation, and so forth.

- Schedule of start-up activities

   A list of steps in starting the business with a target date for completion of each, and a final target date for opening the doors and beginning to operate.

Financial Section

This section of the plan shows, in numbers, what you expect in the way of sales, income, expenses, and other financial aspects of the business.

- Schedule of start-up costs

   A list of expenses you will need to make in order to open the doors and start your business. This may include office equipment, insurance, an initial stock of merchandise, preopening promotion, and so forth.

- Pro forma income and expense statements

   A list of your expected income and expenses, by month for year 1 and by quarter for year 2. You should have another table to show how you obtained the sales figures (i.e., x units per month of product y at z dollars per unit, and so on with your other products). Make sure the total volume is realistic. Also, make sure you are allocating enough money for promotion and selling expenses to support the projected volume of sales.

- Pro forma cash flow statements

  Similar to the income and expense statement, but showing only cash income and cash expenses, by month for year 1 and by quarter for year 2. Depreciation would not be included, for example, because it is a noncash expense.

- Pro forma balance sheets

  A list of your assets, liabilities, and proprietorship at start-up, at the end of year 1, and at the end of year 2. Assets are usually divided into fixed and current assets, and liabilities into long-term and short-term debts. Then, assets minus liabilities equals proprietorship.

- Main assumptions used in preparing the financial projections

  Assumptions you have made in preparing the financial projections, especially in calculating your income from sales. For example, you might assume no new competition or no increase in the prices you pay for merchandise.

- Financial analysis

  Calculations of break-even analysis (the number of dollars or units you must sell to break even), sensitivity analysis (how sensitive is your bottom line to changes in sales), and basic financial ratios. These can be found in any book on business finance.

Supporting Documents

This section can contain any document that will establish that the information in your plan is correct or that will be useful to the reader, for example:

- Pictures of your products
- A summary of your market study

- Sample promotional literature
- Owners' résumés
- Detailed costs for a sample import or export transaction
- Lease agreement for office space
- Detailed sales forecasts
- Letters of intent from suppliers

Appendix C

Possible Sources of Financing for Your Business

Potential sources of financing for your new business are equity (shares of the business) and debt (loans). Equity investors will look for potential profits and increases in value, whereas lenders will be concerned about cash flow, which for them boils down to generating enough cash every month to make your principal and interest payments.

In general, you cannot get financing without putting some of your own money into the business (usually at least a quarter of the total). Both investors and lenders look at the ratio of debt to equity, or leverage, to make sure it is not dangerously high.

1. Your Own Resources:
   - *Equity*: Your personal savings
   - *Debt*: Personal loans, especially home equity loans
     Note 1: It is usually quicker, easier, and cheaper to use personal loans for a business start-up than to try to get a loan to the business itself. Home mortgages are an easy solution, but in the worst case you could lose your house.
     Note 2: Try to avoid using credit cards. The interest rate is too high, and it is usually unwise to use short-term debt for a long-term purpose such as a business start-up.
2. Friends, Fools, and Family:
   - *Equity*: Shares in the company (usually requires incorporating)

- *Debt*: Loans from friends, fools, and family

  Note: If the business fails, equity investors usually lose their money (and the entrepreneur may lose their friendship). Lenders expect to be repaid, sooner or later.

3. Small Business Financiers:

- *Equity*: "Strategic" investors, such as suppliers, who will gain if your business succeeds. For example, look on the Internet at www.activecapital.org. Also look into small business investment corporations (SBICs), which are scattered throughout the United States and usually have federal governmental assistance. Go to www.sba .gov/INV and click your state on the map to find an SBIC near you.

- *Debt*: Microcredit organizations, bank loans, loans, and loan guarantees from the U.S. Small Business Administration (SBA). You will normally need to apply for these programs through a commercial bank that works with the SBA.

  - Microloan, up to $35,000, to help you get started, accessed through a nonprofit lending organization

  - Low documentation loan, up to $150,000, with a simplified application process

  - Prequalification lending, which can put your business on a fast track for a loan of up to $250,000

  - SBA Express Loan, up to $350,000, for going businesses

  - Capital Access Program (CAP), up to $500,000, for investment or working capital

  - 7(a) Loan Guaranty Program, up to $2 million, with a fixed or floating interest rate

  - 504 Loan Program, up to $3 million, mainly for job creation

  - Export Working Capital (guarantee for individual transactions)

  - Export Express Loan

  - International Trade Loan (for established businesses)

Alternative Methods of Financing

- *Leasing*: Leasing equipment, such as computers, can save your money for use as working capital.

- *Fixed asset financing*: If you already own land or equipment, you may be able to use it as collateral for obtaining loans.

- *Trade credit*: When you have even a small track record, suppliers will often give you 30 days or more in which to pay them.

- *Export credit*: The Export-Import Bank of the United States, and similar organizations in some states, can lend (or guarantee loans to) your foreign importers so they can buy from you and pay you immediately. Check out the SBA's Web site at www.exim.gov/smallbiz/index.html.

- *Factoring receivables*: If you make large sales on credit, either in the United States or overseas, you may find a factor who will take over the collection process and lend you money before he collects. Sometimes you can even sell a receivable "without recourse," which means that if the buyer does not pay, it is the factor who loses. You can find factors on the Internet by searching for "factoring receivables" or "accounts receivable financing."

Appendix D

Sample Supply Agreements

Becoming an import/export broker or agent, or working with one, is serious business. Business relationships often start informally, but if much money is at stake, their terms should be discussed and set forth in written agreements.

The sample supply agreements that follow were provided for an earlier edition of this book by the New York City law firm of Kaplan, Russin Vecchi & Kirkwood, located at 90 Park Avenue. The first is between a foreign exporter and a U.S. selling agent, and the second is between a foreign exporter and a U.S. importer/distributor. These are given only as examples; each commercial relationship is different and is likely to require special terms and conditions in the enabling agreement. Most are not as extensive as these.

AGENCY AGREEMENT
(between foreign exporter and U.S. selling agent)

THIS AGREEMENT is made this _____ day of _____, 20_____.
BETWEEN A CORP incorporated in _____ with its registered office at: _____

_____

_____

(hereinafter called "<u>A CORP</u>") of the one part
AND: <u>B CORP</u> incorporated in _____ with its principal office at:

_____

_____

(hereinafter called "B Corp") on the other part

WHEREAS

A. A Corp designs, develops, manufactures and sells widgets and ancillary equipment for use in the widget industry.

B. In view of its previous experience in marketing widgets and ancillary equipment for the widget industry in the United States, its valuable contacts in that industry and its general marketing expertise and organization, B Corp wishes to undertake, and A Corp is willing to support, the marketing of widgets and ancillary equipment manufactured by A Corp in the United States under an agency from A Corp.

C. The parties now wish formally to record the terms and conditions which shall govern their association for the purposes outlined in Recital (b) above.

NOW, THEREFORE IT IS AGREED AND DECLARED AS FOLLOWS:

Clause 1. SCOPE

The parties agree that the terms and conditions set forth in this Agreement represent the entire agreement between the parties relating to the Agency of B Corp for A Corp and shall supersede any and all prior representations, agreements, statements and understandings relating thereto. The parties further agree that neither party places any reliance whatsoever on any such prior representations, agreements, statements and understandings except to the extent expressly set forth in this Agreement.

Clause 2. APPOINTMENT OF AGENT

A Corp hereby appoints B Corp to be its exclusive Agent in the United States during the currency of this Agreement for the sale of all widgets and ancillary equipment listed in Schedule 1. All such widgets and ancillary equipment are hereinafter collectively referred to as "The Products." A list of The Products which are standard as at the date of this Agreement is set forth in Schedule 1 to this Agreement and A Corp undertakes to give B Corp prompt written notice of any additions to or deletions from such list.

Clause 3. DUTIES OF THE AGENT

3.1 B Corp shall during the currency of this Agreement:

   3.1.1   Use its best endeavors to promote the sale of The Products to customers and potential customers throughout the United States and solicit orders for The Products to be placed with A Corp as per Clause 9 hereof. Without prejudice to the generality of the foregoing B Corp shall:

   3.1.1.1   maintain close marketing relationships with customers and potential customers so that their relevant equipment needs and future plans are ascertained.

        3.1.1.2 draw the attention of customers and potential customers to The Products suitable to their needs and ascertain the equipment and technical commercial proposals being offered by A Corp's competitors.

        3.1.1.3 B Corp shall not, during the currency of this Agreement, act as agent or distributor for any products directly competitive in price and specification to The Products.

    3.1.2 Establish and maintain a product support service having the capacity of:

        3.1.2.1 dealing with routine service enquiries from customers either by telephone or telex advice or in the field.

        3.1.2.2 maintaining liaison with customers.

        3.1.2.3 assisting customers in the implementation of the A Corp Warranty for The Products.

    3.1.3 Promptly draw to the attention of A Corp any new or revised legislation, regulation or orders affecting the use or sale of The Products in the United States of America as and when such legislation, etc. come to its attention.

    3.1.4 Employ such technically competent sales, commercial and service staff as may be reasonably necessary.

    3.1.5 Receive within its B Corp's offices temporary visiting staff of A Corp and afford to such staff reasonable office, secretarial and communications services.

3.2 Recognizing its obligations to protect the reputation of A Corp, B Corp undertakes that it shall not undertake any obligations in respect of the performance of The Products in excess of the limits specified by A Corp in respect of The Products concerned and shall not offer any time for delivery earlier than that given by A Corp pursuant to the inquiry and order procedure provisions of this Agreement.

Clause 4. SUPPORT OBLIGATIONS OF A CORP

During the term of the Agreement, A Corp shall:

4.1 Continue to develop The Products to meet the requirements of the United States Market.

4.2 Supply at its own cost B Corp with all reasonable requirements for technical data in reproducible form for use in catalogues, sales literature, instruction books, technical pamphlets and advertising material relating to The Products including developments of The Products as envisaged under Clause 4.1 above, and will pay the equivalent of _% of the prior 12 months' gross billing, in every year, for the preparation of such material.

4.3 Make potential customers within the United States aware of the support available from B Corp as agent of A Corp and of A Corp's support of such agency.

Clause 5. DELIVERIES BY A CORP

5.1 Throughout the term of this Agreement A Corp shall assist the sales efforts of B Corp by holding a stock of certain of The Products in an authorized warehouse within 50 miles of B Corp's headquarters at a level not lower than that set forth in Schedule 2 annexed hereto, which schedule may be changed from time to time by the signature of both parties on the revised version thereof.

5.2 A Corp shall provide adequate and suitable storage accommodations for such stock at its authorized warehouse and all deliveries will be dealt with through that warehouse. The costs and charges of the warehouse company shall be billed directly to and settled by A Corp.

5.3 All stock belonging to and warehoused by A Corp as set forth is and shall at all times remain the exclusive property of A Corp, and neither title or possession thereof or in part thereof, shall pass to B Corp or to any third party customer of B Corp save or until the precise terms and conditions of Clause 5.4 herein below have been completely and exclusively complied with.

5.4 B Corp shall have the authority to instruct A Corp's warehouse to release not more than 5 widgets on any given day. As to widgets released and shipped in accordance with the above authority, B Corp must receive payment in one of the following alternative ways: (a) By cash payment for the widget within 48 hours of such shipment; or (b) by delivery to Barclays Bank, N.Y., Jericho branch, within 48 hours of such shipment, of an irrevocable 45 day Letter of Credit, in the amount of the payment due.

Clause 6. PRICE

6.1 Customers solicited by B Corp shall pay the prices agreed or to be agreed from time to time and annexed as an Exhibit A hereto. Payment shall be made in accordance with paragraph 5.4 herein above. The parties hereto further agree that the said prices shall be reviewed every six months beginning on the date of this Agreement.

6.2 A Corp undertakes that it will give not less than three months' notice of any changes to its United States Dollar prices for the sale of The Products. A Corp further undertakes that any non-standard Products and agreed modifications to The Products shall be priced on a basis consistent with its normal pricing arrangements under this Agreement.

Clause 7. COMMISSIONS EARNED

Upon delivery of, and payment for, each Product pursuant Clauses 5 and 6, B Corp shall be entitled to a commission in the amount of _____ percent (_____%) of the list price of each of The Products as set forth in

Exhibit _____ hereto less any discounts or other allowances made by B Corp in these prices to achieve the sale and any freight, packing, insurance, or other charges. Commissions shall be calculated at the end of each calendar month based upon deliveries during the preceding month. Payment shall be made within 10 days of the end of the calendar month to B Corp.

Clause 8. DIRECT SALES AND FOREIGN ORDERS

A Corp agrees not to solicit sales for use within the United States during the currency of this Agreement. However, nothing in this Agreement is intended to operate nor shall it be construed as operating to prevent A Corp from selling, should it receive direct orders from and to any customer within the United States or to any customer outside the United States which customer whether within the knowledge of A Corp or not, intends to resell or actually resells to a customer within the United States. In the event of a direct sale by A Corp to a customer within the United States then A Corp shall grant B Corp a commission upon such sale in an amount of _____ percent (_____%) of the sale price charged by A Corp to such customer provided always that thereafter The Product support obligations of B Corp pursuant to this Agreement shall apply in respect of the sale of The Product so made by A Corp to the said customer. A Corp shall notify B Corp of each and every such sale. Further and in addition, if B Corp obtains any order for A Corp's products for shipment outside the United States, A Corp shall grant B Corp the same commission on each sale.

Clause 9. PROPRIETARY RIGHTS

9.1 The due and proper performance of its obligations and the exercise of its rights hereunder by B Corp shall not be deemed to be a breach of copyright or infringement of patent trademark or other proprietary right owned by A Corp.

9.2 B Corp shall not under any Circumstances acquire any rights whatsoever in any copyright, patent, trademark or other proprietary right of A Corp nor shall B Corp acquire any rights whatsoever in relation to the design of The Products.

Clause 10. DELIVERY

10.1 A Corp reserves the right to specify and change delivery dates and shall not be responsible for any delay in delivery or failure to meet delivery schedules where such delay or failure arises due to any cause outside the reasonable control of A Corp.

10.2 The parties hereto agree that, in the event that delivery of Products is delayed by an act or omission of a customer, B Corp shall invoice such customers for the reasonable storage charges incurred by A Corp as a result thereof, and will use reasonable efforts to effect collection.

Upon receipt of payment against such invoice, B Corp shall remit such payment to A Corp after deduction of B Corp's commission and costs of such collection.

Clause 11. WARRANTY

11.1 A Corp's warranty on all of The Products is limited to the following: A Corp will repair or replace at its option any Product at its own expense, save as to freight as to which it shall pay 50% of the round-trip cost for all validated warranty claims, as to which Product any defect in design, material or workmanship arises within a period of one year from commencement of operation of such Product or eighteen (18) months from the date of delivery of such Product, whichever shall first occur.

11.2 The warranty contained in Clause 11.1 above is subject to:

11.2.1 the Product not being used for any purpose other than the normal purpose for its specifications.

11.2.2 the observance by the user of all operating instructions and recommendations issued by A Corp in relation thereto.

11.2.3 prompt written notice being given to A Corp within 30 days following discovery of such defect.

11.3 B Corp shall promptly issue a report to A Corp in respect of each warranty claim brought to its attention.

Clause 12. PATENT INDEMNITY

12.1 In the event that any claim should be brought against B Corp that The Products infringe letters patent or other protected proprietary right, valid at the date of acceptance by A Corp of B Corp's order for such Product, owned by any third party, not being an employee or officer or shareholder of B Corp and not being a subsidiary or associated company of B Corp, then A Corp shall indemnify B Corp against and hold B Corp harmless from any and all damages which may be awarded against B Corp by any Court of competent jurisdiction provided that:

12.1.1 B Corp notifies A Corp in writing within 30 days of learning of any such claim as aforesaid.

12.1.2 B Corp permits A Corp to conduct the defense to any such claim as aforesaid and the negotiation of any settlement thereof.

12.1.3 B Corp provides at the expense of A Corp such assistance as A Corp may require in the defense or settlement of such claim as aforesaid.

12.1.4 such indemnity and undertaking as aforesaid shall not apply if the infringement relates to any use other than a use authorized by A Corp.

12.1.5 such indemnity and undertaking as aforesaid shall not apply where the infringement relates to the combination of The Products with equipment not designed, manufactured or sold by A Corp, unless A Corp specifically was aware of and approved such combination in advance thereof.

1.2.2 A Corp reserves the right to settle any such claim as aforesaid on the basis of substituting noninfringing Products for the alleged infringing Products providing that such substituted Products are capable of performing substantially the same functions as The Products so replaced.

1.2.3 Such indemnity and undertaking as aforesaid shall not apply in the event the designs, the subject of such claim as aforesaid, were supplied by B Corp's customers. In that event B Corp shall request such customers to indemnify A Corp against any claims made against A Corp alleging the infringement of letters patent or other protected proprietary rights arising out of the use of such designs or the manufacture or sale of Products utilizing such designs.

Clause 13. LIMITATION OF WARRANTY

13.1 The parties hereto agree that the express undertakings of A Corp pursuant to the provisions of the Warranty contained in Clause 11 constitute the only warranties of A Corp and the said undertakings of Clause 11 are in lieu of and in substitution for all other conditions and warranties express or implied INCLUDING WITHOUT LIMITATION ANY WARRANTIES AS TO MERCHANTABILITY OR FITNESS FOR PURPOSE and all other obligations and liabilities whatsoever of A Corp whether in contract or in tort or otherwise, and B Corp shall so information customers and potential customers. B Corp shall not offer or assume nor authorize anyone to offer to assume for or on behalf of A Corp any other Warranty or similar obligation in connection with The Products other than as authorized by Clause 11 and this Clause 13.

Clause 14. CAPACITY OF THE PARTIES

14.1 B Corp undertakes that it will at all times material to this Agreement make clear to customers and potential customers that it acts in the capacity of agent of A Corp. Except as specifically authorized under the terms of this Agreement, B Corp is not authorized to bind or commit or make representations on behalf of A Corp for any purpose whatsoever, and B Corp shall make this clear to customers and potential customers.

14.2 This Agreement is not intended nor shall it be construed as establishing any form of partnership between the parties.

Clause 15. ASSIGNMENT

The obligations and duties of B Corp hereunder are personal to B Corp and shall not be subcontracted to any third party without the prior written consent of A Corp nor shall B Corp assign this Agreement or any part thereof to any third party without the prior written consent of A Corp.

Clause 16. CONFIDENTIALITY

Any information which may during the currency of this Agreement be divulged by either party to the other on the express written basis that such information is confidential shall be so regarded and be protected whether in storage or in use. Furthermore, any such information shall not be used by the party receiving same otherwise than for the express purpose for which it is divulged and shall not further be divulged except to such of the said party's own servants and agents as may have a "need to know" for the purposes of this Agreement.

Clause 17. DURATION AND TERMINATION

17.1 This agreement shall commence on the date of signature hereof and shall continue unless and until terminated by either party giving to the other not less than 30 days written notice to such effect.

17.2 Any termination in accordance with the provisions of Clause 17.1 above shall not affect the obligations of the parties to fulfill the terms of orders placed and accepted prior to the effective date of such termination.

17.3 If either party should enter into any liquidation, bankruptcy or receivership whether compulsorily or voluntarily or should enter into any Agreement with creditors compounding debts or should suffer the imposition of a receiver in respect of the whole or a material part of its assets or should otherwise become insolvent, then the other party may by notice in writing, forthwith terminate this Agreement.

17.4 Upon termination of this Agreement:

17.4.1 B Corp shall return at its own expense to A Corp any catalogues, sales literature, instruction books, technical pamphlets and advertising material relating to The Products which may have been supplied by A Corp.

17.4.2 B Corp shall immediately cease to trade as an agent of A Corp and shall cease to represent itself in such capacity.

17.4.3 Recognizing that the financial and other commitments to be made by the parties in order to operate this Agreement will be put at risk by a termination pursuant to Clause 17.1 above at any time, the parties agree that any termination by A Corp pursuant to the terms of Clause 17.1, other than a termination pursuant to the terms of Clause 17.3, and other than a termination for cause (which shall include but specifically not be limited to fraud, negligence, breach of the terms of this Agreement), shall entitle B Corp to receive, in addition to sums actually due pursuant to the terms of Clause 17.2 and 17.4.4 herein, an amount equal to the net commissions received by B Corp under this Agreement, during the twelve months immediately preceding the date of notification of such termination, such sum to be paid at the expiration of the 30 day notice period. In the event that termination is by reason of Clause 17.3 herein, or for cause as defined hereinabove, or if termination is at the request or by the notice of B Corp, B Corp shall be entitled only to the amount due to it pursuant to the terms of Clause 17.2 and 17.4.4 herein above. Since the exercise of such right to termination would not constitute any breach of this Agreement such amount as shall be payable as aforesaid shall not be deemed a penalty.

17.4.4   A Corp shall continue to pay commissions on those orders obtained prior to the date of termination as invoices are paid and widgets delivered.

17.4.5   Subsequent to termination of this Agreement by either party in any manner and for any reason whatsoever, neither party shall be prevented or restricted from doing business with any person, corporation, partnership or other business entity within the United States or elsewhere, specifically including but not limited to persons, corporations, partnerships and business entities who have previously purchased A Corp's products, whether through B Corp or otherwise; except that if A Corp terminates this Agreement under circumstances which entitle B Corp to the payment of compensation pursuant to the terms of paragraph 17.4.3 hereinabove, then A Corp agrees that it will not solicit orders from any customers who received the products, or who requested a quotation therefor from B Corp during the currency of this Agreement, for a period of two years from the date of such termination.

Clause 18. NOTICES

Any notice required to be given hereunder shall be sufficiently given if forwarded by any of the following methods: registered mail, cable, telegraph or telex to the registered office of A Corp or the principal office of B Corp as the case may be and shall be deemed to have been received and given at the time when in the ordinary course of transmission it should have been delivered or received at the address to which it was sent.

Clause 19. WAIVER

Failure by either party at any time to enforce any of the provisions of this Agreement shall not constitute a waiver by such party of such provision nor in any way affect the validity of this Agreement.

Clause 20. AMENDMENT
This Agreement may not be amended except by an instrument in writing signed by both parties and made subsequent to the date of this Agreement and which is expressly stated to amend this Agreement.

Clause 21. HEADINGS
The clause headings of this Agreement are for reference purposes only and shall not be deemed to affect the interpretation of any of the provisions of this Agreement.

Clause 22. LAW
This Agreement shall be subject to and interpreted in accordance with the Laws of _____.

IN WITNESS WHEREOF, the parties have caused this Agreement to be signed on their behalf by the hand of a duly authorized officer.

FOR A CORP
_____ (Title)

FOR B CORP
_____ (Title)

DISTRIBUTORSHIP AGREEMENT
(between foreign exporter and U.S. importer/distributor)

AGREEMENT made this _____ day of _____, 20_____, by and between A Corp, a company organized under the laws of C Country with its principal place of business located at _____ (hereinafter called the "PRODUCER") and B Corp, located at S State (hereinafter called the "DISTRIBUTOR");

WITNESSETH:

WHEREAS, the PRODUCER is engaged in the design, manufacture and marketing of, among other things, widgets (the "Product"); under the brand name "Widgets."

WHEREAS, the DISTRIBUTOR maintains a marketing organization and markets widgets in the United States; and ss

WHEREAS, the PRODUCER and DISTRIBUTOR desire to cooperate for the purpose of marketing the product in the United States to civilians under the terms hereinafter set forth;

NOW THEREFORE, in consideration of the foregoing premises, the mutual covenants and agreements contained herein and other good and valuable consideration, the receipt, sufficiency and adequacy of which is hereby acknowledge, the parties hereto agree as follows:

SECTION 1. APPOINTMENT

The PRODUCER hereby appoints the DISTRIBUTOR to be its exclusive Distributor of the Product to civilians in the Territories as defined below, and the DISTRIBUTOR hereby accepts that appointment and agrees to act as the exclusive Distributor for the PRODUCER. PRODUCER specifically reserves to itself the right to market the Product to all Local, State and Federal organizations and entities, and the term "civilian" shall not include any such organizations or entities.

A. As used herein, Territories shall mean the States of _____

B. In addition to paragraph A, Section 1 above, Territories shall also mean all other states east of the Mississippi River at such time as the DISTRIBUTOR delivers to the PRODUCER a marketing plan acceptable to the PRODUCER. DISTRIBUTOR shall have _____ months from the date of this Agreement to deliver such plan.

C. In addition to paragraphs A and B of Section 1 above, the DISTRIBUTOR shall be given the first option to include all States west of the Mississippi River in the above defined Territories, at such time as the DISTRIBUTOR delivers to the PRODUCER a business and marketing plan acceptable to the PRODUCER for all States west of the Mississippi River. The option shall expire if such a plan is not delivered within _____ months from the date of this Agreement.

SECTION II. SALES AND PROMOTION

A. Energetically and faithfully use its best efforts to promote the sale of the Product to civilian customers and potential civilian customers throughout the Territories;
B. Carry continuously and have readily available sufficient quantities of the Product to enable it to promptly meet current demands of all customers;
C. Agree to price the Product at competitive levels, at wholesale and at retail, to sell the Product in accordance with the customs in the trade and will abstain from using selling methods or practices which, in the PRODUCER'S opinion, are harmful to the reputation of the Product or the PRODUCER;
D. Employ such technically competent sales, commercial and service staff as may be reasonably necessary;
E. Vigorously advertise and promote the Product within the Territories and bear all expense therefrom, which shall not be less than US$-per year;
F. Attend and participate annually in all significant trade shows and exhibitions, which includes, at the minimum, having a booth for demonstrations, promotions and advertising to all attendees of such shows or exhibitions. The booths should be staffed with technically qualified people. Such trade shows and exhibitions shall include, but is not limited to the following shows:
G. Not undertake any obligations or promote/advertise the performance of the Product in excess of the limits specified by the PRODUCER.
H. Be expressly permitted to make public announcements in the press of its appointment as the exclusive Distributor of the PRODUCER in the appropriate Territories.
I. Pay for and send the appropriate personnel of the DISTRIBUTOR to the PRODUCER's manufacturing plant for necessary technical update or general orientation should the PRODUCER find it necessary.
J. Not sell outside of the authorized Territories and if the Product is destined for outside the authorized Territories, the DISTRIBUTOR shall take all necessary and appropriate steps to stop such sales.

SECTION III. TERM

This Agreement shall be for a term of three years from the date first written above and shall continue from year to year thereafter until either of the parties shall give _____ months written notice to the other prior that this Agreement shall terminate. Should the DISTRIBUTOR not purchase the minimum quantities set forth below, the PRODUCER may, at any time, terminate this Agreement upon _____ days written notice.

SECTION IV. MINIMUM QUANTITIES

Throughout the term of this Agreement, the PRODUCER shall sell and the DISTRIBUTOR shall purchase from the PRODUCER (and from no other source) such minimum quantities of the Product at the minimum prices hereafter set out:

A. In the first year of this Agreement, DISTRIBUTOR shall purchase at least US$_____ of the Product from the PRODUCER;

B. In the first year of this Agreement, the DISTRIBUTOR shall purchase from the PRODUCER at least _____ pieces of the Product kits;

C. In the second year of this Agreement and every year thereafter, the PRODUCER shall have the option of increasing the above minimum requirements for price and quantities; however, in no event shall any increase by over US$_____ per year, or _____ pieces per year.

SECTION V. PAYMENT AND TERMS

A. Payment shall be made by the DISTRIBUTOR to the PRODUCER (unless otherwise directed by PRODUCER) by irrevocable Letter of Credit in US dollars.

B. The PRODUCER shall sell and the DISTRIBUTOR shall purchase the Products E.O.B. the manufacturing plant at the following prices for the first year:

After _____ months from the date of this Agreement, the PRODUCER shall have the option to raise or lower these prices by giving _____ days notice. However, in no event shall any price be raised by more than—percent (_____%) per year of the above prices.

C. Any duty, tax or other charge the PRODUCER may be required by any Federal, State, County,

Municipal or other law, now in effect or hereafter enacted, to collect or pay with respect to the sale, delivery or use of the Product shall be added to the prices provided herein exclusive of Paragraph B above and be paid by the Distributor.

Distributor shall also maintain and pay for Product Liability Insurance of US_____ million dollars.

SECTION VI. LEGAL COMPLIANCE

A. The DISTRIBUTOR shall comply with all Local, State and Federal laws concerning the Product.
B. The DISTRIBUTOR shall promptly information the PRODUCER of all aspects of any new or revised legislation, regulation or orders affecting the use, sale or promotion of the Product in the United States of America.

SECTION VII. TRADEMARKS, PATENTS, COPYRIGHT AND BRAND-NAMES

A. Any and all trademarks, patents, copyrights and brand-names now in effect, created, applied for or received in the future, of the Product shall always be and remain the property of the PRODUCER.
B. The DISTRIBUTOR shall not under any circumstances acquire any rights whatsoever in any trademark, patent, copyright, brand-name or other proprietary right of the PRODUCER.

SECTION VIII. NONCOMPETITION

A. The PRODUCER shall, at its discretion, repair or replace any Product at its own expense found by the DISTRIBUTOR to be defective, provided that:
  (1) In the case of visible and apparent defects, immediate written notice is given by the DISTRIBUTOR to the PRODUCER of such defects and the defective Products are returned to the PRODUCER within _____ weeks of the date of their shipment by the PRODUCER;
  (2) In the case of functional or non-apparent defects, written notice is given by the DISTRIBUTOR to the PRODUCER of such defects and the defective Products are returned to the PRODUCER within _____ months of the date of their shipment by the PRODUCER;
B. The PRODUCER shall pay fifty percent (50%) of the round-trip cost for all validated warranty claims.
C. The above limited warranty is subject to:
  (1) The product not being used for any purpose other than the normal purpose that it was manufactured for;
  (2) The observance by the user of all operating instructions and recommendations provided by the PRODUCER; and

The DISTRIBUTOR's cooperation in and with any investigation by the PRODUCER or its representative with respect to said defects, including but not limited to any reports of the circumstances surrounding the defect.

SECTION IX. CONFIDENTIALITY

A. The DISTRIBUTOR shall not, either directly or indirectly, in whole or in part, except as required in the marketing of the Product, or by written consent of an authorized representative of the PRODUCER, use or disclose to any person, firm, corporation or other entity, any informationrmation of a proprietary nature ("trade secrets") owned by the PRODUCER or any of its affiliated companies, including, but not limited to, records, customer lists, data, formulae, documents, drawings, specifications, inventions, processes, methods and intangible rights.

B. Any information regarding the Product which, during the term of this Agreement is divulged by either party to the other is confidential and shall be protected from disclosure.

C. The prohibited use or disclosure, as used herein, shall be for the term of the Agreement and at any time within five (5) years after the termination of this Agreement.

SECTION X. ASSIGNMENT

The obligations and duties of the DISTRIBUTOR hereunder are personal and shall not be subcontracted or assigned to any third party without the prior written consent of the PRODUCER.

SECTION XI. TERMINATION AND GOODWILL

A. In the event that the DISTRIBUTOR shall default in the performance of any of its obligations hereunder, or shall fail to comply with any provision of this Agreement on its part to be performed, and if such default or failure shall continue for days after written notice hereof from the PRODUCER, the PRODUCER may terminate this Agreement and the rights granted to the DISTRIBUTOR hereunder upon written notice to the DISTRIBUTOR, and neither waivers by the PRODUCER nor limitations of time may be asserted as a defense by the DISTRIBUTOR for any such failure or default. Such right of termination shall be in addition to any other rights and remedies of the PRODUCER at law or in equity.

B. Upon expiration, termination or cancellation of this Agreement pursuant to the provisions of Section III, Section XI, or for any other reason, with or without cause, the PRODUCER will not be liable for, and the DISTRIBUTOR will not be entitled to, any compensation of any kind for goodwill or any other tangible or intangible elements of damages or costs, nor shall the PRODUCER be liable to the DISTRIBUTOR for any special or consequential damages of any kind or nature whatsoever.

C. Upon the expiration *of* the term *of* this Agreement or any renewal thereof, the Products in the DISTRIBUTOR'S inventory may be sold, with the PRODUCER'S trademarks or' brand names thereon, only for one year after such expiration, subject *to* all the terms, covenants and conditions *of* this Agreement (other than the right *of* renewal), as though this Agreement had not expired. Any *of* the Products in the DISTRIBUTOR'S inventory upon the termination or cancellation *of* this Agreement for any reason other than the natural expiration *of* its term, as set forth in Section III hereof, shall remain the property *of* the DISTRIBUTOR and may be sold only upon the removal *of* the PRODUCER'S owned trademarks and brand names from the Products.

SECTION XII. RELATIONSHIP OF PARTIES

Nothing in this Agreement shall constitute or be deemed *to* constitute a partnership between the parties hereto. It is understood and agreed that the DISTRIBUTOR is an independent contractor and is not, nor ever will be, an agent or an employee *of* the PRODUCER. The DISTRIBUTOR shall not have the right, power or authority, express or implied, *to* bind, assume or create any obligation or liability on behalf *of* the PRODUCER.

SECTION XIII. CAPTIONS

The captions in this Agreement are inserted *solely* for ease *of* reference and are not deemed *to* form a part *of*, or in any way *to* modify, the text or meaning hereof.

SECTION XIV. NOTICE

Any notice required *to* be given shall be deemed *to* be validly served *if* sent by prepaid registered or certified airmail *to* the address(es) stated below or *to* such other address as may be designated by either party in writing. Said notice shall be effective when posted by either party *to* said address(es), postage prepaid.
A. PRODUCER: (address).
B. DISTRIBUTOR: (address).

SECTION XV. DIVISIBILITY

The provisions of this Agreement contain a number of separate and divisible covenants. Each such covenant shall be construed as a separate covenant and shall be separately enforceable. If a court of competent jurisdiction shall determine that any part of any paragraph or any part of any separate covenant herein contained, is so restrictive as to be deemed void, the remaining part or parts, or the other such separate covenants, shall be considered valid and enforceable, notwithstanding the voidance of such covenant or part of a separate covenant. If certain covenants of this Agreement hereof are so broad as to be unenforceable, it is the desire of the parties hereto that such provisions be read as narrowly as necessary in order to make such provisions enforceable.

SECTION XVI. GOVERNING LAW

This Agreement shall be deemed to have been made in, and the relationship between the parties hereto shall be governed by, the laws of the State of, United States of America.

SECTION XVII. PRIOR AGREEMENTS

This Agreement contains a complete statement of arrangements among and between the parties hereto with respect to its subject matter, supersedes all existing agreements among them concerning the subject matter hereof and cannot be changed or terminated except in writing signed by all parties to this Agreement.

IN WITNESS WHEREOF, the parties hereto have executed this Agreement in duplicate by their duly authorized representatives and affixed their corporate seals (if any) the day and year first above written.

(SEAL) PRODUCER

By: _____

Title: _____

(SEAL) DISTRIBUTOR

By: _____

Title: _____

Appendix E

U.S. Export Assistance Centers

The U.S. government has personnel in many field offices of the U.S. Department of Commerce who can assist exporters. The list as of January 2007 is as follows.

ATLANTA

Territory: Georgia, Alabama, Mississippi, Northern Florida
Ray Gibeau
Regional Manager, International
  Trade Programs
Sunbelt U.S. Export Assistance
  Center
75 Fifth Street, NW, Suite 1055
Atlanta, GA 30308
Tel: (404) 897-6089
Fax: (404) 897-6085
E-mail: raymond.gibeau@sba.gov

BALTIMORE

Territory: Maryland, District of Columbia
Patrick Tunison
Chief International Lending Officer,
  International Trade Programs
U.S. Export Assistance Center
300 West Pratt Street, Suite 300
Baltimore, MD 21201
Tel: (202) 205-6426
Fax: (202) 205-7272
E-mail: Patrick.Tunison@sba.gov

BOSTON

Territory: Maine, Vermont, New Hampshire, Massachusetts, Connecticut, Rhode Island
John Joyce
Regional Manager, International Trade
  Programs
U.S. Export Assistance Center
World Trade Center, Suite 307
Boston, MA 02210
Tel: (617) 424-5953
Fax: (617) 424-5992
E-mail: john.joyce@mail.doc.gov

CHARLOTTE

Territory: Virginia, North Carolina, South Carolina, Tennessee
Dan Holt
Regional Manager, International Trade
  Programs
U.S. Export Assistance Center
521 East Morehead Street, Suite 435
Charlotte, NC 28202
Tel: (704) 333-4886
Fax: (704) 332-2681
E-mail: dan.holt@mail.doc.gov

CHICAGO

**Territory: Wisconsin, Illinois,
Nebraska, Iowa**
John Nevell
Regional Manager, International Trade
Programs
U.S. Export Assistance Center
200 Adams Street, Suite 2450
Chicago, IL 60606
Tel: (312) 353-8065
Fax: (312) 353-8098
E-mail: john.nevell@sba.gov

CLEVELAND

**Territory: Ohio, Kentucky, Western
New York, Western Pennsylvania,
West Virginia**
Patrick Hayes
Regional Manager, International Trade
Programs
U.S. Export Assistance Center
600 Superior Avenue, Suite 700
Cleveland, OH 44114
Tel: (216) 522-4731
Fax: (216) 522-2235
E-mail: phayes@mail.doc.gov

DALLAS

Territory: Texas, Louisiana
Rick Schulze
Regional Manager, International Trade
Programs
North Texas U.S. Export Assistance
Center
1450 Hughes Road, Suite 220
Grapevine, TX 76051
Tel: (817) 310-3749
Fax: (817) 310-3757
E-mail: richard.schulze@sba.gov

DENVER

**Territory: Wyoming, Utah,
Colorado, New Mexico, Arizona**
Dennis Chrisbaum
Regional Manager, International Trade
Programs
U.S. Export Assistance Center

1625 Broadway Avenue, Suite 680
Denver, CO 80202
Tel: (303) 844-6623, ext. 18
Fax: (303) 844-5651
E-mail: dennis.chrisbaum@sba.gov

DETROIT

Territory: Michigan, Indiana
John O'Gara
Regional Manager, International Trade
Programs
U.S. Export Assistance Center
8109 E. Jefferson
Detroit, MI 48214
Tel: (313) 226-3670
Fax: (313) 226-3657
E-mail: john.ogara@sba.gov

MIAMI

Territory: Florida
Mary Hernandez
Regional Manager, International Trade
Programs
U.S. Export Assistance Center
5835 Blue Lagoon Drive, Suite 203
Miami, FL 33132
Tel: (305) 526-7425, ext. 21
Fax: (305) 526-7434
E-mail: mary.hernandez@sba.gov
Northern Florida
Ray Gibeau
Tel: (404) 897-6089

MINNEAPOLIS

**Territory: Minnesota, North Dakota,
South Dakota**
Nancy Libersky
Regional Manager, International Trade
Programs
U.S. Export Assistance Center
U.S. Small Business Administration
100 North Sixth Street 210-C
Butler Square
Minneapolis, MN 55403
Tel: (612) 348-1642
Fax: (612) 348-1650
E-mail: nancy.libersky@sba.gov

NEWPORT BEACH

Territory: Southern California, Nevada, Arizona, Hawaii, Guam
Martin Selander
Regional Manager, International Trade Programs
U.S. Export Assistance Center
3300 Irvine Avenue, #305
Newport Beach, CA 92660-3198
Tel: (949) 660-1688, ext. 115
Fax: (949) 660-1338
E-mail: martin.selander@sba.gov

NEW YORK CITY*

Territory: Five Boroughs
John Miller
Marketing & Outreach
SBA New York District Office
26 Federal Plaza, Suite 3100
New York, NY 10278
Tel: (212) 264-7770
E-mail: john.miller@sba.gov
(*handled by SBA's New York District Office)

PHILADELPHIA

Territory: Eastern Pennsylvania, New Jersey, Eastern New York, Delaware, Eastern Maryland
Robert Elsas
Regional Manager, International Trade Programs
U.S. Export Assistance Center
The Curtis Center
601 Walnut Street, Suite 580 West
Philadelphia, PA 19106
Tel: (215) 597-6110
Fax: (215) 597-6123
E-mail: robert.elsas@mail.doc.gov

PORTLAND

Territory: Oregon, Southern Idaho, Montana
Inga Fisher Williams
Regional Manager, International Trade Programs

U.S. Export Assistance Center
One World Trade Center
121 Southwest Salmon Street, Suite 242
Portland, OR 97204
Tel: (503) 326-5498
Fax: (503) 326-6351
E-mail: inga.fisherwilliams@mail.doc.gov
Online help:
Idaho: www.sba.gov/id/id_itresources.html
Montana: www.sba.gov/mt/mt_itresources.html
Oregon: www.sba.gov/or/or_itresources.html

SEATTLE

Territory: Washington, Alaska, Northern Idaho
Pru Balatero
Regional Manager, International Trade Programs
U.S. Export Assistance Center
2601 4th Avenue, Suite 320
Seattle, WA 98121
Tel: (206) 553-0051, ext. 228
Fax: (206) 553-7253
E-mail: pru.balatero@mail.doc.gov
Seattle U.S. Export Assistance Center
Web site: www.buyusa.gov/seattle

ST. LOUIS

Territory: Oklahoma, Arkansas, Iowa, Kansas, Missouri
John Blum
Regional Manager, International Trade Programs
U.S. Export Assistance Center
8235 Forsyth Boulevard, Suite 520
St. Louis, MO 63105
Tel: (314) 425-3304
Fax: (314) 425-3381
E-mail: john.blum@mail.doc.gov

Avoiding Import/Export Scams

This appendix is a compendium of things to watch out for. It is taken, with considerable editing, from a short essay titled, "Import Export Scams: What to Watch Out for and How to Avoid Them." The original essay was written by Nick Taylor of Blue Star International Brokerage, which represents manufacturers and acts as a finder for people who are looking for products. You can find him on the Web at www.alibaba.com/company/10674167.html.

In the example below, country X is a nation in West Africa that has developed quite a reputation for the kinds of activity discussed in this appendix.

The import/export business is exciting and has many possibilities of making lots of money. Import/export is a huge moneymaking business, and you can bet that there are a lot of people in the game who are, shall we say, "not honest."

Yes, scams are rampant in the import/export industry and getting more and more ridiculous!

On average I blacklist at least 5 to 10 e-mails a day that are scam letters and offers. In this article I will list the ones I have received so you can avoid them. Hopefully you haven't fallen for any of them. Here are the scams I have recently seen.

Country X scam letters and offers.

1. One country X scam letter tells how a relative, friend, prince, or king has passed away and has millions of dollars in an account that they want to transfer to your account and then have you transfer it back to them, keeping a portion for yourself. This is a trick to get your bank account

information. Never ever give out your bank account information, and completely disregard these letters!

2. Country X import/export offers. I get them sometimes simply stating, "I want to buy your products." Inside, the message will typically say, "I saw your product listed and want to buy it. Send prices right away." Usually they don't have any company information, but sometimes they do. I have just made it a point not to do business with country X at all. Sorry, but too many scams come from country X and have ruined it for everyone.

3. Bank wire fee scam. These are very common. Fake banks are set up, typically just a Web site or not even one at all. The scam artists will tell you they want to buy a high dollar amount of products. Then, when it comes to buying, the bank will tell you that a fee must be paid first to transfer the funds into your account. Do *not* pay this fee! You will never see your money again, and you certainly won't get an order from them, either!

4. Also watch out for forged and fake money orders, fraudulent checks, and fake Western Union payments.

5. Check scams. I got several of these while I was selling high-dollar diamond jewelry. A message comes in and says, "I want to buy your item. Do you mind if I pay with an e-check?" An e-check is an electronic check. E-checks typically get transferred from one bank to another. What the scammers do is tell you it's easy; all you have to do is go to a print shop or office supply store and pay for the printing material and ink. Then the check is printed and you have a check that you can cash. The problem is that the e-check will be no good. If someone writes me a check for a large order, I won't ship the products until the check completely clears! One company inquired about buying a large quantity of items from me and sent a company check to pay for the order. I deposited the check in my company account and waited for it to clear. A week and a half later my bank called and said the check was fake. Good news and bad

news. The good news is I didn't send them the items. I was waiting for the check to clear. The bad news is that my bank closed my account because of the check that was sent to me. To avoid this from happening, you can get a machine that clears or rejects checks. Some banks offer this machine.

6. COD scams. I got one scam in which a guy asked me to ship the product COD and said he would pay with a check. The problem was this guy could have had the package delivered to an anonymous address and written a hot check or even a fake check for it. While he gets the product, you find your check is fake and it's too late. They have your product and you have a worthless piece of paper. Watch out for this one. A lot of these scams come while selling stuff on craigslist.org.

7. Payment agent scams. This one is common in online job post boards. The scammers will say they are hiring payment agents to collect payment from foreign companies they do business with. They want you to collect the money, deposit it into your bank, send them the money, and keep 10 percent for yourself. Sounds pretty easy, but here's what happens: They have a fake business write a fake check and send it to you. Once you put the fake check in your account, you send them 90 percent, and keep 10 percent for your work. What happens is they get the money, but by the time the fake check is caught by your bank it's too late, and now you owe the amount that you sent the scammers and, of course, the nice 10 percent commission you kept for your work. You can actually go to jail for this, considering your bank might think you were in on the scam. Don't even bother with these offers!

Steps and precautions to avoid these pitfalls.

1. When I get offers for large orders from people or companies, the first thing I do is a company background check. Here are some places to check a company's background and history:

- Dun & Bradstreet for credit reports/financial information
- www.Hoovers.com.

2. Check to see if they have a Web site. Most companies that try to place large orders have valid Web sites. A few may not. If they don't, at least ask for their business license information and business registration, office address, phone number, and Web site to see if they are licensed to do business in their country.

3. Watch out for people asking you to reply to a personal e-mail address! If I see a message that says, "Reply to my personal e-mail address," I won't even bother. A personal e-mail address will end with @hotmail.com, @yahoo.com, @excite.com, @myway.com, and so on. To see if it is a personal e-mail address and not a business e-mail, copy the words after the @ sign and paste them into your browser to see what kind of site it is. If it's an e-mail provider or a Web developer, don't waste your time!

4. Google. I will copy the name of the supposed company and go to www.google.com. I will paste into the search box the name of the company with a comma and then the word "scam." Here's an example: "johndoe inc, scam." Or, if they have a Web site, I will type in "www.johndoeinc.com, scam." This will pull up any scam reports about the company or its Web site. If they don't have a Web site or you're not getting any information on the business name, you can type in the business address or e-mail address they gave you to see what you get.

5. E-mail backtrack—to find a person's real identity and IP address. I am relentless! There are online services you can pay for that will give you all of the information on someone from their e-mail address or Web site. Here is one URL to use for this: www.abika.com.

6. Don't be afraid to ask the company or the person for their complete company information before you even consider doing business with them. If they are a legitimate com-

pany, they will have no problem giving you their information, especially if they contacted you!

7. Go through government trade sites and forums to find potential buyers. Typically, smart scammers will stay away from government sites.

8. Follow your gut and look for red flags! Some sites and offers will throw up lots of red flags, while others are trickier and more complex. Remember that if it sounds too good to be true, it probably isn't true.

9. Even if you have been corresponding with someone for days or even weeks on a deal, if at the last minute they try and pull something that you're not sure about, *don't* do it! It's not worth it! Some scammers will do this. They will agree to all of your terms until it comes time to pay. They will say things like, "If we can't do it this way, then you are wasting my time," "You must not want this deal," or "I will go somewhere else." Let them go somewhere else!

10. If you post in trade forums, it won't hurt to put in your company description warnings for scammers. Here are some ideas for description warnings.

   • Before you solicit us or request a price list, have all of your company information ready to submit including business license number, reseller's tax number, and county or country office where you obtained your business license. Otherwise, we will not respond.

   • Scammers beware, don't waste your time. We will track your IP address and report you to the proper authorities!

Here are some Web links to look at for information about common scam letters, e-mails, job offers, work at home, bank, and investment money scams:

   • www.scambuster.com
   • www.419eater.com
   • www.Dont-Get-Scammed-Again.com

- www.FraudPolice.com
- www.scamorama.com
- www.scam.com

I hope this information has been of great help and will prevent you from losing any money to scammers! Remember, the due diligence and research is more than worth the effort!

Appendix G

Letters from Store Owners

In May 2007, a member of the Coop America Business Network (CABN) sent a letter to the membership. In the letter she asked a series of questions about selling to small stores. Two of the answers she received provide a clear picture about selling to retail stores. They are from Fred Wilson Horch, the owner of F. W. Horch Sustainable Goods & Supplies in Brunswick, Maine, and Miranda and Baptiste Paul, the owners of Worldgoods, LLC, in Green Bay, Wisconsin.

The questions and the answers are given here.

FROM FRED WILSON HORCH

How do you choose products to sell in your retail store?

We have a product screening process to evaluate each potential product. We have a tight focus on practical products that our customers can use to conserve resources, protect our environment, and save the planet. If we can't sell it as a way to save the planet, we don't bring the product into the store. Most smaller retailers have a focus and can tell you what kinds of products they sell. Listen and move on if the store owner isn't interested. With small stores you'll be talking directly to the owner. In larger stores, you'll be talking to a buyer.

Do you prefer that potential vendors e-mail, call, or stop by with product samples? Why?

Definitely e-mail first. Calls are okay, but we're often busy. Unannounced drop-ins are a very bad idea; I have other things to do. When you e-mail, provide a link to your Web site, and on your Web site provide as much information as you possibly can about why your product will sell. Anyone who owns a retail store will want to know the following:

- Minimum order quantities
- Margin (wholesale cost and suggested retail price)
- Point-of-sale displays and product literature
- Warranty support
- Returns policy
- Comparison to competing products

Put the above on your Web site; don't bog down your initial e-mail with these details—your initial e-mail should just be a short introduction, sales pitch, and heads-up that you'll be giving us a call. If you get back a "not interested" e-mail, don't bother calling. Move on to your next prospect. If the call goes well, then you can set up a time to come in and show your product.

If a vendor stops by to introduce his or her product, how likely are you to place an order right then?

Never.

What quantity of an item do you feel comfortable stocking the first time around?

If I can return the product if it doesn't sell, then I don't really care. I will want to stock enough product to make a good display. I will listen to the vendor about how much to stock; I figure they know their product better than I do the first time around. If I have to buy more than $300 worth of product, can't return it, and I don't have a great feel for whether it will sell, then I'll probably pass on it.

What advice would you give to a potential vendor who is trying to sell his or her product in your store?

Make it easy to do business with you. Have your wholesale price list ready to go and easy to understand. Have a rational and obvious system for your item codes and product names. Provide low minimums. Offer to take back product on the first order if it doesn't sell. Give net 30 terms. Offer to drop ship. Provide good point-of-sale display options and good packaging. Give good margins. Limit the number of retailers you sell to in a given market. Respect our time, especially if you cold call. We are always too busy to talk and often need to attend to customers, so be super nice and efficient on the phone. Also, do your research before you call. If the store has a Web site, review it so you know what kind of store you're calling and can explain why you think your product would be a good fit.

How helpful are trade shows for finding new products and getting new accounts?

The right shows are extremely helpful. The wrong shows are dreadful. Know your target market and be at the trade show that will attract the kinds of stores you want to sell to.

What are some of your pet peeves when dealing with vendors whose products you sell?

Inferior products. Make sure your product really is good and does everything you claim it does. Test it. Get testimonials. Get third-party certifications.

Make sure you have enough stock. Nothing is worse than trying out a new product that turns out to be a hit with customers and then not being able to get a reorder filled.

High minimums are a problem for some of my vendors—I'd like to sell their products, but I can't afford to spend $500 each time I order.

Don't undercut me by selling your product for below MSRP (manufacturer's suggested retail price) on your own Web site or on a featured retail partner.

Do send a confirmation after receiving an order and send a tracking number once you ship an order. Put your invoice with prices with the order. I hate getting packing slips with no prices and separate invoices. I understand why vendors do it (so they can ship out products efficiently and then charge different accounts different prices), but it's a waste of paper and my time, because I have to wait for the invoice to complete my receiving to make sure my cost and prices are correct. Design your shipping and invoicing processes to make my life easier.

What information do you need from a vendor before placing an order for his or her products, besides wholesale and retail costs? Do you also want to see the vendor's marketing plan, press kit, etc.?

I really want a sample of the actual product. I need to know what it will look like in my store (packaging, presentation, etc.). For items I sell on my Web site, I need a high-quality picture (hire a professional photographer), good copy, and specifications (depending on the product).

Beyond that, I need a terms sheet (minimum order quantities, methods of placing orders, shipping times, price breaks, etc.).

I don't think I've ever seen a marketing plan or a press kit for any of the products I sell. Coop advertising and slicks are nice but not essential. I do appreciate vendors who have retail store locators on their Web sites; let me know if you offer that. Send me the link when you've added me so I can verify that my store information is correct and that the link works. I track my Web site traffic and will know when customers call me through a vendor referral.

FROM MIRANDA AND BAPTISTE PAUL

How do you choose products to sell in your retail store?

First and foremost the products have to be fair trade and/or environmentally sustainable/responsible. I look for products and vendors listed on the FTF (Fair Trade Federation) Web site, TransFair, IFAT (International Federation of Alternative Trade Organizations, Coop America, and so on. I have a pool of customers who review several products and/or product photos to determine if I will carry something. I also ask almost all of my customers what items they'd like to see more of in our store and I listen to their suggestions, and that has done very well for me. Occasionally I just simply ask vendors to give me statistics on a product's success. My market is largely women.

Do you prefer that potential vendors e-mail, call, or stop by with product samples? Why?

E-mails are great. I can read them any time. I don't have vendors stop by too often; I feel that there aren't as many in my area, but dropping in could be very time-consuming. I have had a few salespeople who prefer talking on the phone, which is actually very time-consuming for me as I am dealing with customers and doing work during regular business hours. Some of the salespeople who have contacted me are very long winded. So, I prefer e-mail, and I will call when I need more information.

If a vendor stops by to introduce his or her product, how likely are you to place an order right then?

Probably not, but I did have someone call me and tell me they would send me a free sample and if I didn't like it I could send it back for free. I ended up really liking the items and made a purchase (fair trade jewelry from Mexico).

What quantity of an item do you feel comfortable stocking the first time around?

If I can, I get one of each, that's it. Depending on the item, I guess, I try not to get more than six if I am really unsure. If it's an item similar to something that is already selling well, I will usually get more. I really consider the cost of shipping if I am making a small purchase, though.

What advice would you give to a potential vendor who is trying to sell his or her product in your store?

I love it when vendors offer the products on a display unit that is affordable or even free. It makes my life easier.

How helpful are trade shows for finding new products and getting new accounts?

This is not applicable to me, as I do not attend trade shows at this time.

What are some of your pet peeves when dealing with vendors whose products you sell?

- Really nice pictures that make products look different, higher quality, larger, and so on, than the actual items when they arrive, or getting a surprise about the nature of any product. This is my number-one pet peeve. The best vendors I work with have detailed descriptions and sizes, and they really know their products well. I have stopped buying from a few people already, as I continuously get products that I feel are misrepresented in a catalog or online, and so forth. Salespeople should really know what products are made of and how large or small they are, and skimpy descriptions online or in a catalog should be supplemented by knowledgeable people. We're in the business of being picky and reading labels, and so are our customers. Total honesty is appreciated. I don't want T-shirts that are not made fair trade but are dyed and batiked like fair trade, coat hooks that are really just key hooks and about one-third the expected size, and so on.

- Not being able to get in touch with someone quickly enough, having to leave a message that isn't returned promptly.

- Not being able to order wholesale online or through e-mail.

- A vendor taking a lot of phone time during my business day.

- Being quoted one price but getting another and having to call and follow up. I got charged twice from a music company, got overcharged by a fair trade jeweler, and had my credit card charged for $60 more than my invoice from a fair trade olive oil producer. I spend a lot of time just going through invoices with a fine-tooth comb, dealing with damaged products, etc. All of this takes time from running my shop!

- Not getting informational tags, cards, or other producer information and thus not knowing the country of origin, artisan, etc. This is a big deal to me.

What are things you really like about certain vendors?

- Free shipping on orders of a certain amount or affordable shipping rates that don't leave me wondering what the invoice is going to look like.

- Tons of product information on the Web site: country of origin, what it's made of, how it's fair trade or eco-friendly, the cultural significance, and so on, as well as vendors who send or let me download producer cards or information. My customers will buy items tagged with a story of the artisan who made it over unknown items, two to one. I spend a lot of time making producer cards myself.

- Low minimum orders—$100 is great when you just need to refill, say, a jewelry display or key chains and small items. Many of my orders are much larger than this, but sometimes I am ordering a special item for a customer or trying something new and don't want to make a big order just because I have to.

- Being able to order wholesale online after business hours.

- Offering decent terms and auto-pay. Many people on this (CABN) list, especially new retail shops, know what cash flow is like, and it's really preferable to sell some of the product before you have to pay the invoice. It's also way cool when vendors just keep my credit card on file and charge it after 30 days. This makes my life a lot easier.

- Totally friendly and great customer service when a product is damaged, missing, etc. I have been very surprised at how often products break during shipping. I guess I didn't expect it, but the vendors I deal with have mostly been really great about replacing items.

- I really love when the items come packaged in boxes, recycled material, etc., that I can reuse. I don't buy any shipping or packaging materials, and I get really creative for my 100 percent reused and recycled handmade displays. Many things come in looking nice (Maggie's Organics is one I give great kudos to for recycled packaging) and go out that way. Global Crafts also has its products packaged nicely by Florida Citizens with Disabilities, and the Pakistani Onyx carvings from Bright Hope International come in really nice speckled cardboard gift boxes.

What information do you need from a vendor before placing an order for his or her products, besides wholesale and retail costs? Do you also want to see the vendor's marketing plan, press kit, etc.?

Producer information—country of origin, name of the artisan or Fair Trade Cooperative, a detailed product description, ingredients list if the product is edible, etc.

Index

Figures are indicated in *italics*

documentary drafts for collection, 114–17
international, 23–24, 112–24
methods, 112–32
open account, 113–14
through PayPal, 7
sources of information about, 130–32
PayPal, 7, 13, 113, 122–23
pesticides and toxic substances, importing of, 216
Phoenix Regulatory Associates, 208, 225
PIERS (Port Import and Export Reporting Service), 55, 89
Postal Service, U.S. (USPS), 141–42, 161
Airmail Parcel Post, 142
preferential tariff programs, U.S., *197*
preferential trade agreements, 239–41
price quotation, 11
prices, 77, 86–87, 103
markups, 77, 134
setting of, 8
pro forma invoices, 167
pro forma (projected) income and expense statement, 18
produce broker, 88
products
counterfeit, 59–60
defective, 78
ideas for exporting of, 68–73
ideas for importing of, 56–68
labeling of, 50, 79
as marketing function, 86
modifications to, 62–63, 71–72
patents and trademark, 78–79
pricing of, 77
promotion of, 78
recalling of, 247
relabeling and repackaging, 79
reports on, 78
researching for, 56–61, 70–73
samples of, 60–61
servicing and replacement of, 78
shipping priority, 78

sources of information, 81–85
testing of, 61–63
warranties on, 78
watched, 205
promotion, 22, 78, 86–87, 103
Public Health Security and Bioterrorism Preparedness and Response Act, 212

quotas
absolute, 204
on imports, 204–205
Quota Category Number, 205
source of information, 224
tariff rate, 204
and visas, 205
quotations (trade), 165–66, *166*

radio frequency identification (RIFD) tags, 136
rate books (tariffs), 147–49
rationalization, 146–47
reefer container. *See* refrigerated ("reefer") container
Reference USA (book), 91, 105
refrigerated ("reefer") container, 136
registration identification numbers (RN), 212
regulations. *See* Customs Service, U.S.; trade regulations
release orders, 182
remote location filing (RLF), 172
reports, 78
retailers, 92–94
RIFD. *See* radio frequency identification tags
roll-on, roll-off (ROLO) process, 135

SACU. *See* South African Customs Union
sales, 103–104
sales confirmation document, 167, 169
Salesman's Guide (book series), 92, 105
sales targets, 76

CPSIA information can be obtained at www.ICGtesting.com
Printed in the USA
BVOW02n2326190514

353642BV00024B/35/P